I0813050

IMAGES
of America

GREEN RIVER

ON THE COVER: A crew of tie hacks takes a lunch break. Tie hacks were men who cut and roughed out railroad ties. The ties were transported by floating them down the river to collection points, where they were gathered and loaded onto trains. Green River was such a collection point; a large boom was placed across the river here every spring. These men sit upon railroad ties in varying stages of completion. (Courtesy of Sweetwater County Historical Museum.)

IMAGES
of America

GREEN RIVER

Terry Del Bene, Ruth Lauritzen, Cyndi McCullers,
and the Sweetwater County Historical Museum

ARCADIA
PUBLISHING

ISBN 978-0-7385-4819-7

Published by Arcadia Publishing
Charleston, South Carolina

Printed in the United States of America

Library of Congress Catalog Card Number: 2007930841

For all general information contact Arcadia Publishing at:
Telephone 843-853-2070
Fax 843-853-0044
E-mail sales@arcadiapublishing.com
For customer service and orders:
Toll-Free 1-888-313-2665

Visit us on the Internet at www.arcadiapublishing.com

We dedicate this book to all the men and women from Green River who have served in our armed forces, police departments, fire departments, and emergency services.

Contents

Acknowledgments

We thank the many photographers who reached across time to provide the images used here. The wealth of photographic resources made the selection process a difficult one. Our deepest thanks go to the Sweetwater County Historical Museum, the Union Pacific Museum, the Denver Public Library, the U.S. Army Corps of Engineers, the Church of Jesus Christ of Latter-Day Saints Archives and Intellectual Services, Hays King, and Jim Shaw for allowing us to reprint images from their collections. We also wish to acknowledge the kind assistance of members of the Green River Historical Preservation Commission and the Sweetwater County Historical Society.

INTRODUCTION

The Green River is part of the headwaters of the Colorado River system. Also known as the Seedskadee Agie, which means "Prairie Chicken River "in the Shoshone language, it is a reliable source of water in an arid land. The earliest permanent settlement at the current location of the city was established near the confluence of the Green River and Bitter Creek in 1862, when several crude buildings were erected there as an Overland Stage station. From this modest beginning, a settlement sprouted and grew.

Before 1862, the major east-west route across the West was the corridor of the Oregon, California, Mormon Pioneer, and Pony Express Trails, located 30 miles to the north. That corridor was the superhighway of the time, funneling people, commerce, mail, and telegraphic communications. Green River might have remained just another river crossing on the lesser-traveled Cherokee and Overland Trails had it not been for the 1861 decision to move the mail to a more southerly route. The postmaster general believed that the move was necessary because of depredations by Native Americans in the northern trails corridor. The move resulted in a stage station being built here, at the river crossing near Castle Rock and Man's Face Rock.

The stage station, located on the southern bank of the river, was built mainly of stone. A graveyard was established nearby, where the municipal horse corrals now stand. On the north side of the river, opposite the stage station, additional development became known as "Old Town" or "Adobe Town." Many of the early buildings in this area incorporated mud bricks in their construction.

This small settlement on the banks of the river was destined for greater things. While the stage station was handling its first mail, Pres. Abraham Lincoln signed the Transcontinental Railroad Act, setting the construction of the transcontinental railroad into action. The route for this monumental undertaking eventually was chosen based on the need for water and fuel to feed the steam engines. These factors assured the link between the tiny settlement at Green River Station and the railroad.

The plan was to make the town a rail stop with multiple tracks and a roundhouse where cars and engines could be maneuvered and repaired. The land that the railroad chose for its facilities was not the Green River Station on the south side of the river, but the Old Town area on the northern banks. To the company officials' dismay, when the rails finally arrived in Green River in 1868, the desired site was already owned by someone else. S. I. Field, an early entrepreneur, had arrived in Green River before the railroad and filed a homestead claim on the land. Union Pacific refused to designate a switching point in a town they did not own. The company continued the line through Green River and 13 miles to the west, establishing the switching point at Bryan. Almost overnight, Green River became a ghost town.

It was during this downturn that Maj. John Wesley Powell began the first of two expeditions down the Green and Colorado Rivers. Major Powell was a Civil War veteran and explorer who, in 1869 and 1871, led scientists and surveyors down the rivers through the Grand Canyon, one of the last unexplored areas within the United States. His explorations both began in Green River, near where the railroad intersected the river.

In 1871, Frederick S. Dellenbaugh described Green River as a town of roofless ruins, shanties, a station, a section house, S. I. Fields' store, and a number of canvas-roofed shacks.

Meanwhile, Bryan, where the switching point had been established on the Black's Fork River, was thriving as a tent community. Lawlessness abounded, and murder, theft, and a variety of crimes were common events. Drought caused the Black's Fork River to dry up, and by 1872 the switching point was moved back to Green River. S. I. Field and Union Pacific came to an agreement about the land, opening the way for the growth of the community.

The newly revived town was designated as county seat of Sweetwater County (formerly Carter County) in 1875. Sweetwater County, at that time, was much larger than it is now, reaching as far north as the Montana border. South Pass City, located roughly 76 miles to the northeast, had become the county seat because of a gold rush in 1869. By the early 1870s, the boom was over, and South Pass City's population and influence dwindled. In 1875, the Territorial Legislature ordered the county seat to be moved to Green River. The county records traveled back and forth between the two towns, resulting in the loss of many vital county records.

With the establishment of the county seat in Green River, a courthouse was constructed in 1876, housing the county offices and what remained of the records. The two-story building was built of locally manufactured brick and stood on the same site as the present county courthouse.

Green River in 1876 was primed for development. Many of the buildings in Bryan, including the roundhouse and several residences, were relocated to Green River. Stores, rooming houses, and even a brewery sprang up. The community became a supply hub for outlying areas, servicing the new livestock, mining, and timber (tie hack) industries. The Union Pacific Railroad remained the primary employer in town. Throughout the early years, the town was dominated by the red-painted Union Pacific buildings. The railroad was the incentive for most new construction, including housing, stores, a hotel, and a meeting hall.

Several employees of the railroad served as mayors of early Green River. Thomas Seddon Taliaferro Jr., a station agent, was mayor from 1893 to 1896. Dr. Jacob W. Hawk, a company physician, served three nonconsecutive terms as mayor between 1900 and 1925. Dr. John Gilligan, another company physician, was mayor from 1901 to 1902.

The railroad provided early medical care in Green River. Dr. Gilligan arrived during the 1880s, and he served as physician until he was discharged for speaking to striking railroad workers. Doctors Jacob and Charlotte Hawk, a husband-and-wife team, arrived in 1896. Both had graduated from the University of Illinois Medical School. Charlotte Hawk was one of two women in her class, and she had suffered abuse and discrimination at school for stepping outside the strict gender roles of the period. With her arrival in Green River, things did not change, as the men who worked the rails were opposed to having a female doctor. "Dr. Charlotte," as she became known, was relegated to the role of nurse until she discovered her niche as the local obstetrician and gynecologist. She took care of much of the region's female population, from the leading ladies of Green River to the "working girls" at the Green House brothel, and was well loved by her patients.

The first school was established in the early 1870s and consisted of two small buildings. With time, Green River constructed a variety of public schools. Soon there was a water system and electrical service, though the latter operated only at night for some time. At first, all public and church activities took place in the Sweetwater County Courthouse. Dances and other social events were held there, as well as a community Sunday school.

The earliest church building in Green River was the Union Congregational Church. The building was dedicated on December 6, 1885, and boasted a congregation of seven members served by the Reverend Timothy Thirloway. In 1892, the Episcopalians built their church, which still stands. The Catholic church was built in 1884 on the present site of the Green River City Hall.

Green River's importance as a rail center grew in 1884, when the Oregon Short Line, a branch of the Union Pacific main line that served the Pacific Northwest, was completed. Green River was designated as the terminus of the short line and as the division point on the main line. This resulted in the addition of repair shops and the enlargement of the roundhouse.

The oldest financial institution in the county, the State Bank of Green River, was established in 1883. This financial institution returned to Green River after being sold to another bank. In the early 1890s, the incorporation of the town under the new state of Wyoming spurred further development. New businesses, including Robert Freedman's Wyoming Saloon and the Morris Mercantile, took advantage of the growing prosperity of the region. The Morris Mercantile was established by Edward J. Morris, son of Esther Hobart Morris, who was known as the mother of women's suffrage in Wyoming. The building housed the store, the post office, and the Morris State Bank. The second story contained offices and was serviced by an elevator, the first in Green River.

In 1896, Green River took the first step in the development of a minerals industry. During the drilling of a test oil well on the north shore of the Green River, soda brine was discovered. This mixture of saline mineral substances in solution was processed by the Green River Soda Works into sal soda or washing soda for use as a general cleanser. The soda works operated intermittently until World War II, when it closed and the well was capped.

Transportation routes other than the railroad served the town. Though the coming of the railroad ended the days of the Central Overland Express Stage Line, small feeder roads were still needed to connect outlying areas to the railroad. The Green River–South Pass stage road was one such line. Green River businesses, such as the Sweetwater Brewing Company, shipped their products north to Lander and Riverton and south into the Uinta Mountains.

In 1908, the Green River Navigation Company launched its flagship, the *Comet*, on its voyage from Green River to Linwood, Utah. The 40-ton stern-wheeler, built by Danish shipbuilder Holger Larsen, was launched with much ceremony on July 7. The downstream trip took about eight hours. However, due to river currents and trouble with sandbars, the return trip took about 33 hours, and supplemental coal had to be packed in by mule to fuel the craft. In spite of the troubles, the trip was deemed a great success by the *Green River Star*, which proclaimed, in typical flowery style, "The project is an assured fact, so let every enterprising citizen of Green River City and Sweetwater County aid the new enterprise by every word of encouragement." Commercial hauling on the river proved impractical, and the *Comet* soon became an excursion boat. Eventually, the ship was stripped, and the metal hull was sunk in the river. The remains were dredged out when gravel was taken from the river in the 1960s for the construction of the Flaming Gorge Dam.

Early mayors promoted city improvements, forwarding ordinances for the protection of trees, sidewalk construction, snow removal, the establishment of a fire department, the construction of a park, the construction of a bridge across the river, and the creation of a telephone company. Among them were Edward J. Morris (1891–1893 and 1896–1898), Thomas Seddon Taliaferro (1893–1896), Elmer E. Peters (1896–1898), and Robert H. Lawrence (1898–1900).

The world wars and the Great Depression brought changes to Green River. Another attempt was made at establishing a minerals industry. During World War I, Germany was one of the leading producers of potash, a strategic mineral then in short supply within the United States. The Liberty Potash Company was established in 1919 to process potash made from Wyomingite and limestone quarried in southwestern Wyoming. The venture was not long-lived, as the end of the war erased the shortages. After operating sporadically for several years, the plant closed in the 1940s.

The adoption of the Green River Ordinance was a response to the increase in door-to-door sales during the Great Depression. Green River's shift workers soon tired of constant knocking on their doors while they were trying to sleep, and they demanded action from the city council, which responded in November 1931 by passing the Green River Ordinance. This prohibited door-to-door selling unless the salesperson was specifically invited to go to a residence. The ordinance was challenged unsuccessfully in the courts by the Fuller Brush Company, and similar laws were adopted by other communities.

The town increased in size dramatically following World War II. Land was acquired on the south side of the river, and veterans' housing was constructed there. The most successful minerals venture also began. In 1938, the Mountain Fuel Supply Company had drilled a test hole for oil and gas 20 miles west of Green River, but had found a solid bed of trona 10 feet thick. Trona is processed into soda ash, a substance widely used in glass and metal fabrication as well as in the chemical industry. Production of soda ash began in 1948, and during the next 35 years, four other mines and processing plants were opened. The trona industry has grown into a major employer in Green River.

The growth of this industry, combined with developments in coal, oil, and gas, resulted in a boom during the 1970s. At this time, the railroad was replaced as the major employer in town. The population of 5,000 tripled in just 10 years, forcing housing, schools, and city services to expand rapidly. Most of the residential and business development happened on the south side of the river. To handle increased traffic, a new bridge was built over the river in 1951, and an overpass was completed over the rail yards in 1976. A new city hall was dedicated in 1982, and a city recreation center opened in 1987.

Green River's quirkiest government action occurred in 1994, when a tongue-in-cheek resolution was passed by the city council proclaiming the city as a refuge for aliens from Jupiter, as that planet was suffering a deluge of meteorites. The municipal airport was officially dubbed "the Greater Green River Intergalactic Spaceport" to facilitate alien refugee landings.

A second energy boom, focusing on natural gas products, began in the late 1990s, swelling the population of the town again. Much of the population of Green River commutes to work in the far-flung gas fields, mines, construction areas, and power-related industries of southwestern Wyoming. With rapid growth comes both opportunity and challenge. Without a doubt, the city will meet these with the same enthusiasm and industry that allowed an insignificant Overland Mail station to become a thriving community.

One

Palisades of the Green River

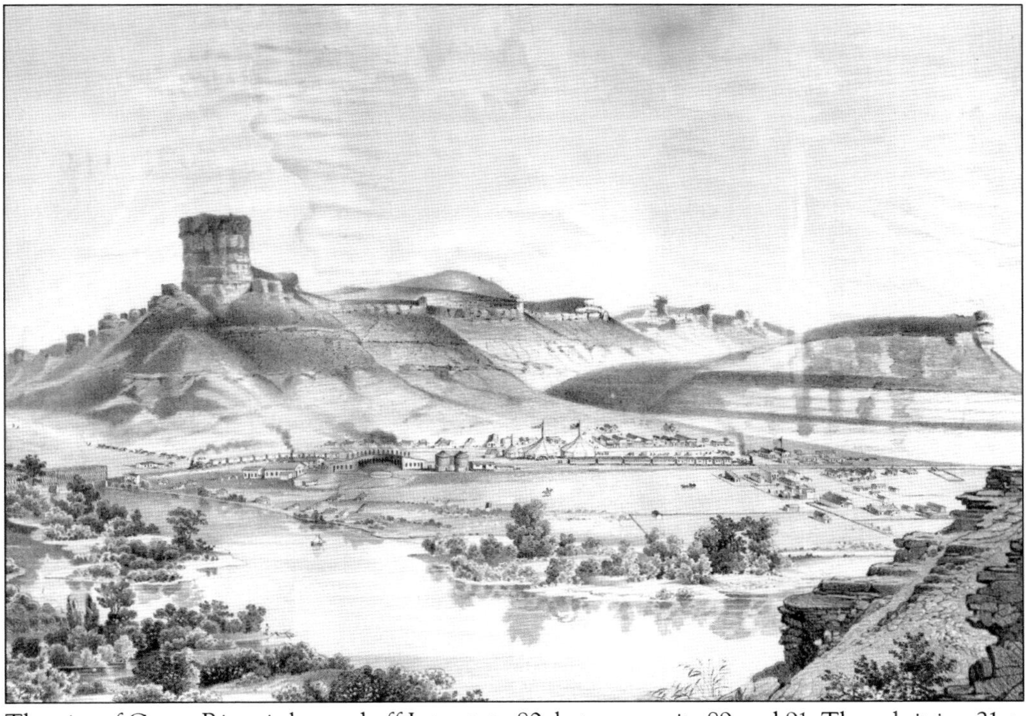

The city of Green River is located off Interstate 80, between exits 89 and 91. Though it is a 21st-century town, Green River owes much of its attraction to its prehistoric past. The industrious river has carved a unique backdrop of colorful stone formations, and the landscape surrounding Green River has been a constant source of inspiration to visitors and inhabitants alike. The majestic palisades of the river have been painted, sketched, and photographed throughout the city's history. These formations remain old friends, peering down and reminding us all of the history that has passed this way. This book documents but a fraction of all they have witnessed.

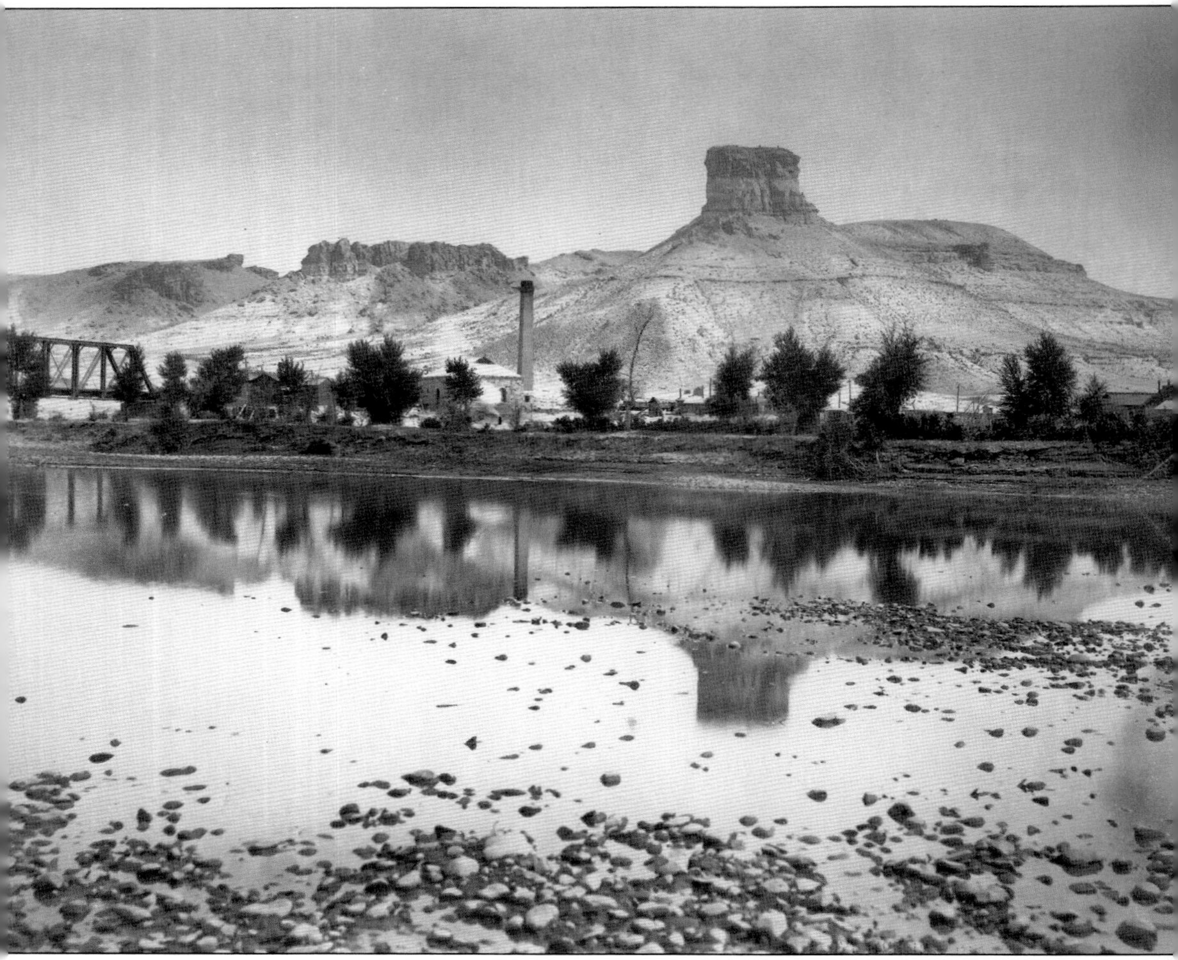

This 1869 image shows Castle Rock's reflection on the Green River. William Henry Jackson's photographic images predated his work as a premier landscape painter and documenter of westward expansion. Jackson worked throughout this area in the late 1860s as a teamster and photographer. His photographic images have much of the same monumental grandeur that characterized his paintings. Castle Rock, also referred to as Citadel Rock, towers directly above the city and is perhaps the defining feature of the city's skyline. As described in the *Pacific Tourist*, "Here is Solomon's temple petrified . . . Sure enough, it seemed as though some great temple once stood here, or several of them, and in the wrecks of time, left their gigantic pillars standing, as a reminder of their former greatness." (Courtesy of Sweetwater County Historical Museum.)

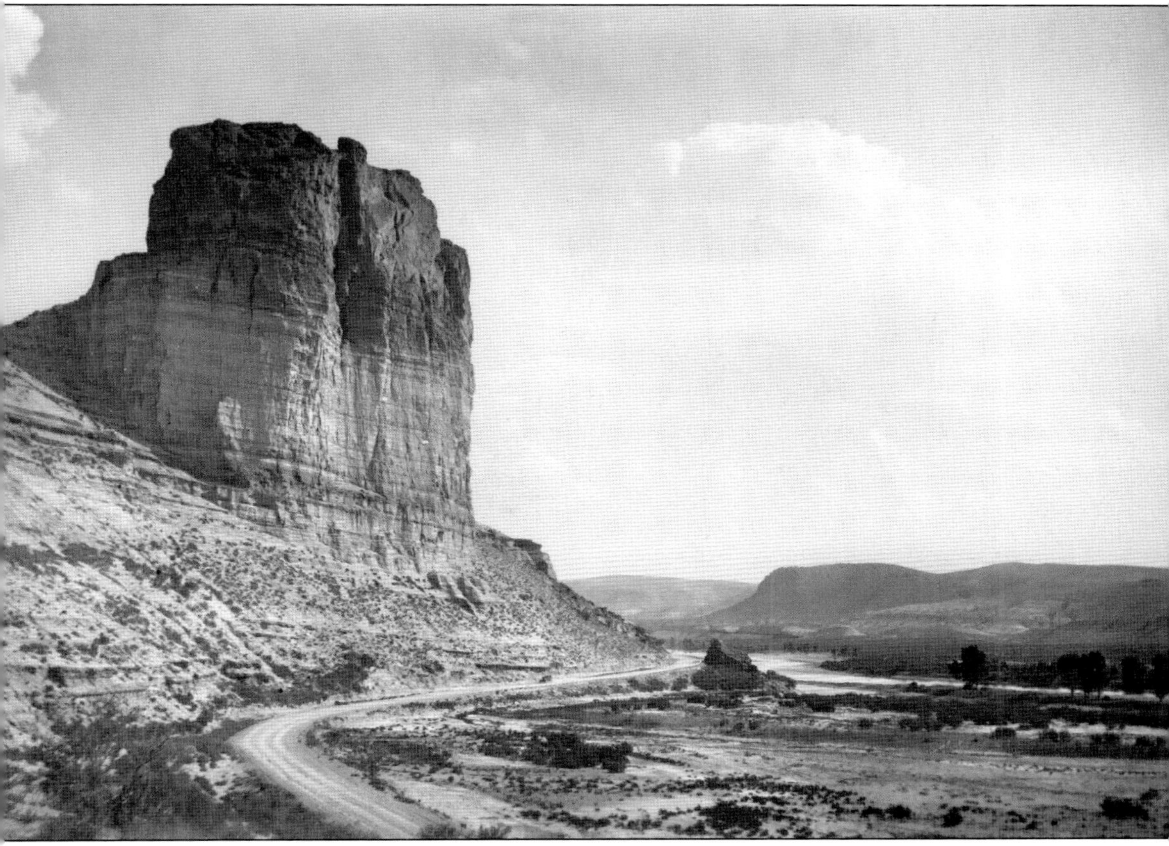

This is a typical view of Tollgate Rock, made famous in the paintings of important western artist Thomas Moran. It is seen here much as the artist might have viewed it in the 1870s when he created his famous paintings. It is fitting that the first subject of Moran's western sketches was Tollgate Rock, also known as Castle Butte, Split Rock, Toll Rock, and the Sleeping Giant. Tollgate Rock was named for the tolls collected by early settlers, who carved a roadway on the south side of the rock and placed a toll chain across the road. In the 20th century, a small outcrop that served as the southern anchor point for the barrier chain was removed when the road was expanded. Much of the material used to construct the community of Green River came from the vicinity of Tollgate Rock. (Courtesy of Sweetwater County Historical Museum.)

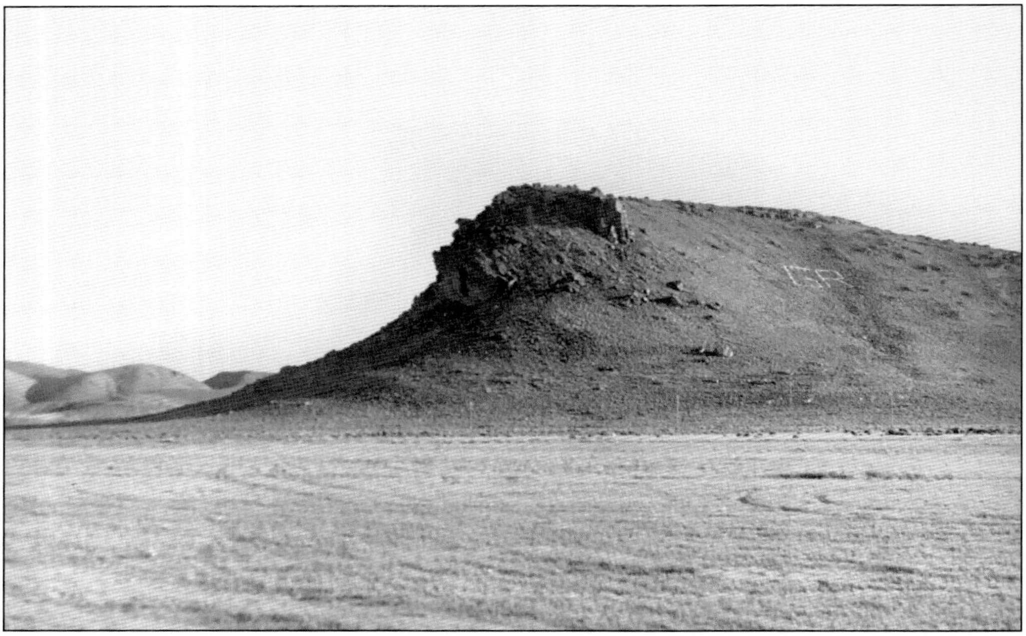

Man's Face Rock is also known as Old Man's Face Rock, Profile Rock, and Face Rock. This curious feature is located within the city limits on the south side of the Green River, near Man's Face Street. The Overland Stage Road, also called the Overland Trail, passed beneath the nose of Man's Face Rock. (Courtesy of Sweetwater County Historical Museum.)

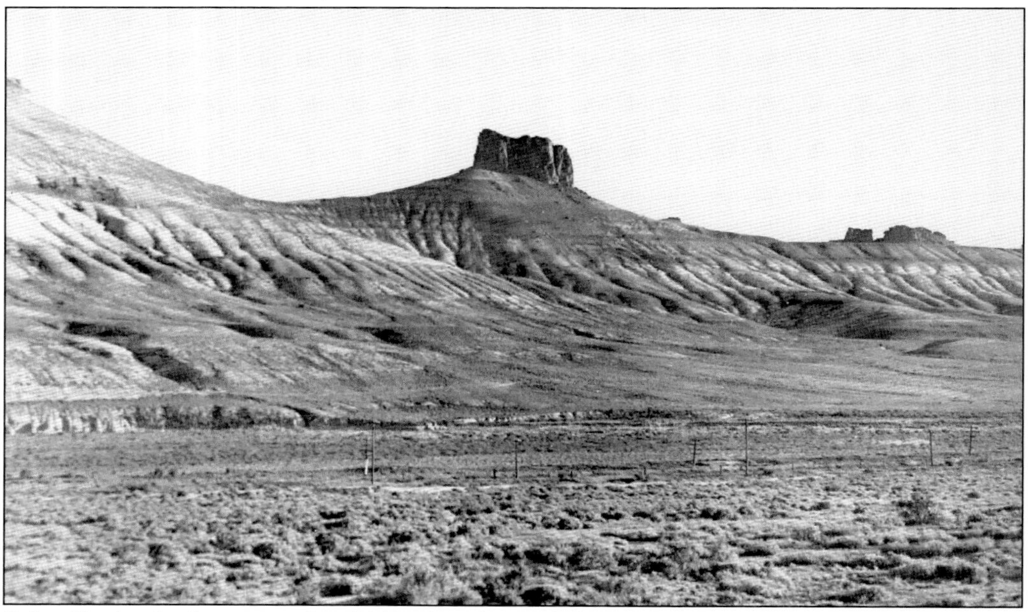

Pulpit Rock, also known as Smith's Rock, is located three miles east of the city of Green River. The story behind the naming of the rock places Brigham Young here in 1847 during the Mormon migration to the Valley of the Great Salt Lake. However, Young likely never passed within 25 miles of this rock during 1847, as his party crossed the river well to the north. Pictured to the right of Pulpit Rock is Kissing Rock. (Courtesy of Sweetwater County Historical Museum.)

Two

STARTS AND STOPS
1862–1889

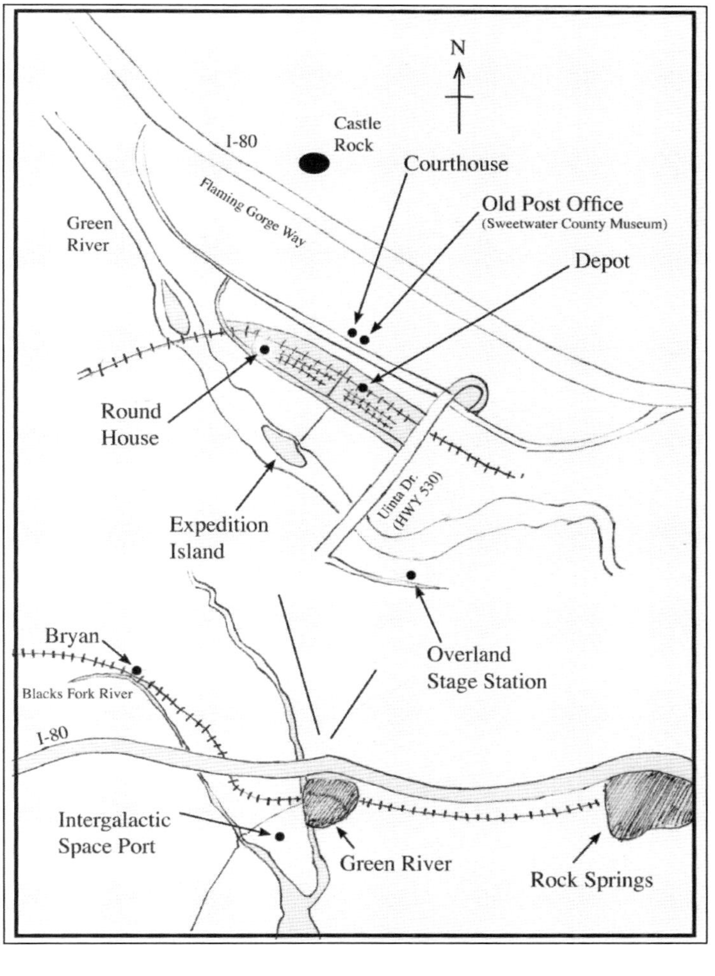

The early days of Green River were characterized by a series of starts and stops in its development. The town began as an Overland Stage station and had great plans to become a railroad switching point. When the railroad bypassed the fledgling community, it withered and almost died. Green River's dreams of growth began anew when a drought forced the railroad to return. This map shows many of the places mentioned in the text. (Courtesy of Sweetwater County Historical Museum.)

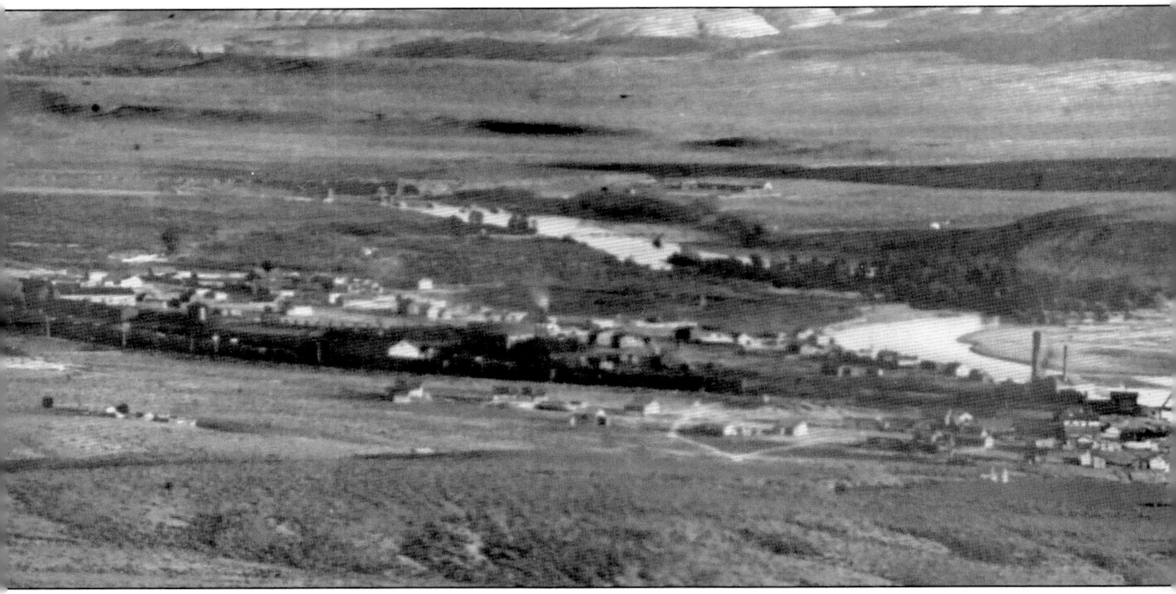

In 1862, the postmaster general of the United States moved the Overland Mail route from the Oregon-California Trail to the Overland Trail, a southerly route through Bridger Pass. A station was placed near the Green River crossing on the south side of what later became the city of Green River. During the height of Native American hostilities, such stations had a telegraph operator and a small military contingent. These buildings were the beginning of the city of Green River. This 1899 image is one of the few surviving views that show the station. (Courtesy of Sweetwater County Historical Museum.)

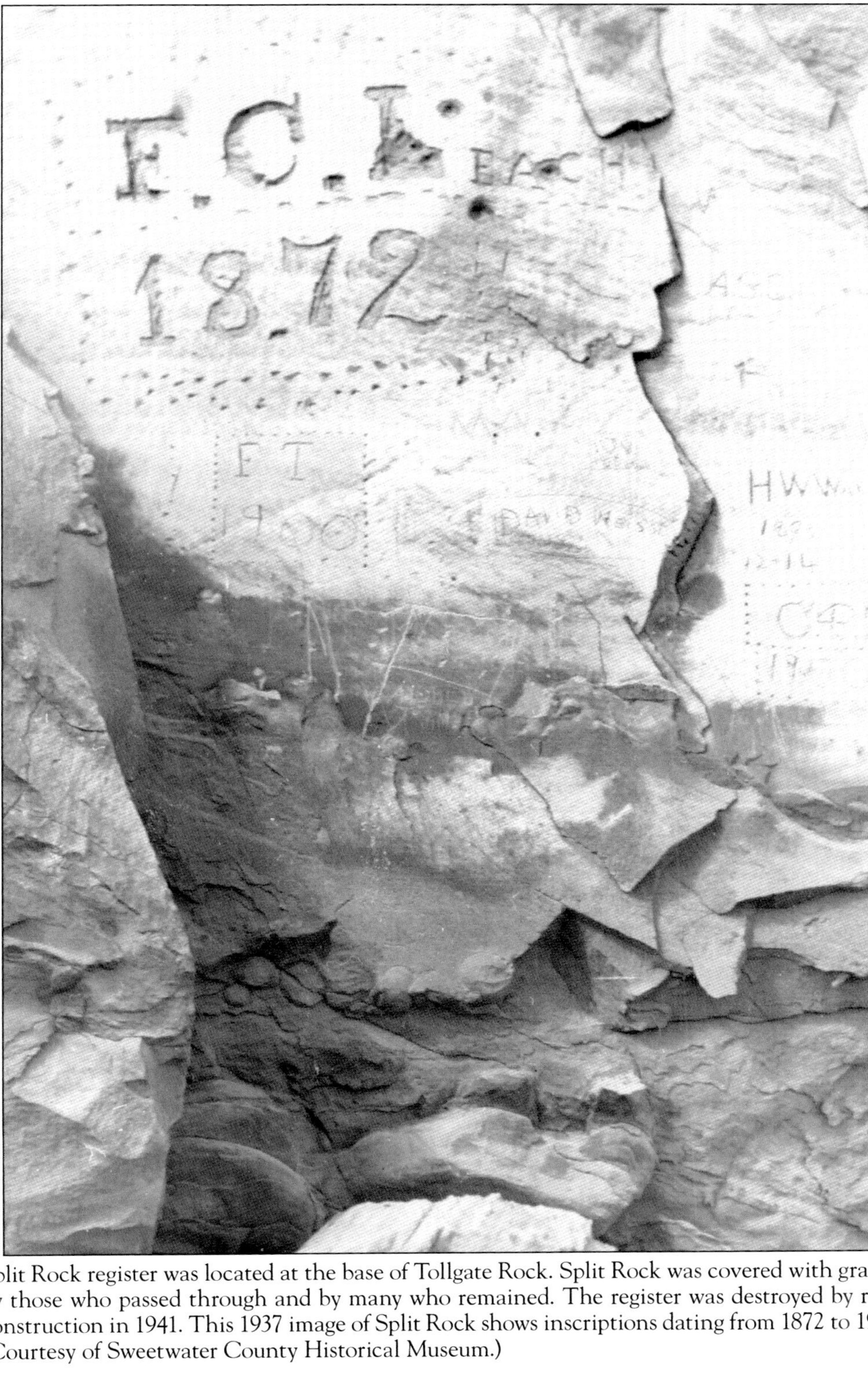

Split Rock register was located at the base of Tollgate Rock. Split Rock was covered with graffiti by those who passed through and by many who remained. The register was destroyed by road construction in 1941. This 1937 image of Split Rock shows inscriptions dating from 1872 to 1914. (Courtesy of Sweetwater County Historical Museum.)

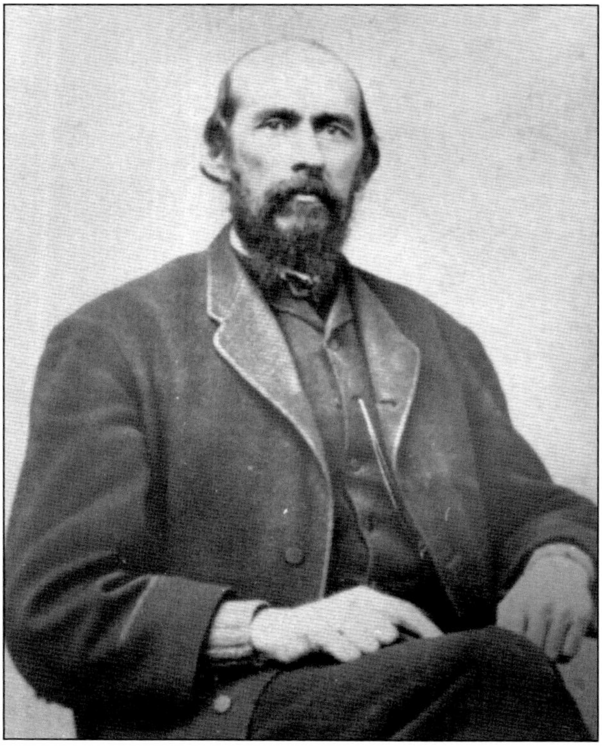

The original owner of historic Green River, Samuel Ichabod Field, was a true entrepreneur. Portions of his 160-acre homestead were purchased by the city of Green River and the Union Pacific Railroad. Field ran a courier company known as the Jackass Express, the Union Pacific Eating House, and the store that outfitted both of the John Wesley Powell expeditions. (Courtesy of Sweetwater County Historical Museum.)

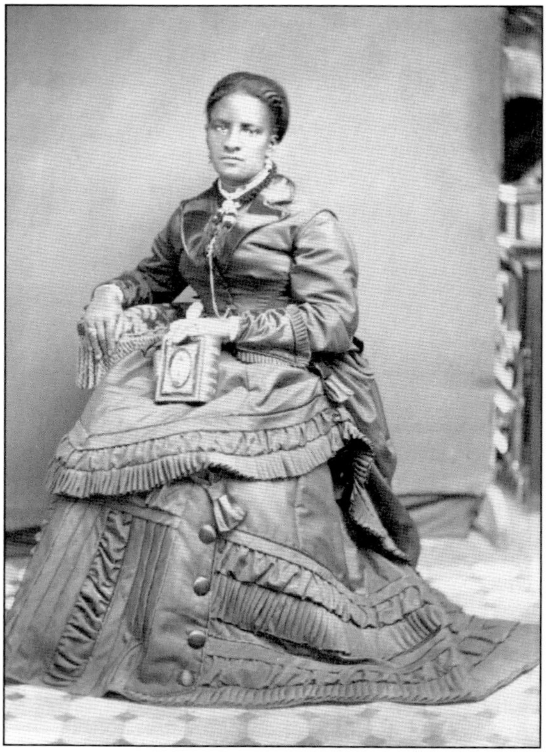

A member of Samuel I. Field's household was his housekeeper, dressmaker, and midwife, "Auntie" Nancy Phillips. She and her family were among the first African American residents of Green River. A former slave, Phillips became an employee at the Field household after leaving an employer in New York who had allegedly tried to poison her and her child. (Courtesy of Sweetwater County Historical Museum.)

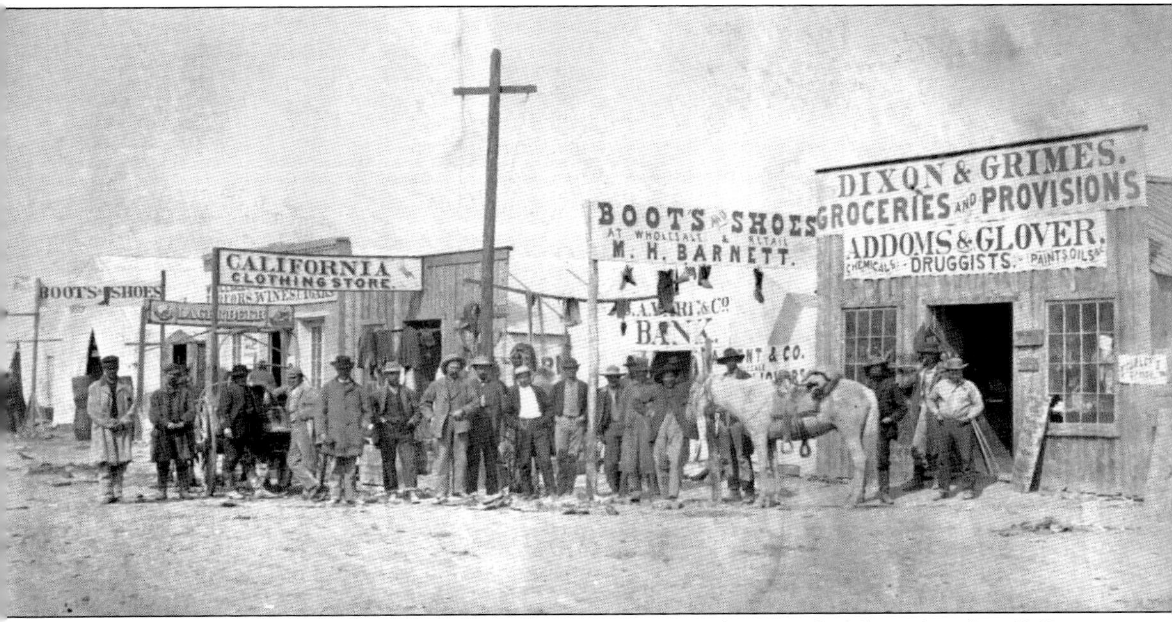

An image by Arundel Hull shows a view of Green River prior to the arrival of the railroad in 1868. In the center of the photograph, just to the left of the telegraph pole, is Jack Morrow, the closest thing that Green River had to an organized crime boss in the 1860s. Morrow came west as a teamster on an ammunition wagon. He sold the ammunition along the route and got himself kicked off the wagon train before the delivery was made. While in Wyoming, Morrow ran a freight company and a coal mine and filled timber contracts for the railroad. To Morrow's right is Leigh Freeman, publisher of the transcontinental railroad's traveling newspaper, the *Frontier Index*. To Morrow's left is a man who appears to be William G. Tittsworth, a local rancher, frontiersman, and author. (Courtesy of Denver Public Library, Western History Collection, Arundel Hull, Z-5795.)

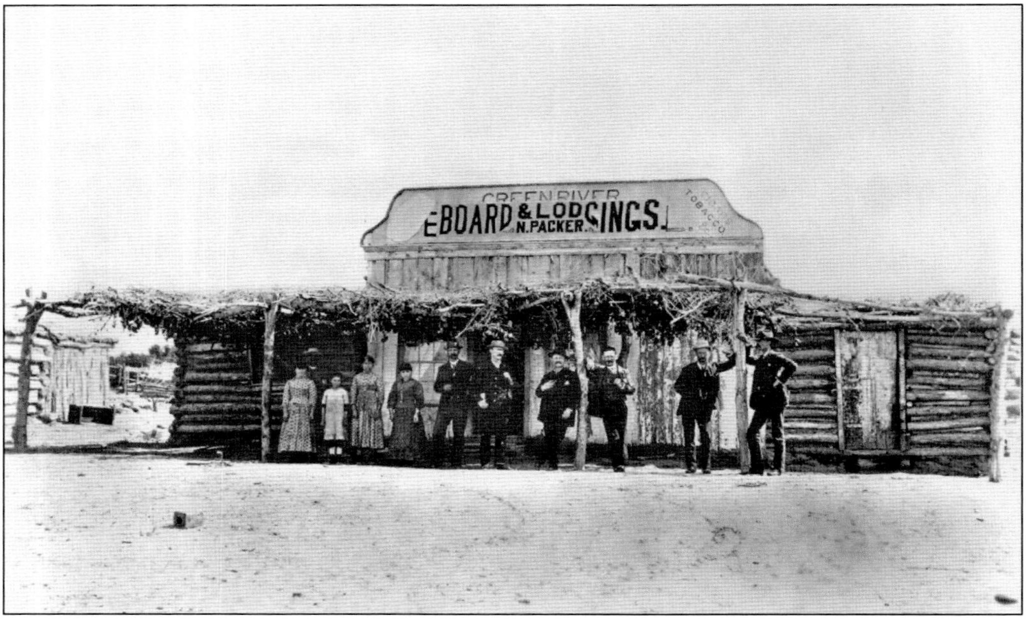

This is an 1868 image of the Green River Board and Lodgings building, run by N. Packer. The structure appears to be the former Empire Hall converted into a boardinghouse. None of the seven men and four girls seen here have been identified. (See if you can find the seventh man.) (Courtesy of Union Pacific Museum.)

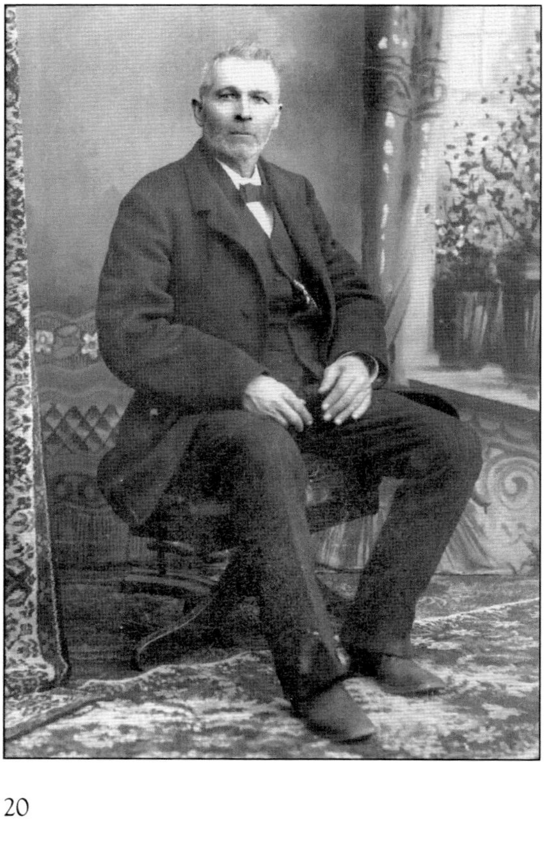

Pat "Paddy" Barrett was one of the pre-railroad inhabitants of Green River who also homesteaded just outside town. Barrett financed the construction of the original Green River building for the Sweetwater County Courthouse in 1875. He was an entrepreneur, running a mercantile and a sheep and cattle business. His business suffered at the hands of famous outlaw Butch Cassidy, who allegedly rustled Barrett's livestock. (Courtesy of Sweetwater County Historical Museum.)

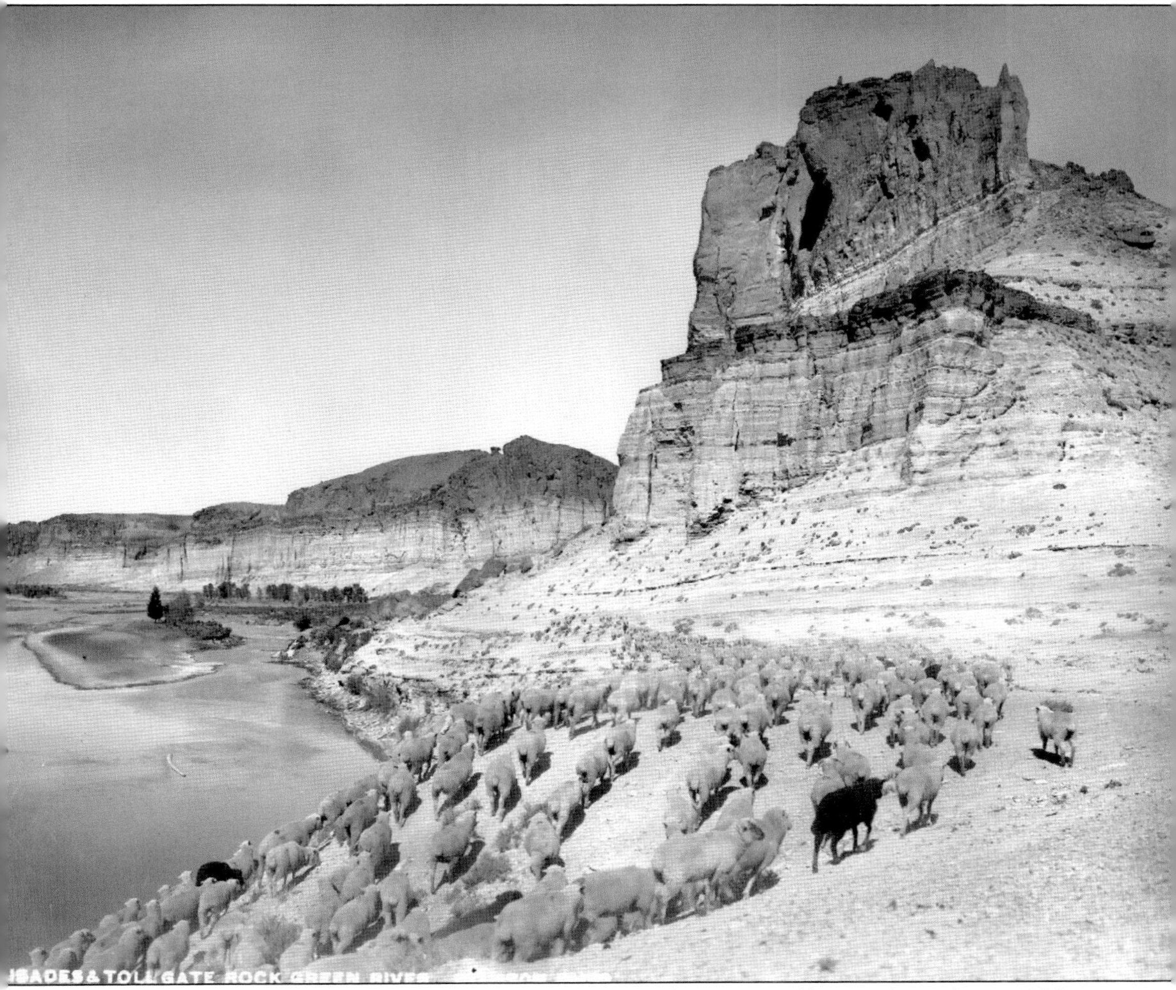

One of the earliest industries in the Green River area was the raising of livestock. In this *c.* 1890 image, a sheep drive passes through the Green River Palisades and Tollgate Rock. This sheep trail eventually became the main road west, and it was followed by the Lincoln Highway in 1924. Many of the founding families of Green River were involved in the livestock industry. Fledgling criminals such as Butch Cassidy are reputed to have gathered some of their ill-gotten gains from the herds in the Green River area. (Courtesy of Wyoming State Archives.)

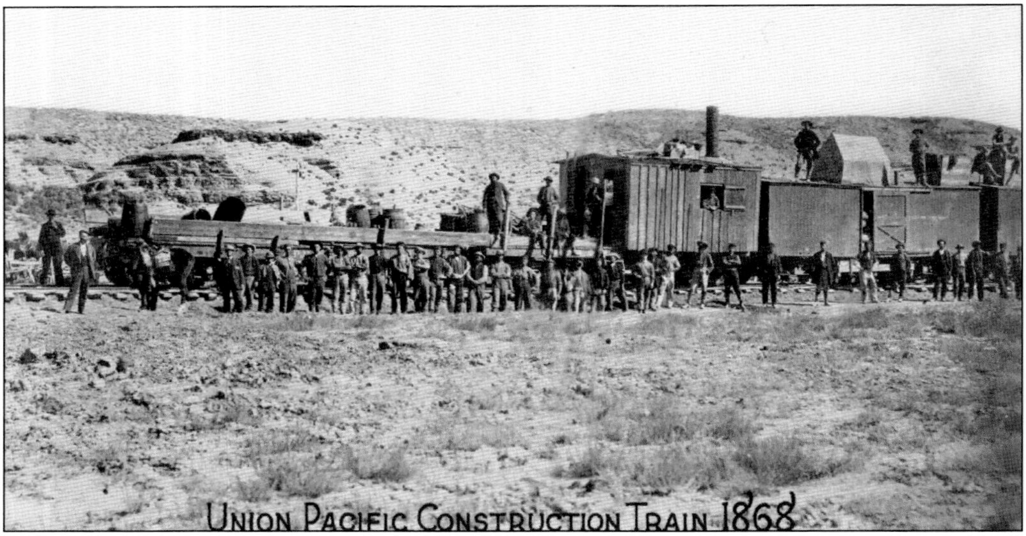

In 1868, the railroad laid track through Green River. The *Philadelphia Bulletin* described the construction: "It is a grand Anvil Chorus that those sturdy sledges are playing across the plains. It is in triple time, three strokes to a spike. There are ten spikes to a rail, four hundred rails to a mile, eighteen hundred miles to San Francisco!" (Courtesy of Sweetwater County Historical Museum.)

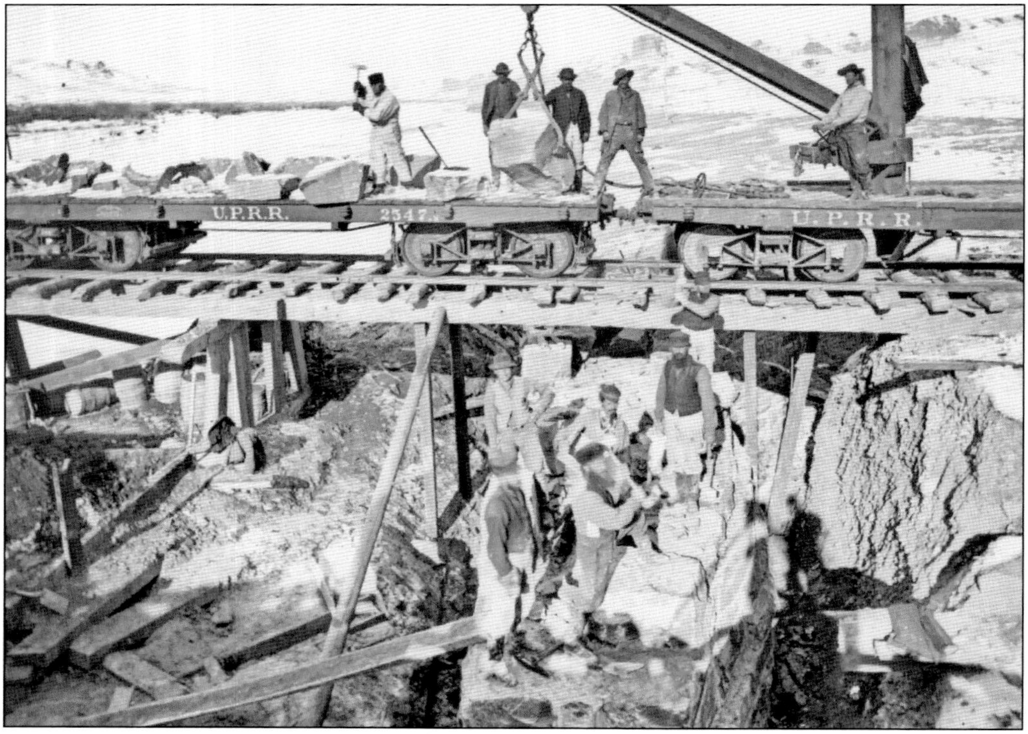

During their epic race against the Central Pacific Railroad in 1868, the Union Pacific Railroad's construction crews placed a temporary wooden bridge, depicted here, within Green River. This wooden edifice carried rail traffic while the permanent bridge was being built adjacent to it. (Courtesy of Oakland Museum.)

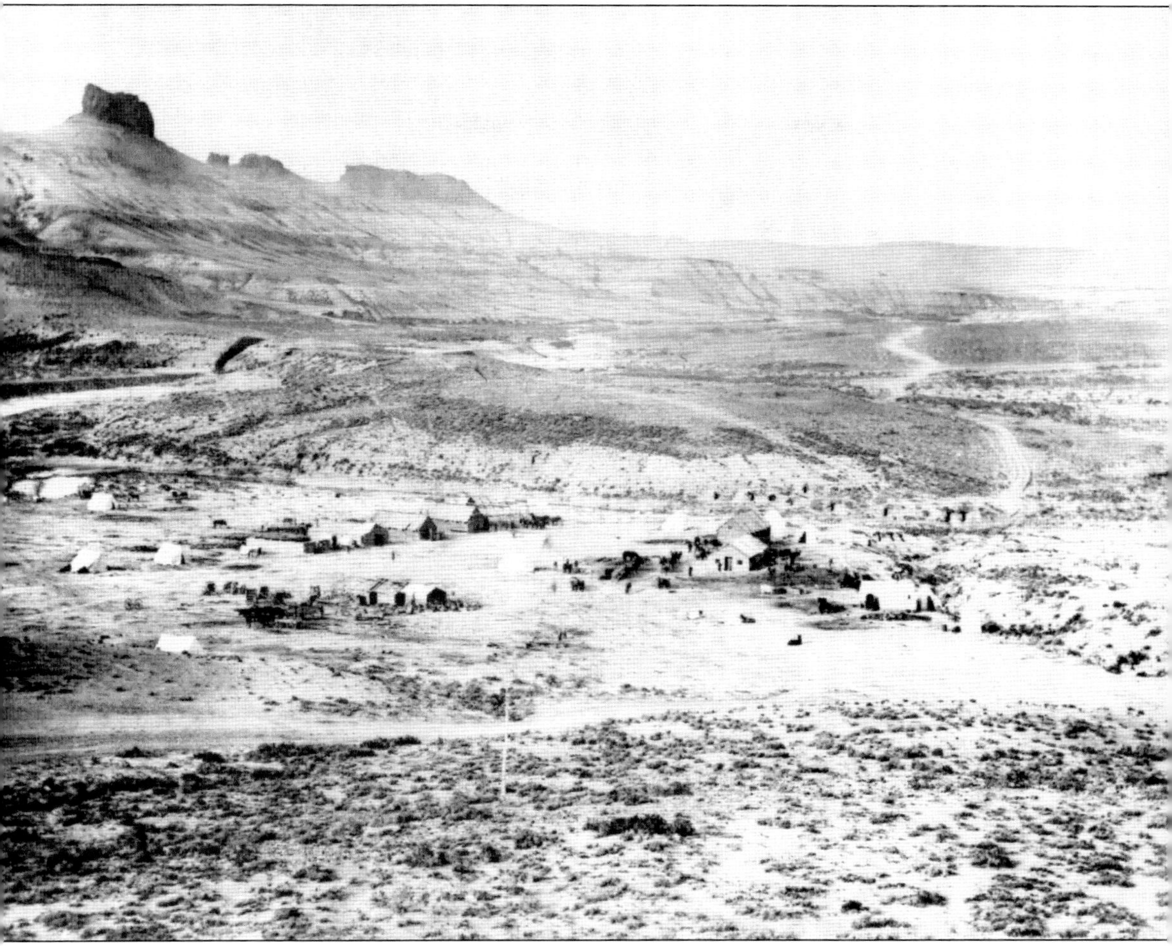

Construction through the Bitter Creek Valley to the Green River involved extensive down-cutting in order to maintain the grade. Lewis Carmichael ramrodded the massive excavations. The temporary construction camp for his crews, located east of Green River, bore his name. (Courtesy of United States Geological Survey.)

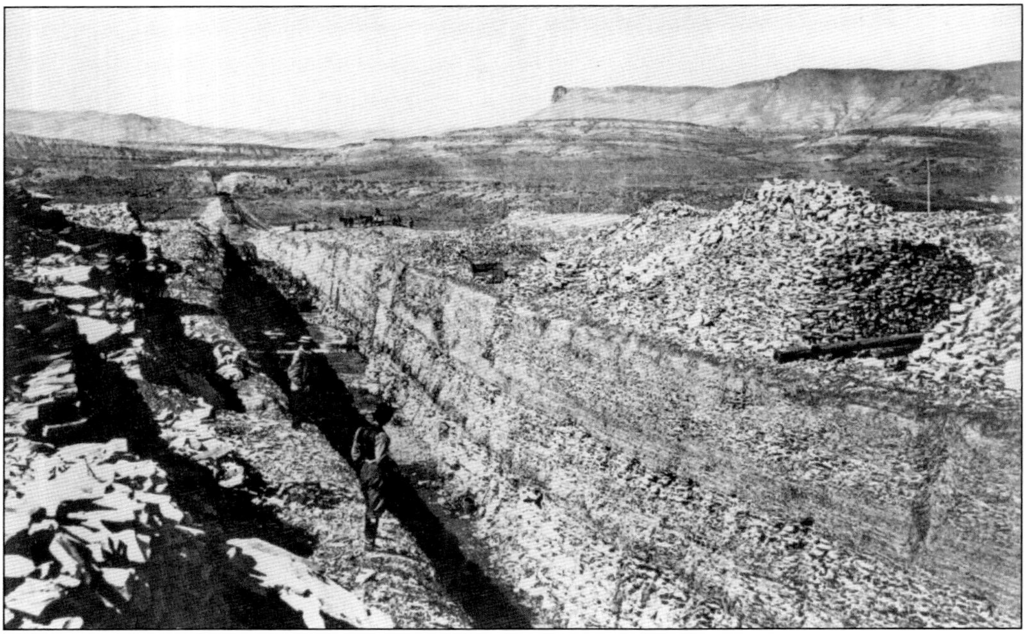

Crews operating out of Carmichael's Camp excavated the steep cut at Burning Rock in 1868. The cut is so named because of the presence of oil shale, which, when ignited, burned for several days. Another nearby cut is called Fish Cut because of the presence of fossil fish. (Courtesy of United States Geological Survey.)

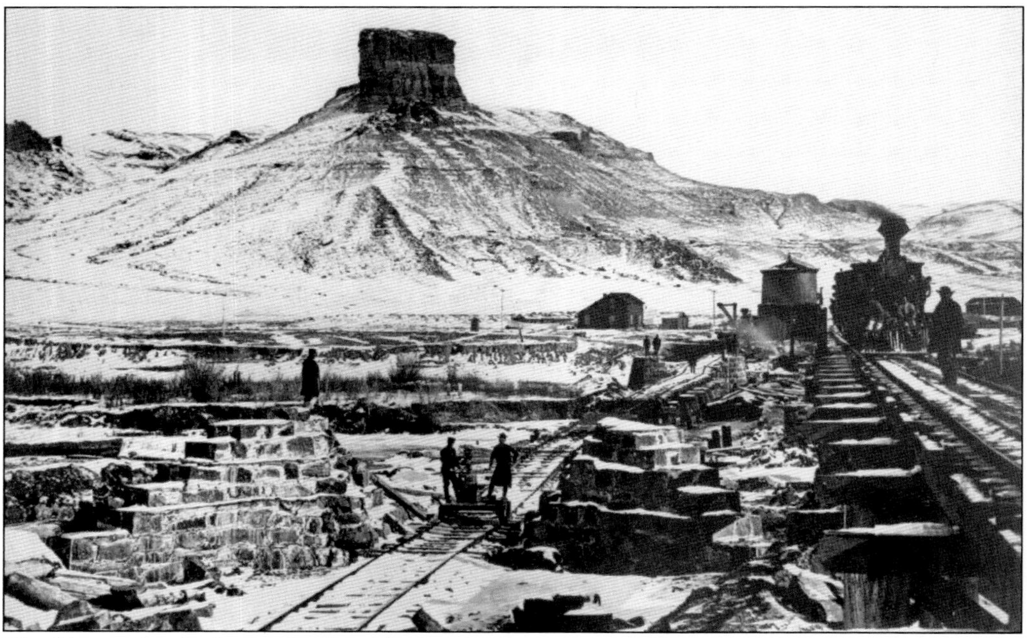

The Union Pacific laid rails through Green River in November 1868. Pictured to the right is one of the first locomotives to cross the newly built permanent bridge. To the left, workers ride a handcar on the temporary wooden structure. Photographer Andrew J. Russell labeled the prominent landmark Castle Rock as Citadel Rock. (Courtesy of United States Geological Survey.)

Andrew J. Russell traveled through this area at least three times between 1868 and 1869, working as a photographer for the Union Pacific Railroad and the U.S. Geological Survey. In this 1868 image, a locomotive is being readied for departure. The engine has yet to be attached to the cars. (Courtesy of Oakland Museum.)

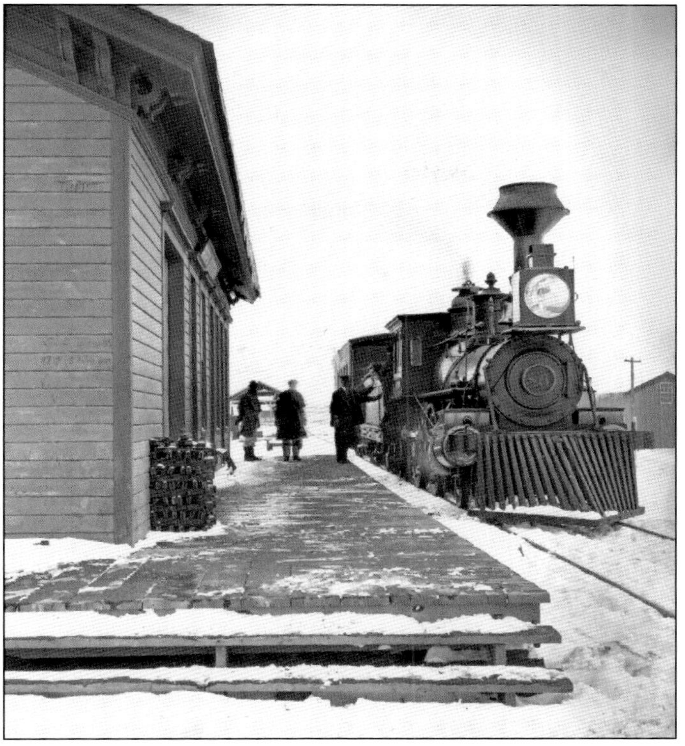

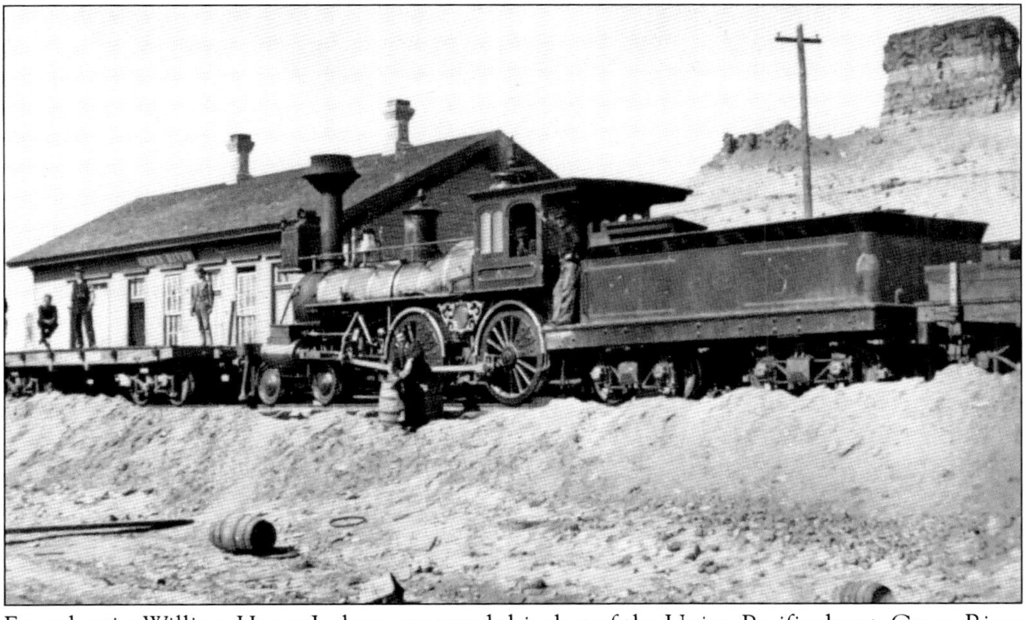

Famed artist William Henry Jackson captured this shot of the Union Pacific depot, Green River Station, in 1868. The earliest engines on the transcontinental railway, such as the one pictured, were wood burners. As western coal reserves were developed, the wood burners were phased out. The wooden-framed depot building was removed in 1910 to make way for a large brick structure, which still stands today. (Courtesy of United States Geological Survey.)

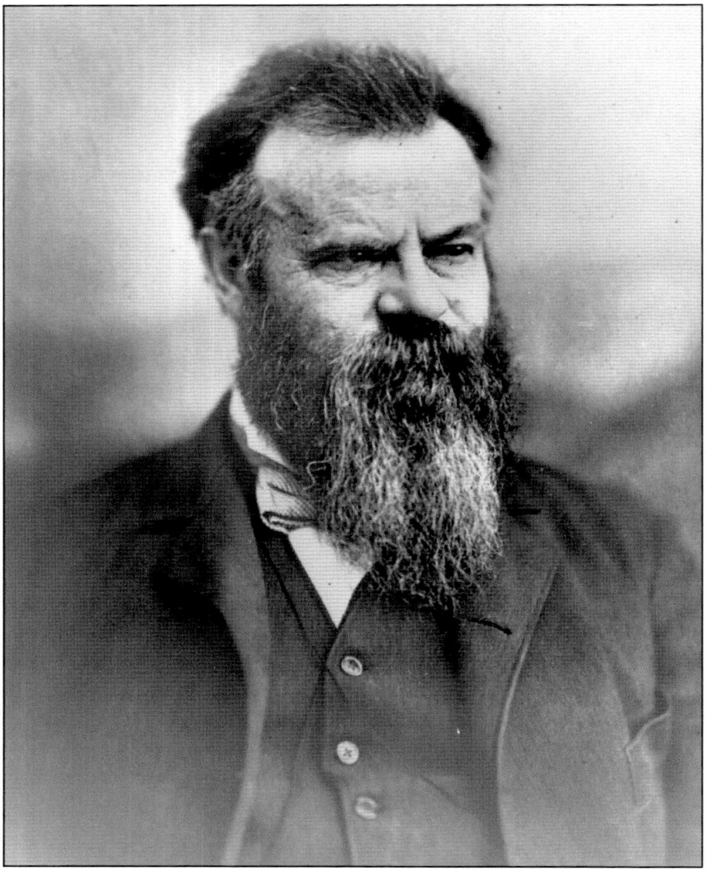

With his explorations of the Green and Colorado Rivers in 1869 and 1871, John Wesley Powell put Green River on the map. Powell was a disabled veteran who had lost his right arm in the Civil War. He was appointed director of the Smithsonian's Bureau of Ethnology and director of the U.S. Geological Survey. He died in 1902 and is buried in Arlington National Cemetery. (Courtesy of United States Geological Survey.)

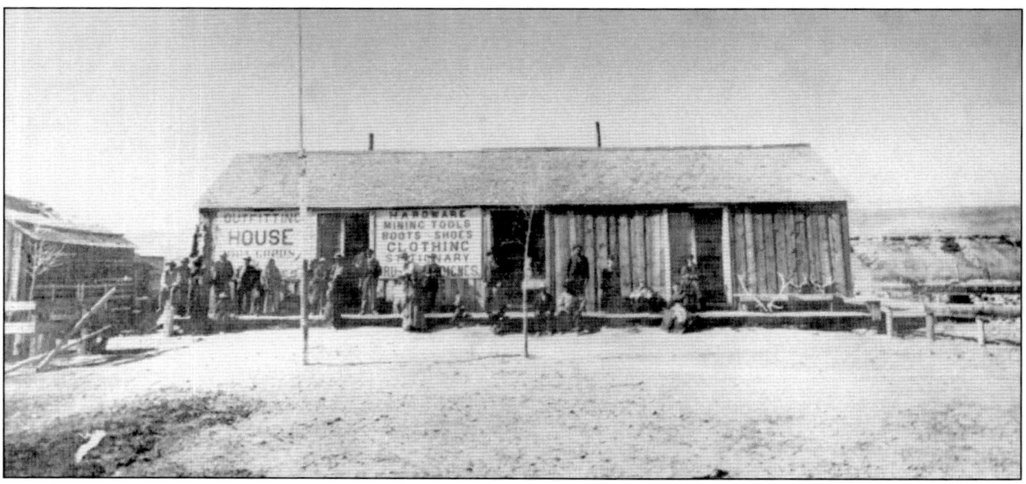

The unofficial headquarters of the Powell expeditions, Samuel "Jake" Field's store, is shown here in 1871. The store provided supplies for the trip, as well as other items necessary for the comfort of the explorers. John Sumner recalled, "We camped and awaited orders and in the meantime tried to drink all the whiskey there was in town. The result was a failure, as Jake Fields persisted in making it faster than we could drink it." (Courtesy of United States Geological Survey.)

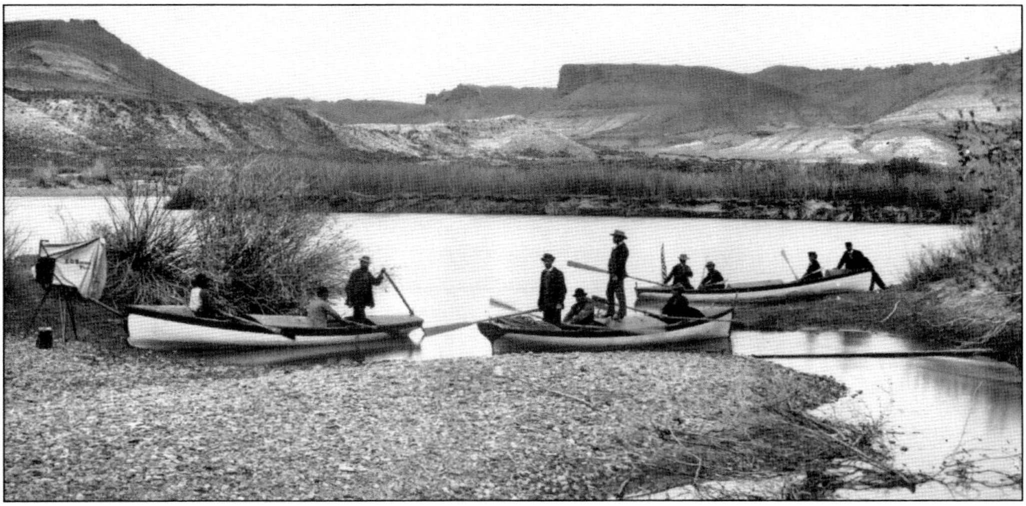

On his quest to explore the Colorado River system, Maj. John Wesley Powell set off from Green River on two separate occasions. This Elias O. Beaman photograph from the 1871 expedition shows the members of Powell's crew with their boats, the *Emma Dean*, the *Nellie Powell*, and the *Canonita*. Powell's men were undaunted by the doomsayers at Field's store, who predicted the expedition's undoing. (Courtesy of United States Geological Survey.)

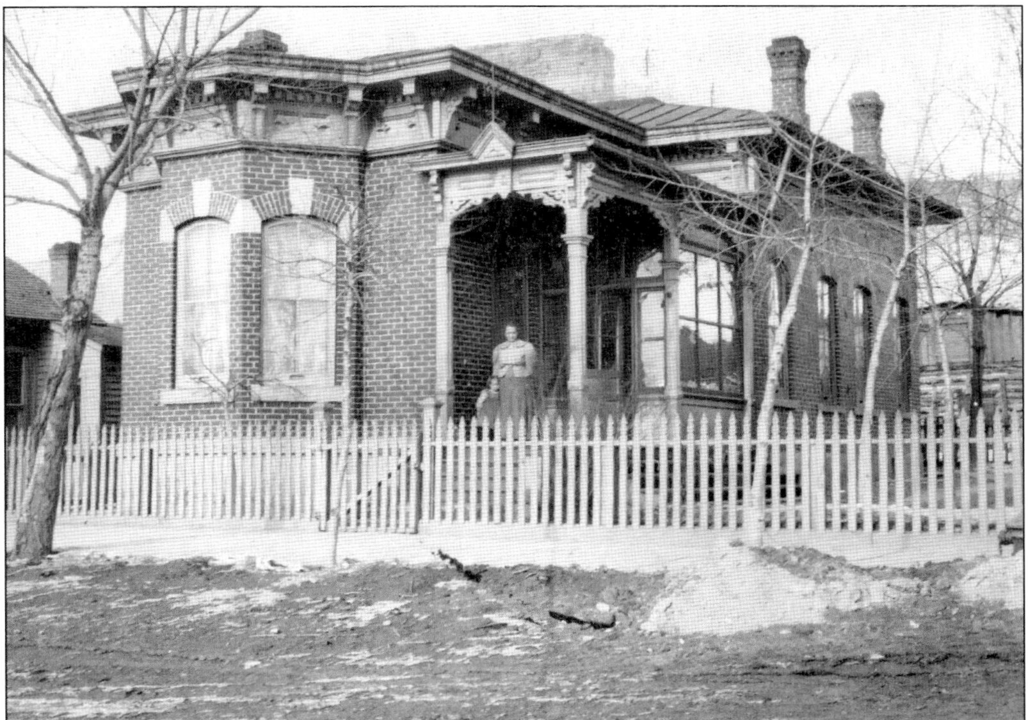

This home was built of locally made bricks by Karl Spinner Sr. in 1880. Spinner came to Green River that year and purchased the Green River Brewery, located just to the east of his home. Hugo Gaensslen was the brewmaster, and he became the owner of this home, as well as the brewery, when Spinner left Green River in 1891. (Courtesy of Sweetwater County Historical Museum.)

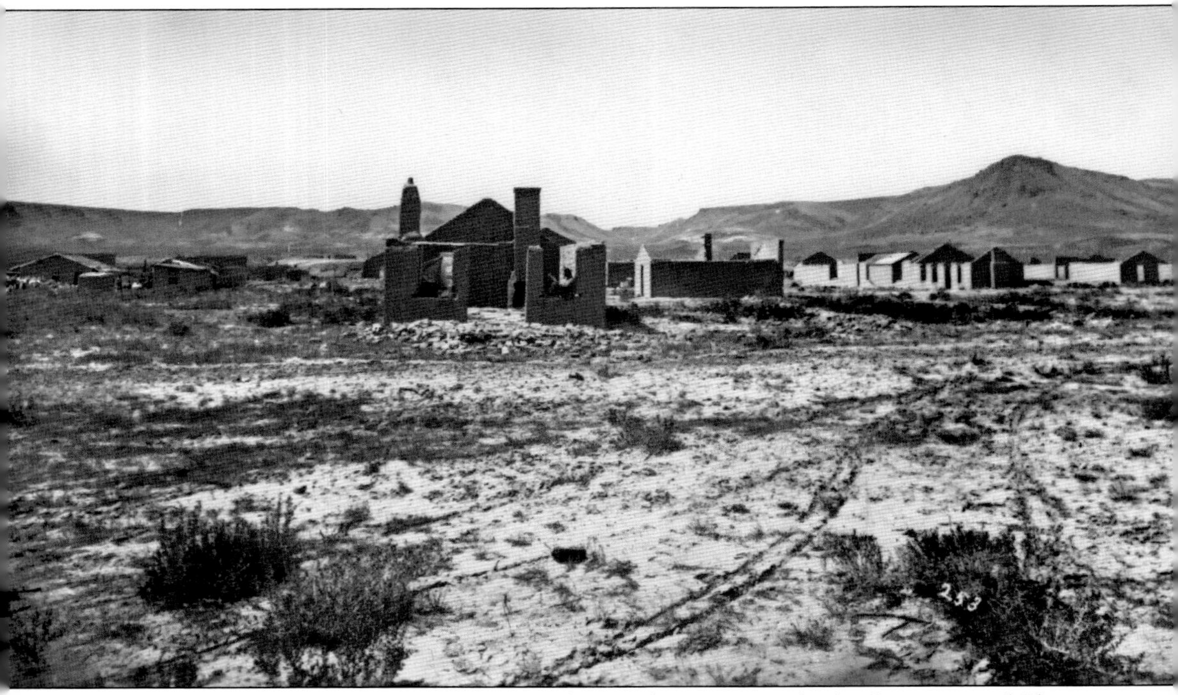

The city of Green River was laid out in July 1868 by H. M. Hook, the first mayor of Cheyenne, shortly before his tragic drowning death at the Red Creek rapids, located south of town. Hook's widow offered $1,000 for information about the location of her husband's grave. At least three supposedly legitimate locations were identified. In September 1868, there were more than 2,000 people in Green River, but by May 1869, it was almost empty. Most of its inhabitants moved west to Bryan with the railroad. Pictured in 1871 are the abandoned adobe structures that were once part of Green River. (Courtesy of United States Geological Survey.)

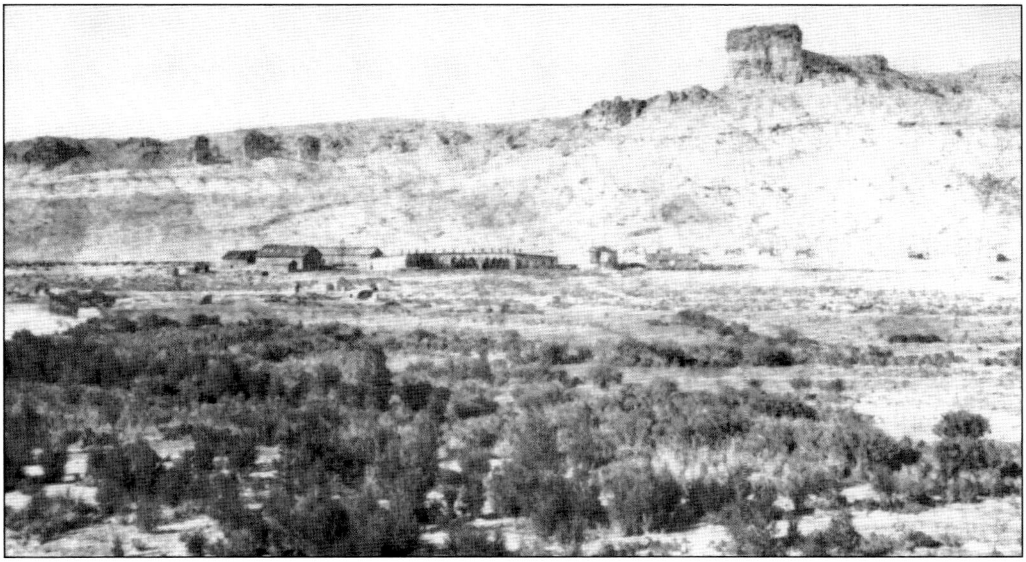

In 1871, the Black's Fork River near Bryan dried up, and the need for water to help power the steam engines drew the Union Pacific Railroad back to Green River. It was Bryan's turn to become a ghost town and Green River's turn to show what it could do. Charles R. Savage photographed Green River with its newly acquired roundhouse, which was dismantled in Bryan and moved within weeks to its new home. The Union Pacific remains a major employer in Green River today. (Above courtesy of Church of Jesus Christ of Latter-Day Saints Archives and Intellectual Services. Below courtesy of Sweetwater County Historical Museum.)

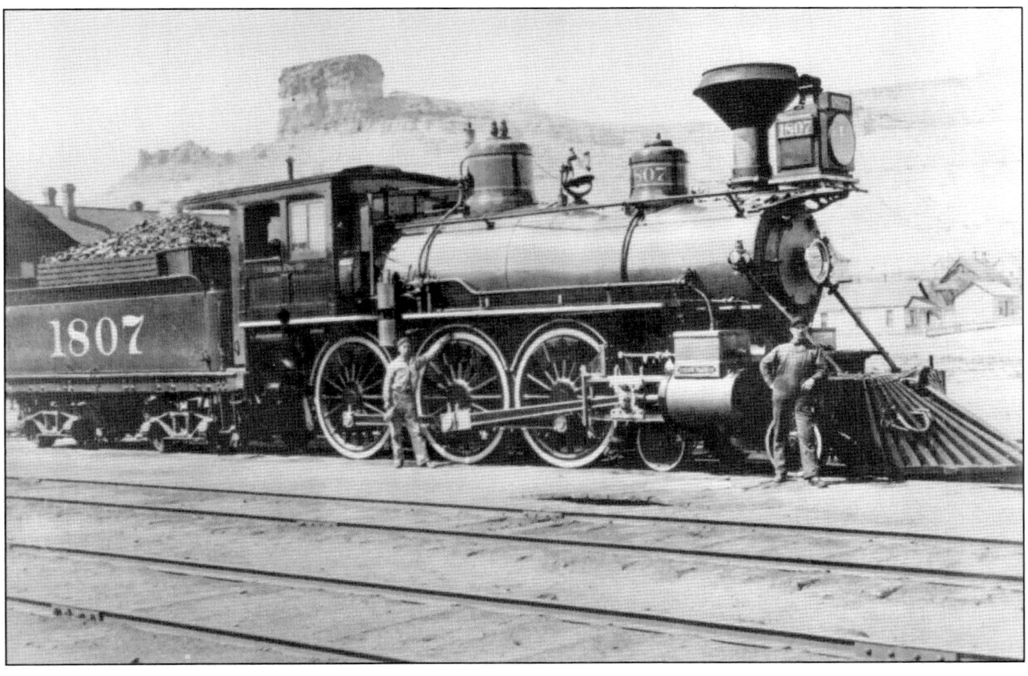

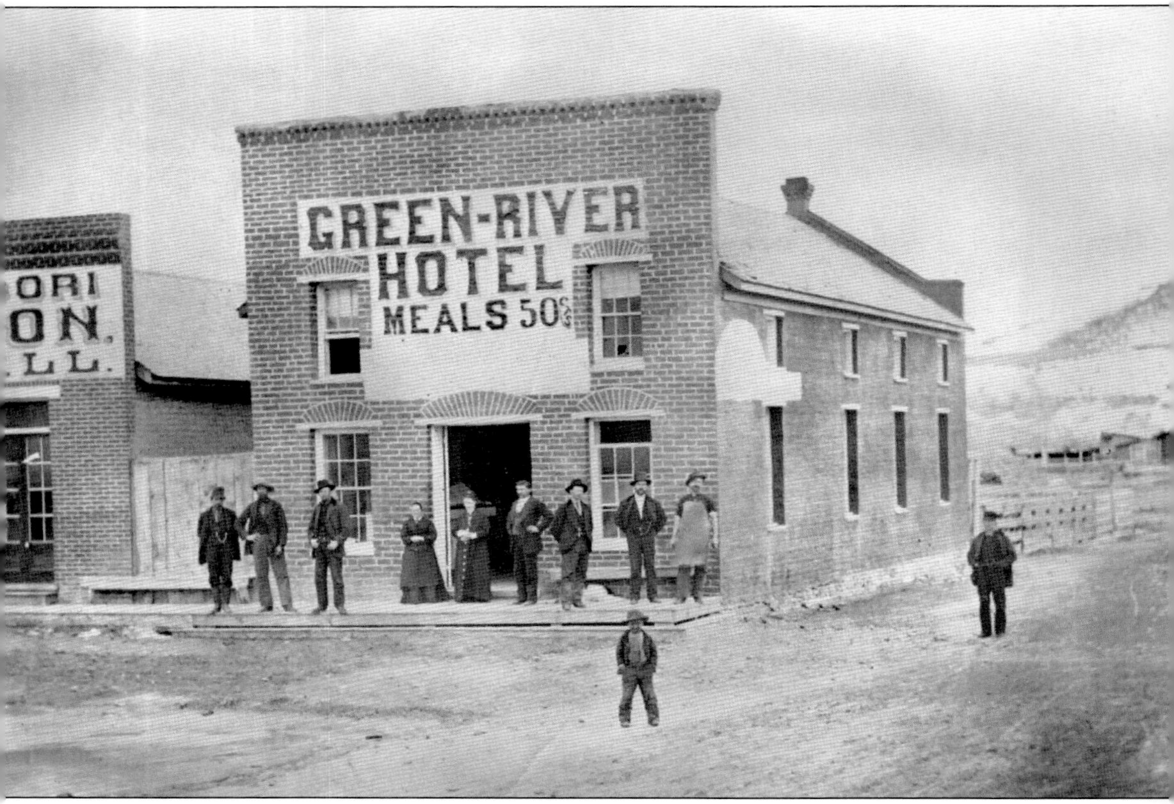

The Green River Hotel, built around 1875 by Peter Appel, provided travelers with a comfortable place to stay. The hotel had a handful of owners over the years. It was demolished when the Union Pacific Railroad expanded the rail yard in 1919, removing an entire block on the south side of the tracks. (Courtesy of Wyoming State Archives.)

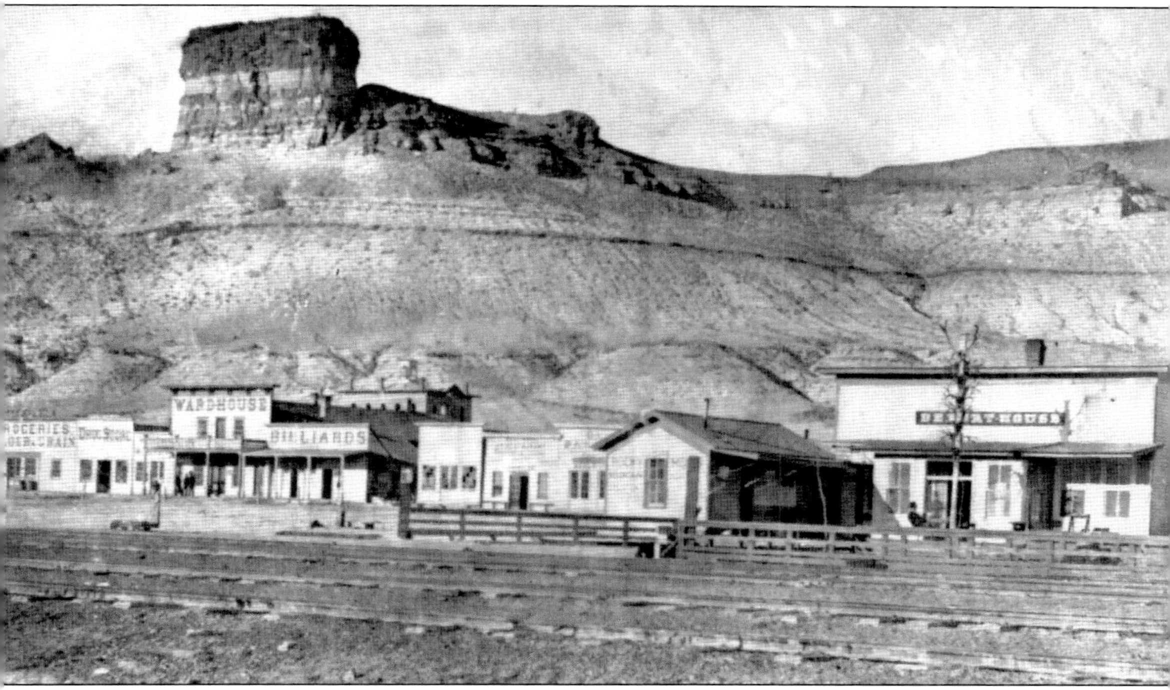

This photograph, taken around 1876, is one of the earliest images of downtown Green River. It depicts the growing community beneath Castle Rock. Businesses seen here include the Ward House (which included a bar and restaurant), the OK Saloon, a restaurant, a grocery store, a rock shop, and the Desert House (which also included a restaurant and bar). The Desert House was the official Union Pacific Railroad eating house and was operated by Samuel I. Field, one of the founders of Green River. The city had become the county seat of Sweetwater County in 1875. The courthouse, under construction, is visible behind the Ward House. (Courtesy of Sweetwater County Historical Museum.)

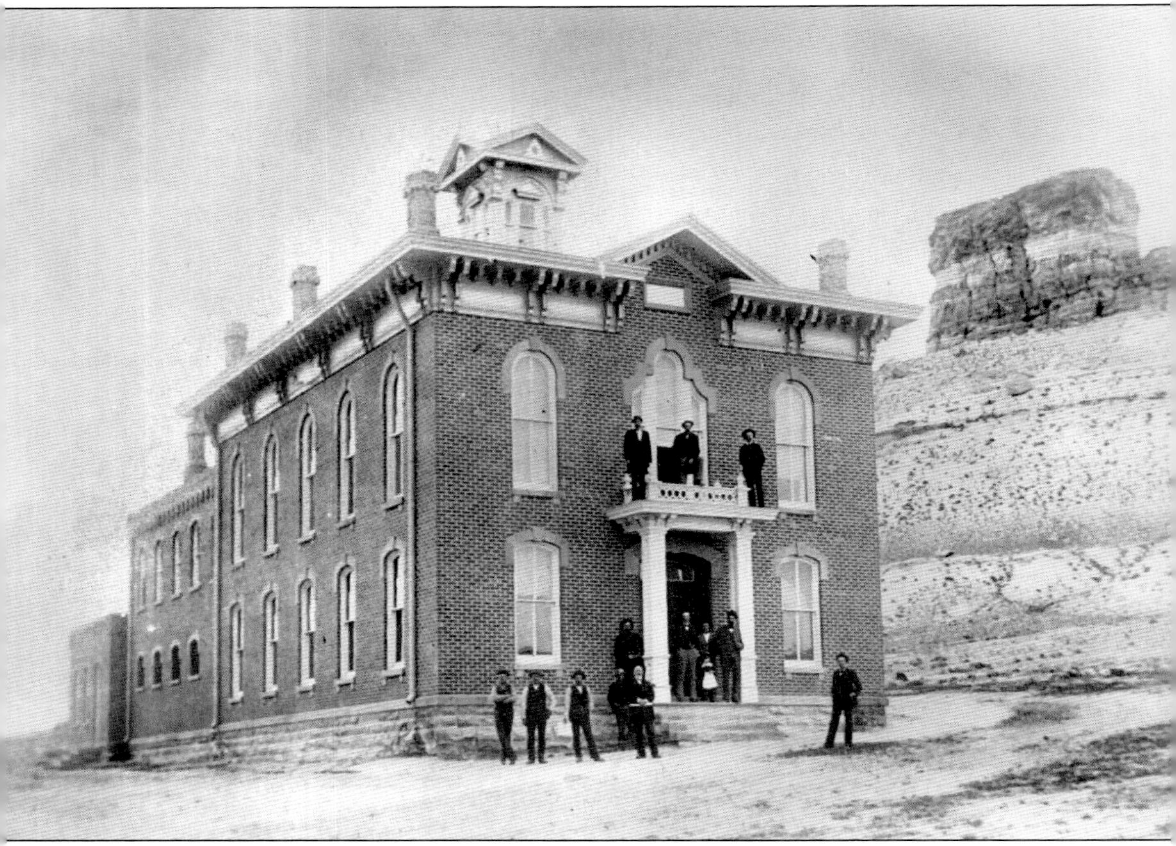

This 1876 view shows the Sweetwater County Courthouse shortly after its completion. The person in the middle of the group on the balcony appears to be Samuel Field. The bricks used in the construction of the courthouse were manufactured locally. The courthouse served as the civic heart of the community, hosting a wide variety of church and social events in addition to performing its governmental functions. (Courtesy of Sweetwater County Historical Museum.)

Born in the 1870s, Martha Gilligan left a written account of her childhood in Green River. She described the first buildings in town as mostly adobe; these were later replaced with wood and brick. She recalled a town where all the Union Pacific buildings were painted red. She also remembered a bear pit and a mountain lion cage located between the hotel and the express office. (Courtesy of Sweetwater County Historical Museum.)

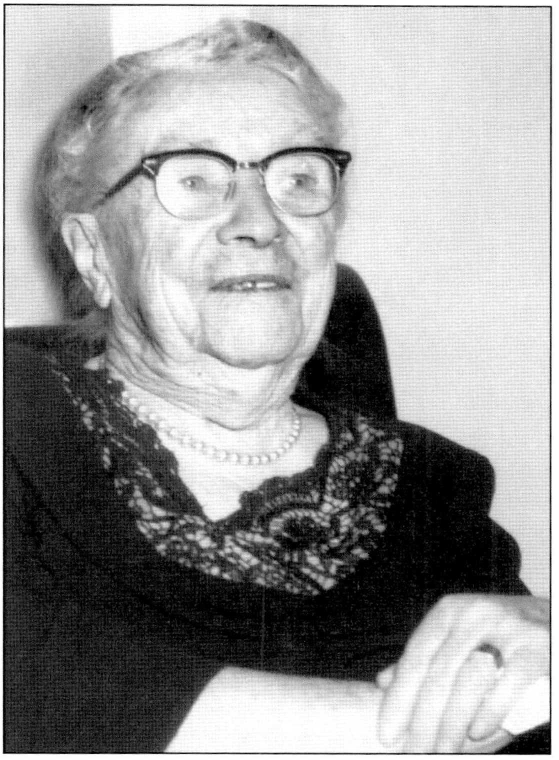

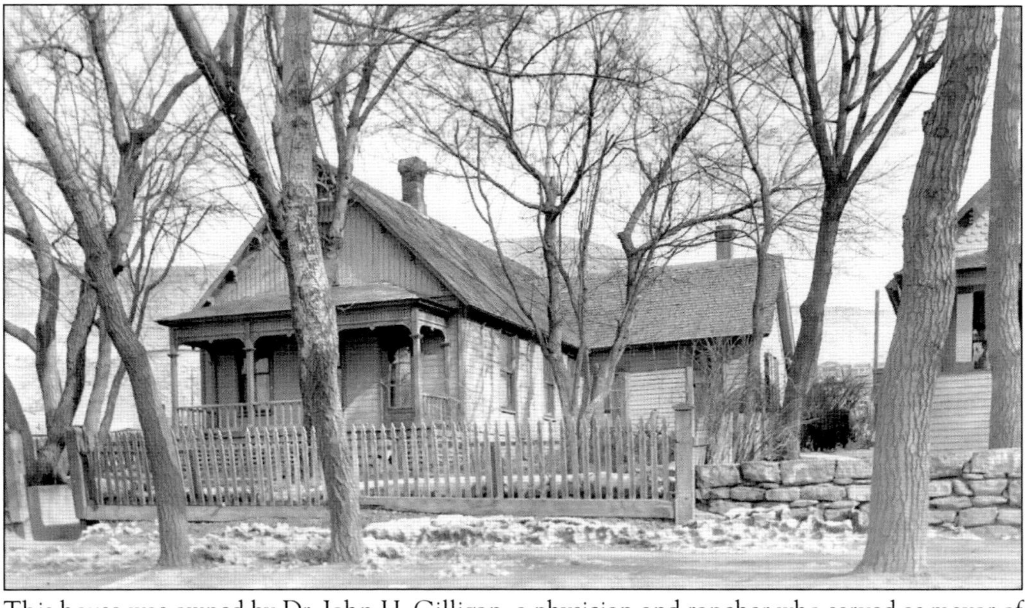

This house was owned by Dr. John H. Gilligan, a physician and rancher who served as mayor of Green River from 1901 to 1902. Dr. Gilligan came to Green River in the 1870s and practiced medicine for roughly 60 years. During his tenure as mayor, he oversaw the completion of a sewage system for the town and cracked down on unlicensed gambling. (Courtesy of Sweetwater County Historical Museum.)

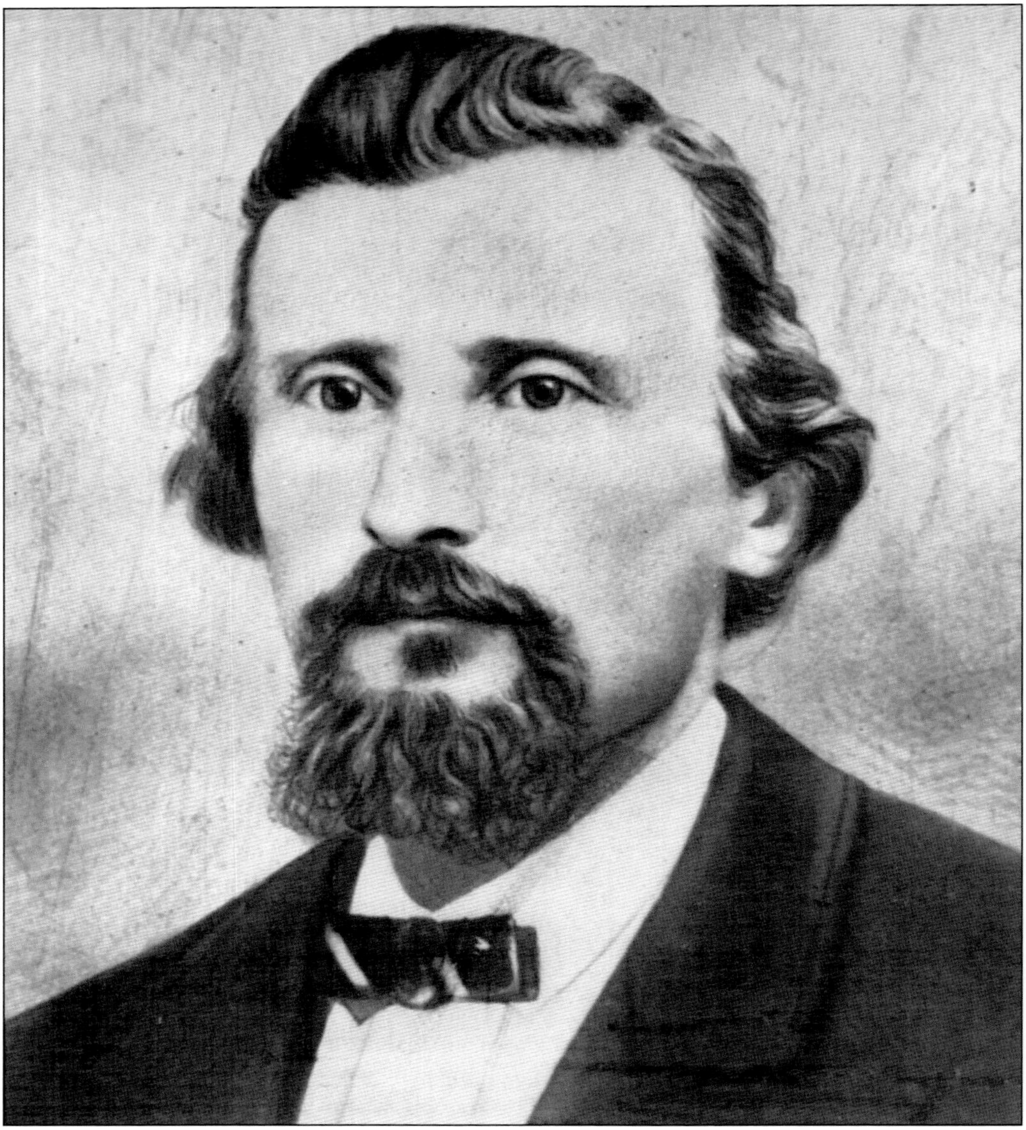

Sheriff William A. Johnson, one of the first settlers in Green River, was the man who "cleaned up" the city. As Sweetwater County sheriff, he struggled to purge the area of its lawless elements. Johnson, a transplanted Texan, was heralded as an expert shot with both pistol and rifle. During his tenure (1878–1879), he killed the notorious and deadly Mountain Jack, a man with roughly 20 notches in his gun. Johnson also served as county commissioner (1873–1874), as county assessor, (1875–1876) and as a state legislator (1875). For about 10 years, he was the owner of Expedition Island, which was then known as Johnson Island and later as Island Park. At the time of his death in 1910, Johnson had lived in Green River for 62 years. Like most founders of the town, Johnson had no monuments or streets named after him. (Courtesy of Sweetwater County Historical Museum.)

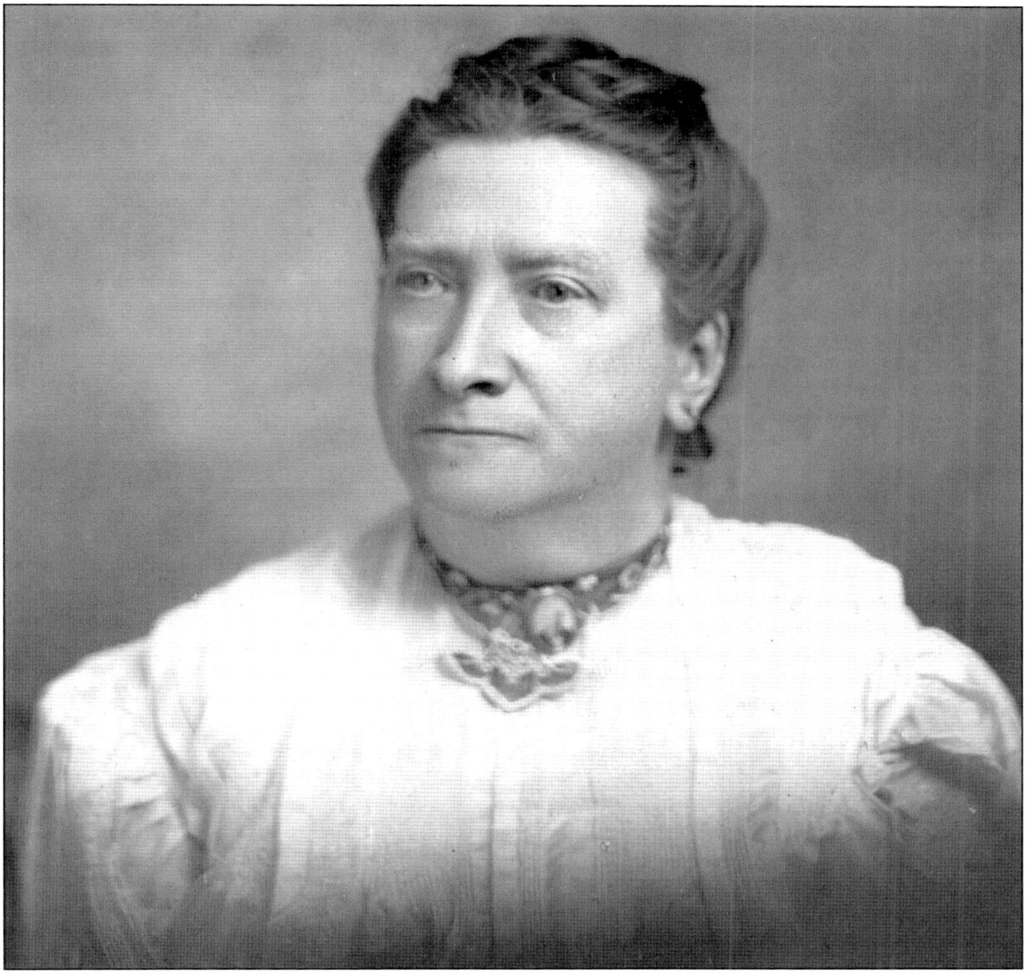

Martha Scott Baker Gravelle Campbell, the not-so-merry widow of Green River, is pictured here. In 1872, she and her first husband, William Baker, moved to Green River from Bryan, where she had buried two sons. William drowned while fishing in 1873, and another son also drowned in the Green River. Martha remarried to George Gravelle, the town apothecary, in 1876. George died of a kidney ailment two years later. Martha continued to run the drugstore, and she married Henry Hudson Campbell, a carpenter, in 1881. They worked at the drugstore together until Henry died suddenly in 1894 while reaching for a bottle of medicine. (Courtesy of Sweetwater County Historical Museum.)

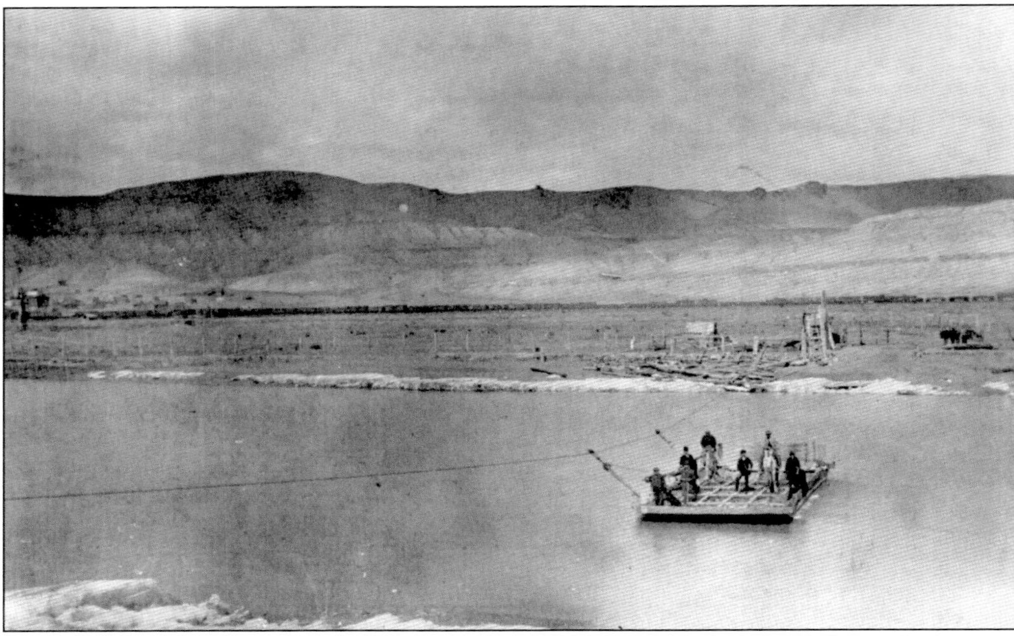

This 1886 image of Peter Appel's ferry, located at the bend of the Green River on the east end of town, is the only known photograph of this important service. From 1862 to 1896, ferries transported stages, wagons, and early automobiles across the Green River when the river was not fordable. In 1896, a bridge was built over the Green River, and the use of this ferry was discontinued. (Courtesy of Sweetwater County Historical Museum.)

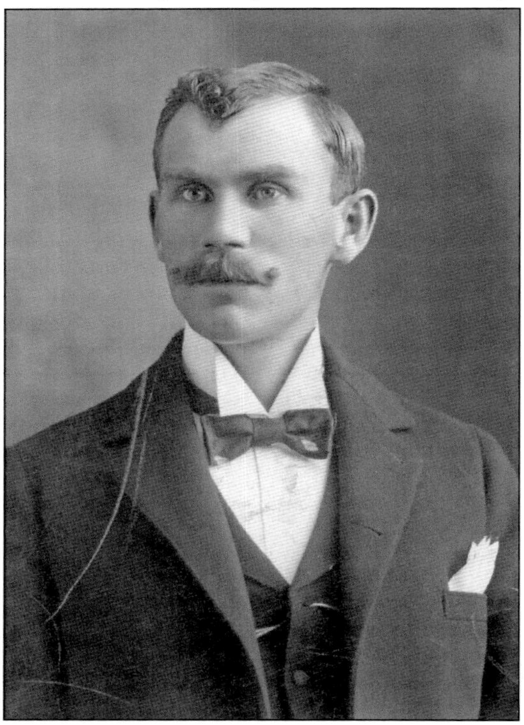

Businessman and rancher Chet Chrisman worked as a freighter. He later moved from the Green River area to ranch near Opal. In 1911, he was shot several times by a man named Crosby. One shot hit Chrisman in the head. Blinded by spurting blood, Chrisman shot his son, Chet Jr., in the arm when the younger man came to his aid. Both recovered from their wounds. (Courtesy of Sweetwater County Historical Museum.)

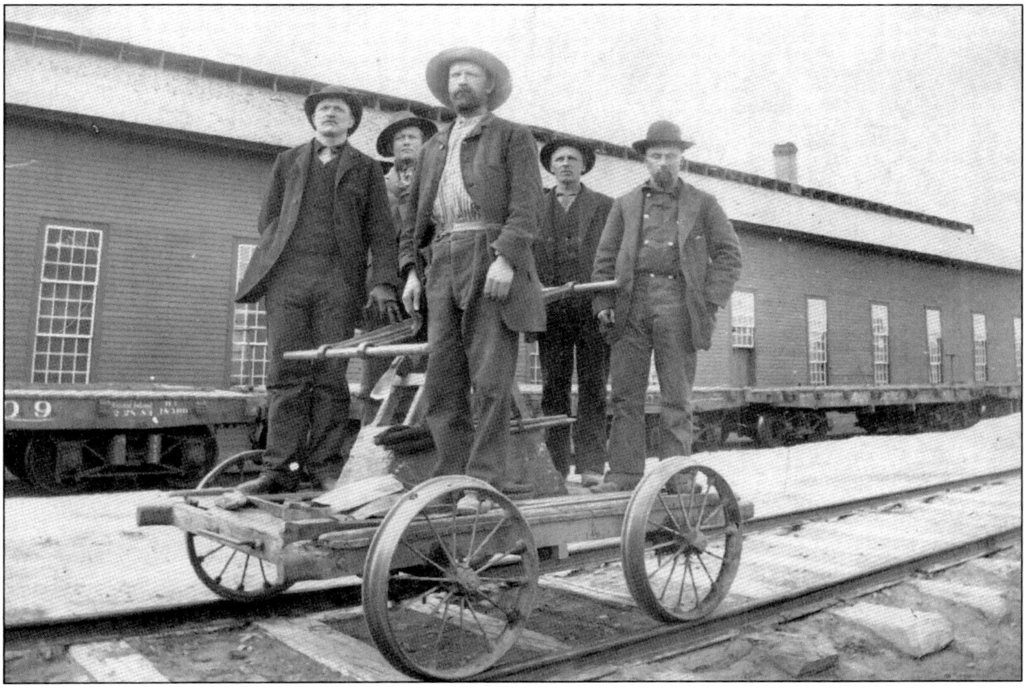

A handcar is a piece of railroad equipment powered by pushing up and down on the bars on each end. Track maintenance, as performed by crews like this, was an ongoing job. The men's blackened hands reveal their labors on the soot-encrusted railroad right-of-way. (Courtesy of Sweetwater County Historical Museum.)

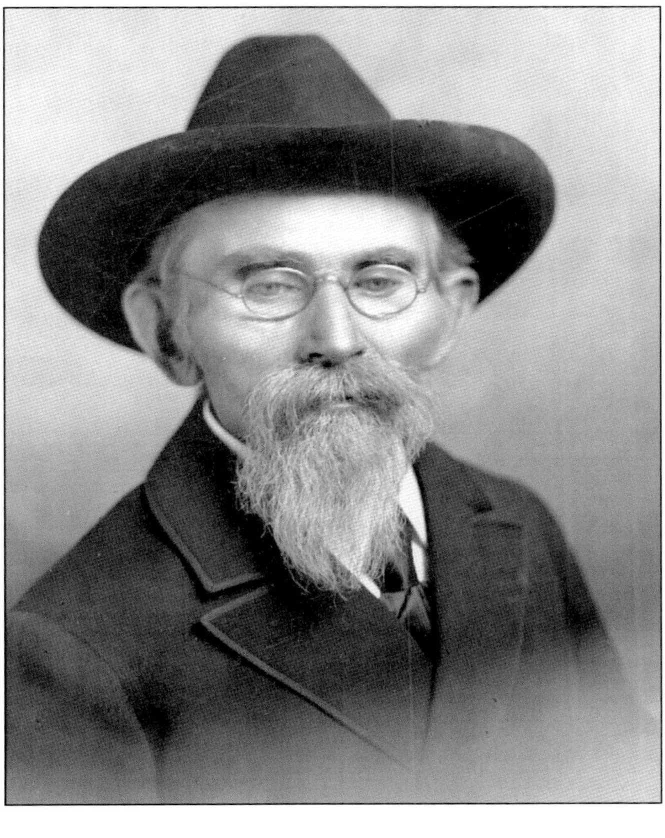

An early German entrepreneur, Bernhardt Spinner, ran a butcher shop in a tent in the wild town of Bryan until a stray bullet disabled him and his partner ran off with the company assets. Recovering from these dual disasters, Spinner started over with a new shop in Green River, which ran under the names Spinner and Viox until 1939. (Courtesy of Sweetwater County Historical Museum.)

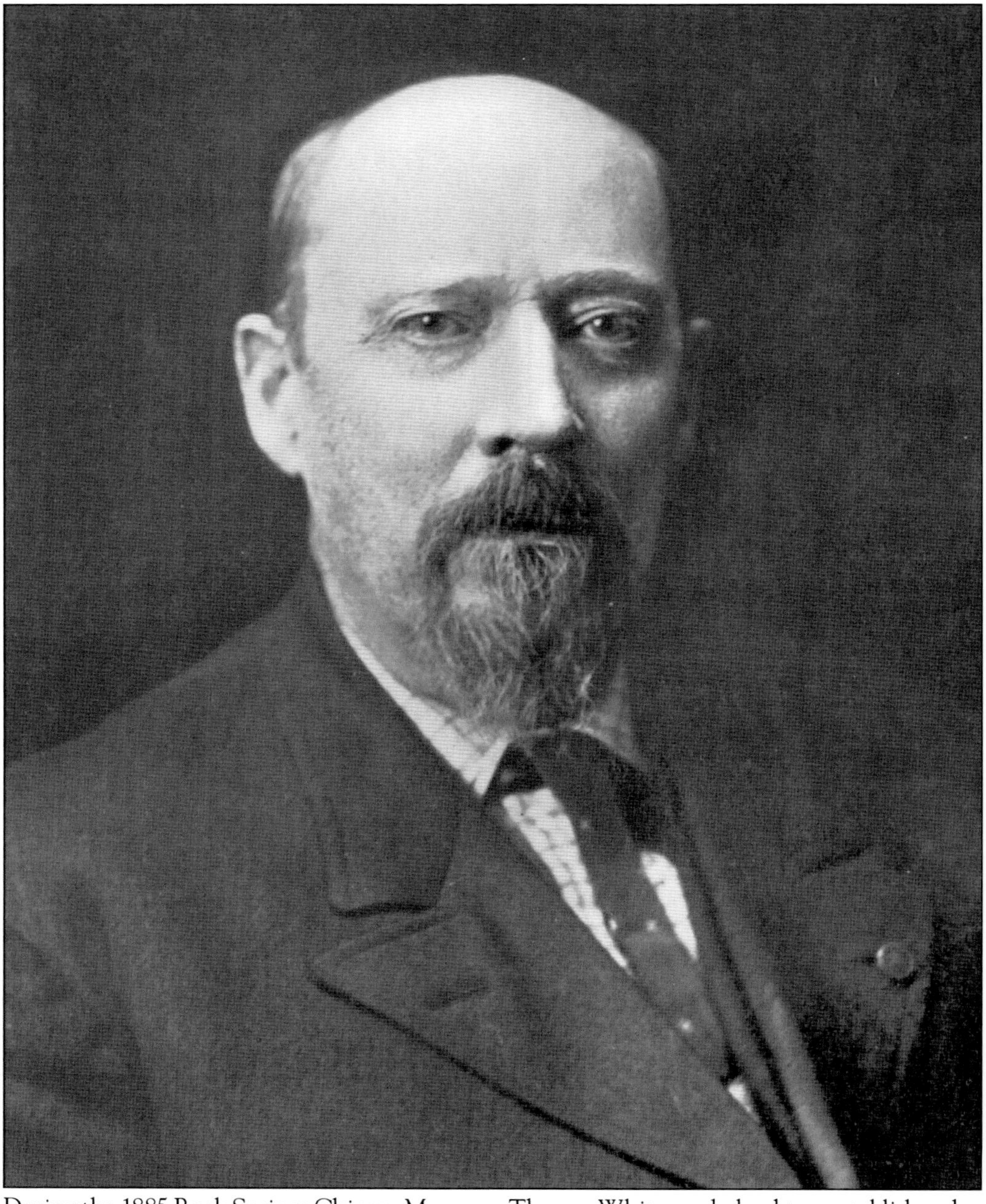

During the 1885 Rock Springs Chinese Massacre, Thomas Whitmore helped to reestablish order. Citizens urged him to run for sheriff, and he won the election to become a territorial sheriff in 1888. He was reelected in 1890 after Wyoming became a state, and he went on to serve six years as sheriff and two years as deputy sheriff. Whitmore remained in Green River until his death in 1923, serving as the clerk of court for 15 years. He was the last living member of the John A. Campbell Post of the Grand Army of the Republic. Whitmore has an American Legion post named after him in recognition of his Civil War service. According to his obituary, Whitmore wore his lawman's badge courageously and was a patriotic citizen, a staunch friend, and a brave enemy. (Courtesy of Sweetwater County Historical Museum.)

Three

FULL STEAM AHEAD!
1890–1918

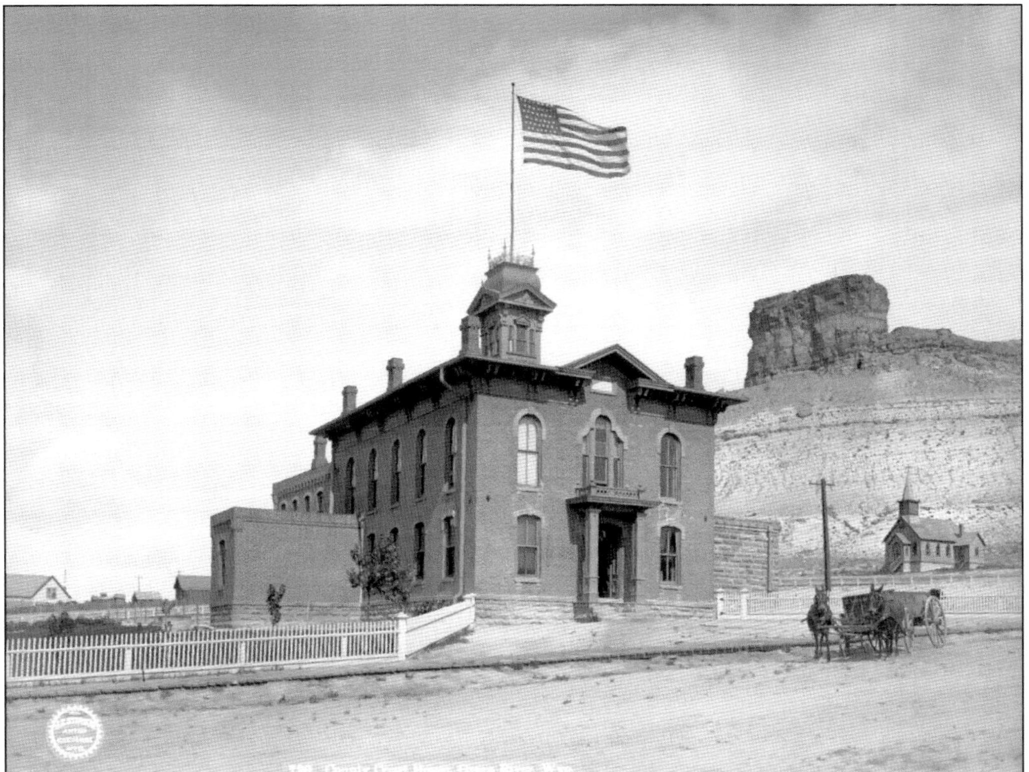

With the coming of statehood, Green River found itself well positioned for economic growth. The railroad town soon became the Sweetwater County seat, and it grew in size and complexity. This is a 1903 view of the Sweetwater County Courthouse. The central tower supported an ornate roof and a flagpole. Additions have been placed on the south and north sides of the building. The Episcopal congregation used to meet in the courthouse prior to the construction of its own building. (Courtesy of Wyoming State Archives.)

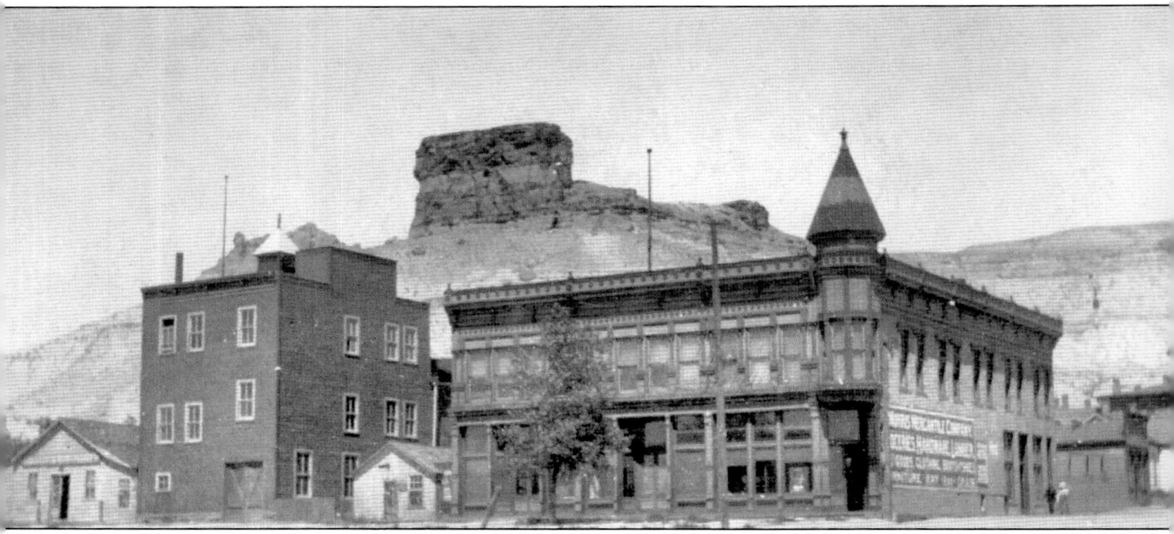

In 1872, W. A. Johnson Mercantile occupied this building. Robert Morris and a partner, who cannot be identified through records, bought out Johnson and established the Hunter and Morris Mercantile in 1888. In 1890, Robert and Edward Morris acquired the Morris Mercantile block, which housed the mercantile, the Morris State Bank, and professional offices. The building was destroyed by a fire caused by a defective furnace in 1917. (Courtesy of Sweetwater County Historical Museum.)

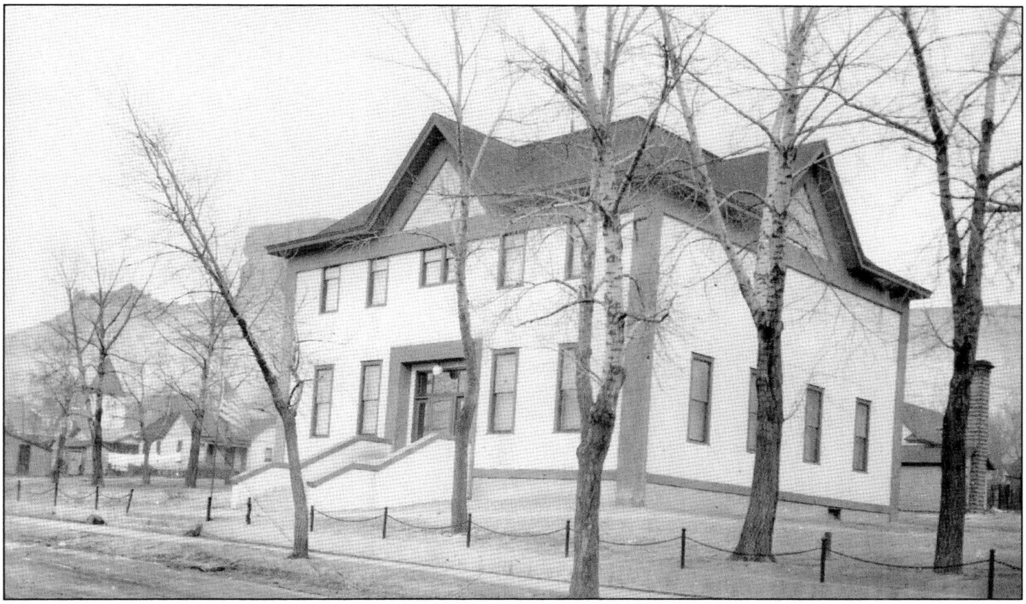

The third public school in Green River was built in 1891 to serve grades one through nine. The frame structure originally had three finished classrooms, with the lower grades located on the ground floor and the upper grades on the second. In 1926, the building was decommissioned and was sold to the Mount Moriah Masonic Lodge. (Courtesy of Sweetwater County Historical Museum.)

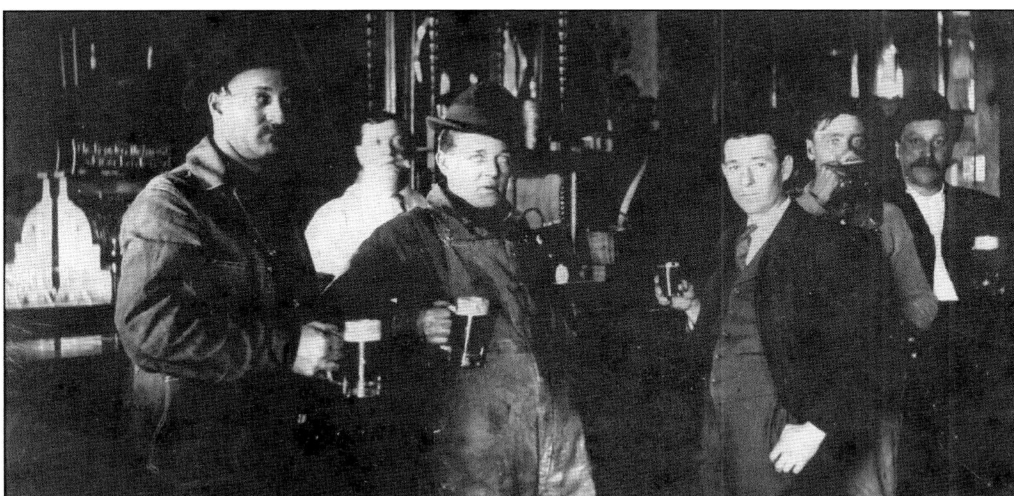

The U. P. Bar was built in 1872, and by 1891 it was nicknamed the "Bucket of Blood." When this photograph was taken in 1904, it was called the Senate Saloon. During Prohibition, a front business, the Candy Kitchen, served ice cream, candy, and legal beverages, while the back room continued to operate as a bar. With the end of Prohibition in 1933, the candy store was replaced by the current occupant, the Green Gander Bar. (Courtesy of Sweetwater County Historical Museum.)

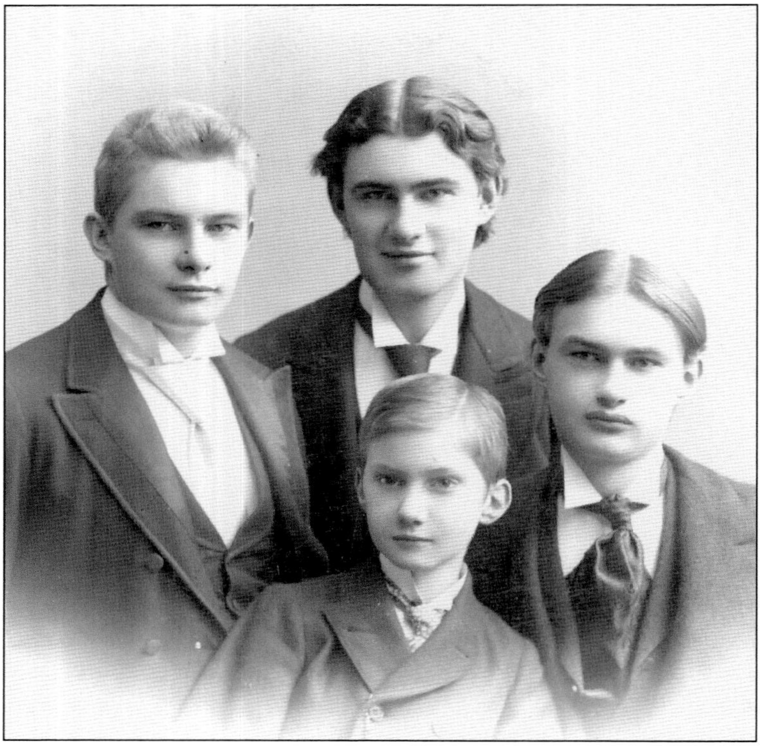

The two eldest Gaensslen brothers, shown here along with their younger siblings, were members of Green River's prominent German community. After 1891, the eldest, Hugo (far left), served as brewmaster and proprietor of the Sweetwater Brewing Company. He was also a councilman, a mayor, and a trustee for the Carnegie Library. Emil (rear center) was the office manager and accountant for the brewing company. (Courtesy of Sweetwater County Historical Museum.)

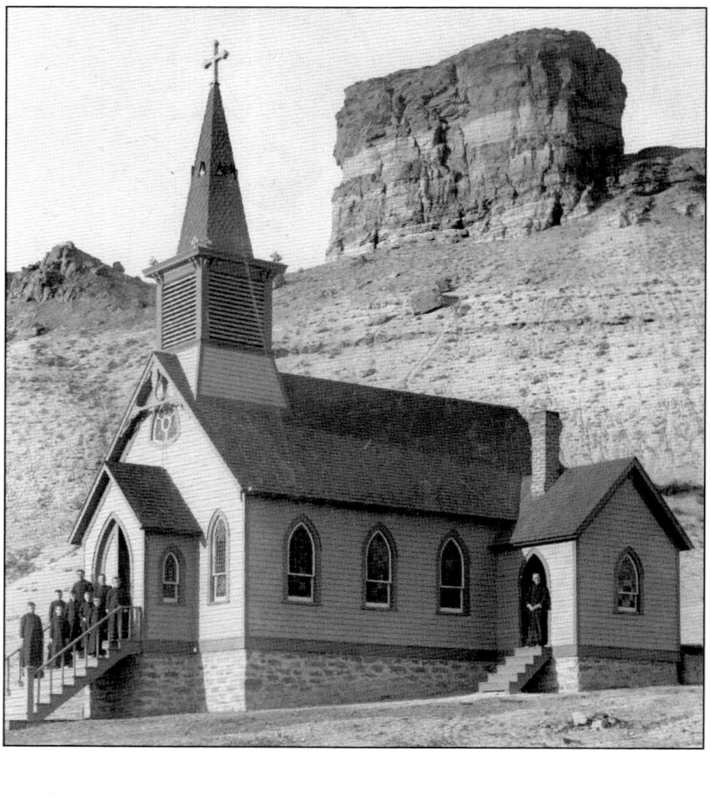

Saint John's Episcopal Church, constructed in 1892, was the third church built in Green River. F. N. Cockcroft and William Doggett, pictured here with the choir, were early lay ministers. Doggett was a former military man who came to the area as a result of the Chinese Massacre of 1885. (Courtesy of Sweetwater County Historical Museum.)

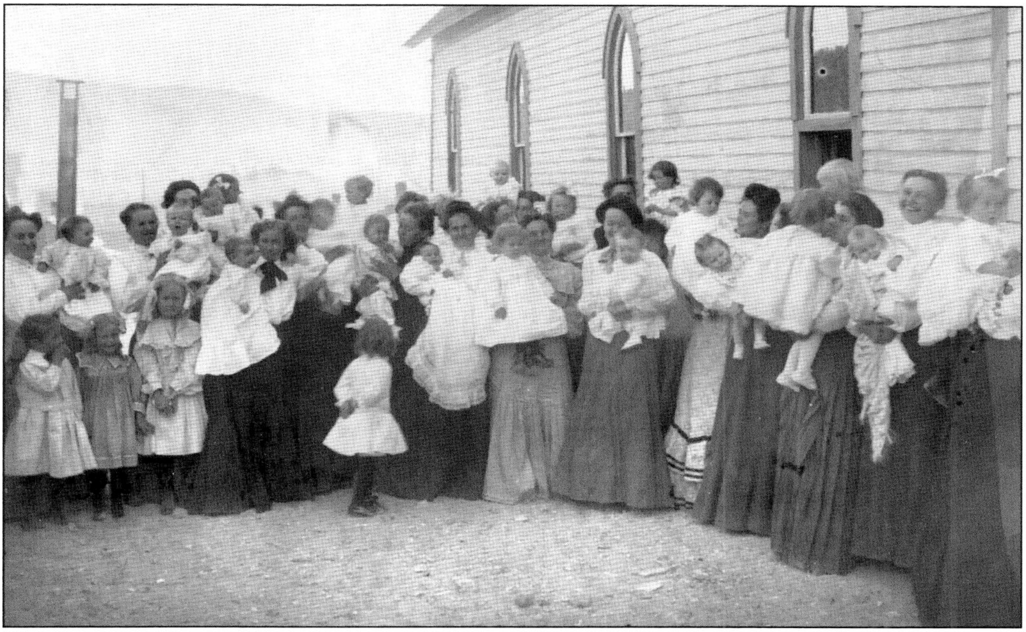

The Ladies' Guild of St. John's Episcopal Church, organized in August 1892, was an active society for good works and fund-raising. The 1892 Christmas fair included sales booths of needlework and baked goods created by the ladies, a fish pond, a fortune teller's booth, and dinner and dancing. (Courtesy of Sweetwater County Historical Museum.)

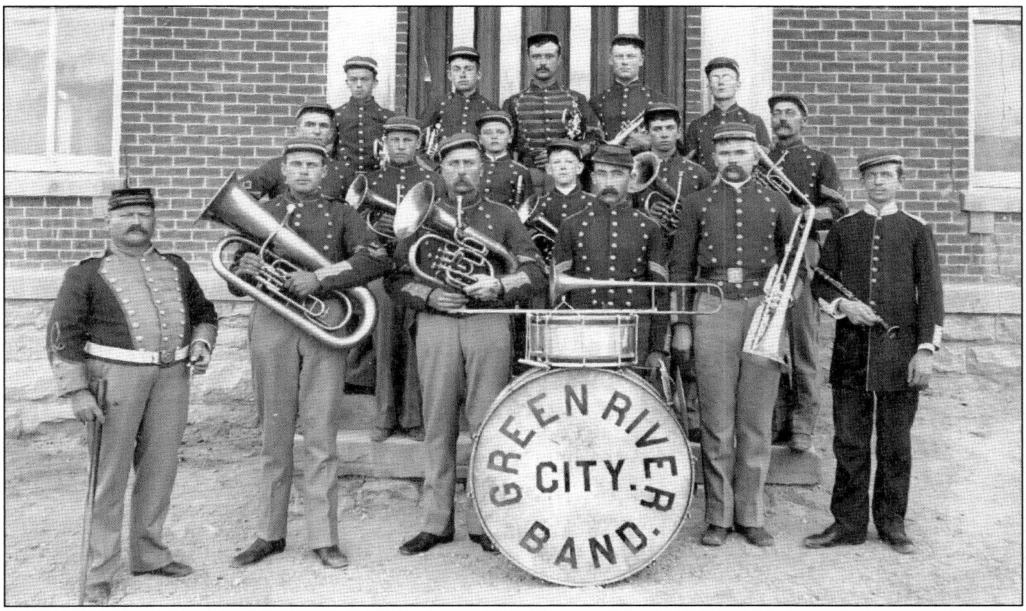

The records are not clear as to when the Green River City Band was established. The band is pictured here on the Sweetwater County Courthouse steps in 1892. Local bands were a great source of civic pride and prestige. These uniforms emulate the military style of the mid-to-late-19th century. Almost all of the men are wearing various forms of sergeants' stripes. (Courtesy of Sweetwater County Historical Museum.)

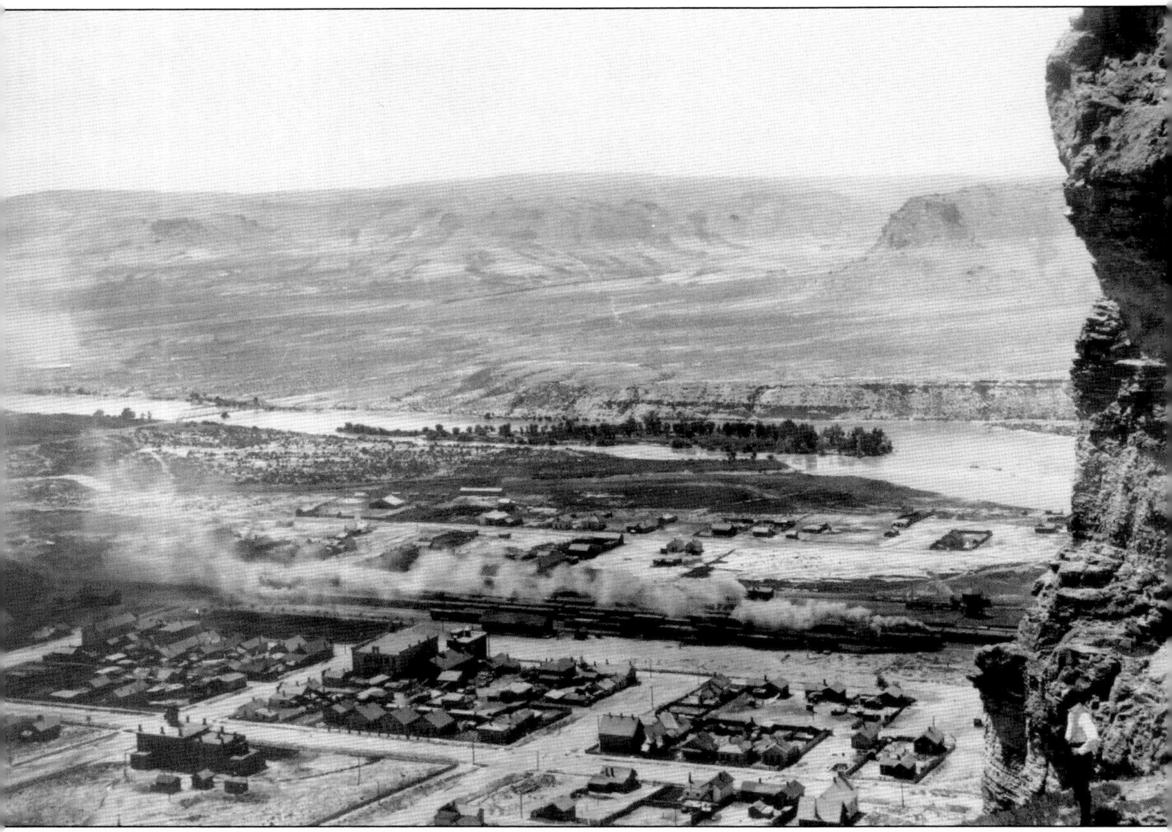

This is Green River as viewed from Castle Rock sometime between 1892 and 1900. By Wyoming standards, modern conveniences arrived early in Green River. A water system was installed in the 1870s, and electricity in 1892. Wooden sidewalks and a fire department were introduced in 1893. In 1895, the first park was constructed. Telephone service was authorized in 1898. The heavily wooded Expedition Island, known as Island Park, was a favorite picnicking locale. (Courtesy of Sweetwater County Historical Museum.)

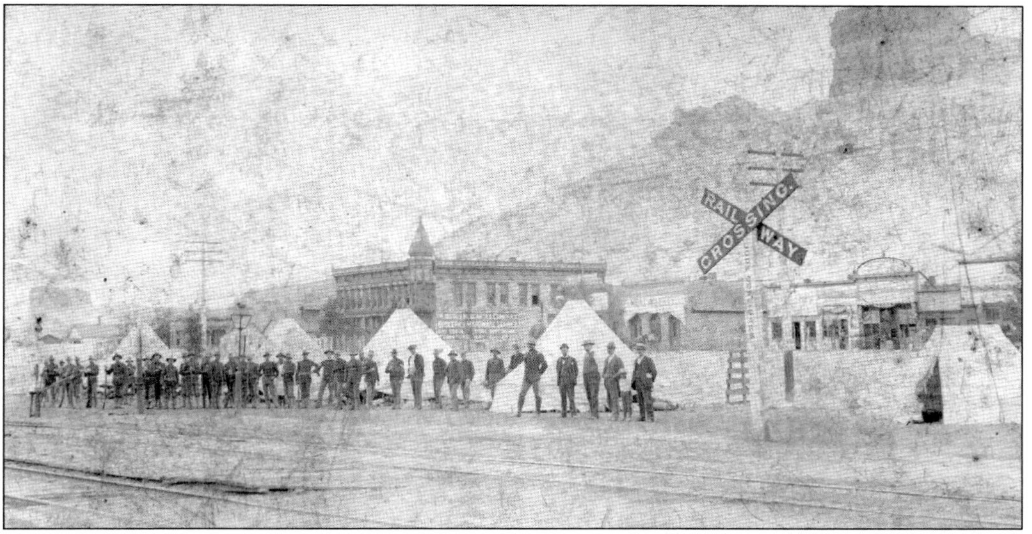

In 1894, the Pullman Company, located near Chicago, laid off nearly one-third of its employees and cut the wages of the rest. In a show of sympathy, railroad workers in Wyoming went on strike. More than 800 Union Pacific employees in Wyoming lost their jobs for participating in the short strike. This image shows a body of soldiers sent to Green River to keep the peace and protect the railroad's property. (Courtesy of Sweetwater County Historical Museum.)

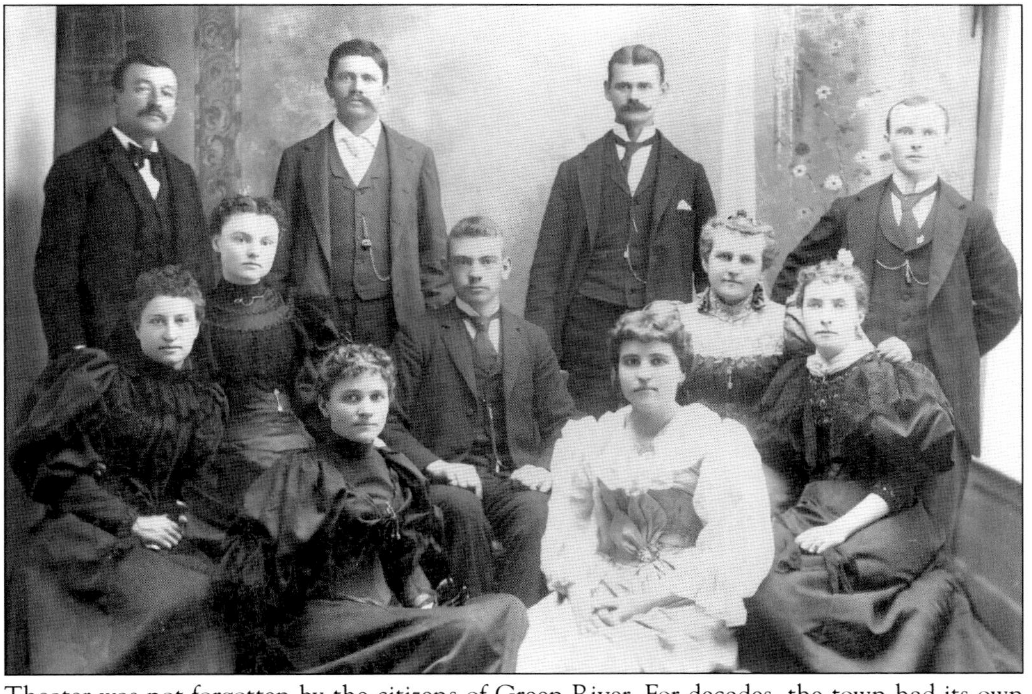

Theater was not forgotten by the citizens of Green River. For decades, the town had its own dramatic club. The Green River Dramatic Club of 1895 included (pictured here in no particular order) Bertha Rumph, Anna Eckert, Eleanor Gaensslen, Mary Gilligan, Ida McDermott Regan, George Gravelle, Edith Tressler, Skinney Roberts, Edward Fisher, Joe Payne, and Martin Cleary. (Courtesy of Sweetwater County Historical Museum.)

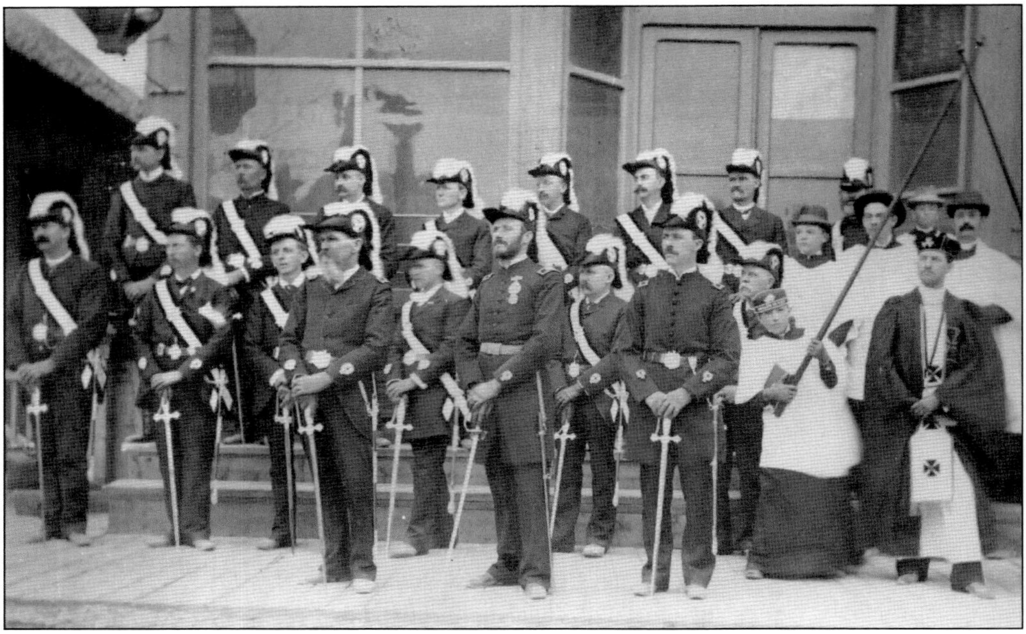

The members of the Ascalon Commandery No. 2 of Knights Templar, a Masonic group, pose after Easter services in 1895. There is no historical link between this philanthropic organization and the Knights Templar of the First Crusade, which started in 1118. The more recent Masonic order was established in the 1700s. (Courtesy of Sweetwater County Historical Museum.)

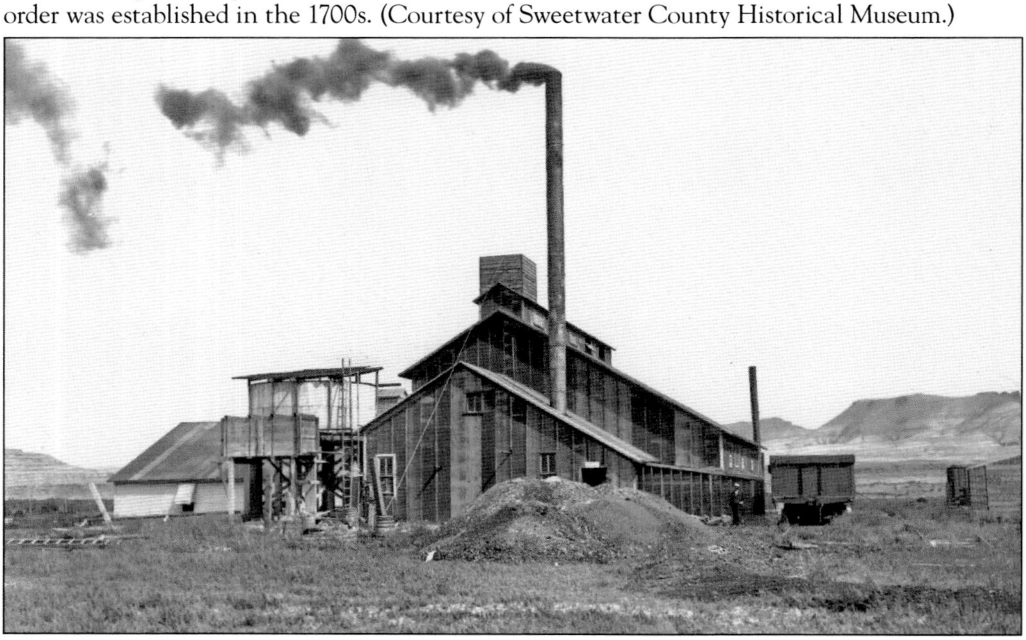

In 1895, the Green River Fuel and Oil Company drilled a well. Instead of oil or even freshwater, soda water came bubbling up from the ground. As a result, the Green River Soda Works was born. The pioneer of the trona industry in Sweetwater County, the Green River Soda Works plant, enjoyed some success until 1939, when it was closed. (Courtesy of Sweetwater County Historical Museum.)

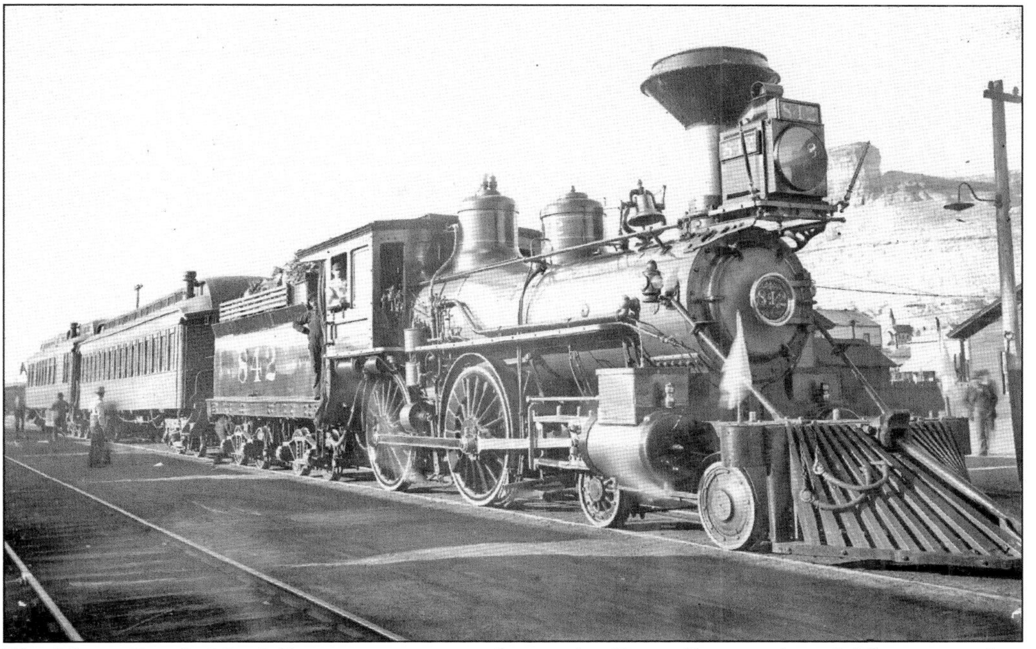

The Union Pacific No. 842 train prepares to depart the Green River rail yard. The engine has taken on a full load of coal and has two passenger cars to haul. Visible in the background on the right is the Episcopal church. Here Castle Rock lacks a flagpole and the town has an electrical system, indicating that this photograph was taken between 1898 and 1902. (Courtesy of Sweetwater County Historical Museum.)

Edward Morris took part in the South Pass Gold Rush of 1868–1869. He then moved to Green River, and he became its first mayor once the town was incorporated under the state of Wyoming. He promoted an ordinance for the protection of growing trees and served as a delegate to the Wyoming Constitutional Convention. (Courtesy of Sweetwater County Historical Museum.)

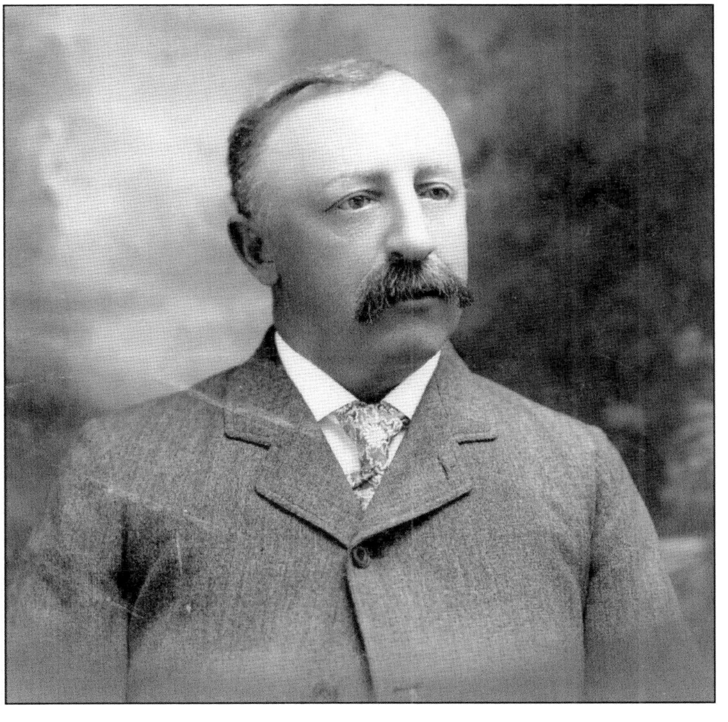

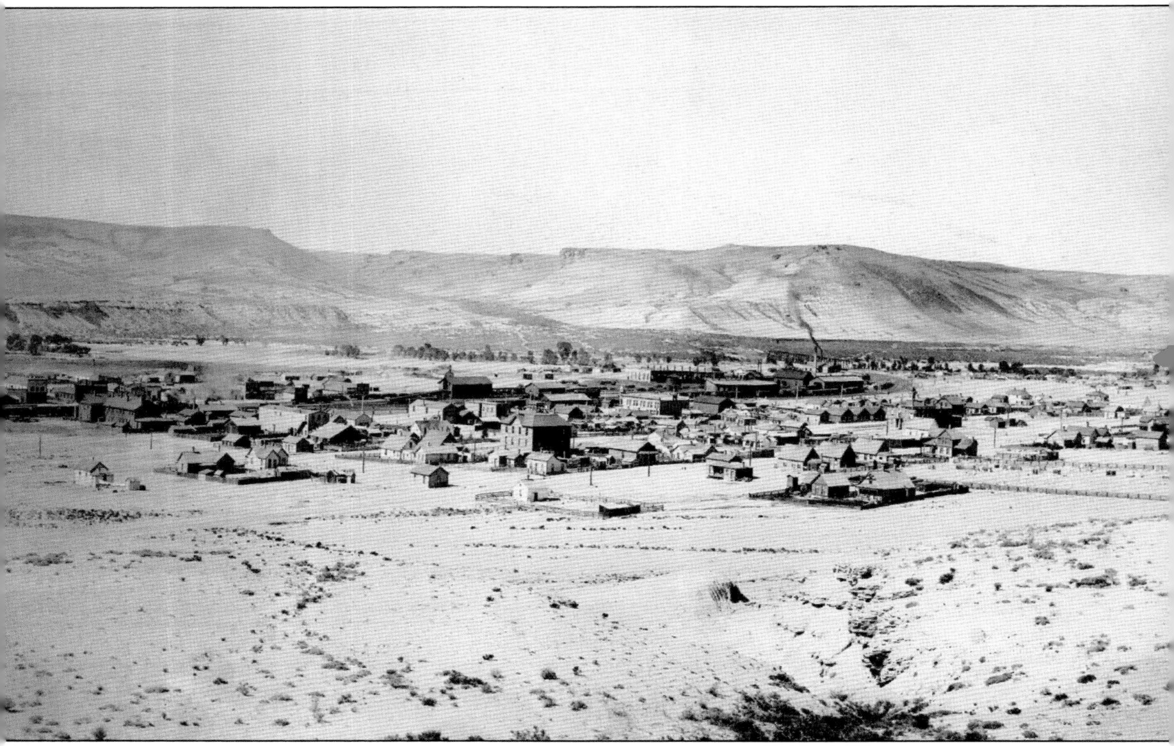

This 1898 view looks southwest at Green River. The cemetery, the courthouse, Union Pacific's roundhouse, and the bridge are among the many local landmarks visible. The Green River runs through the background, and several homes still have outhouses and horse barns. (Courtesy of Sweetwater County Historical Museum.)

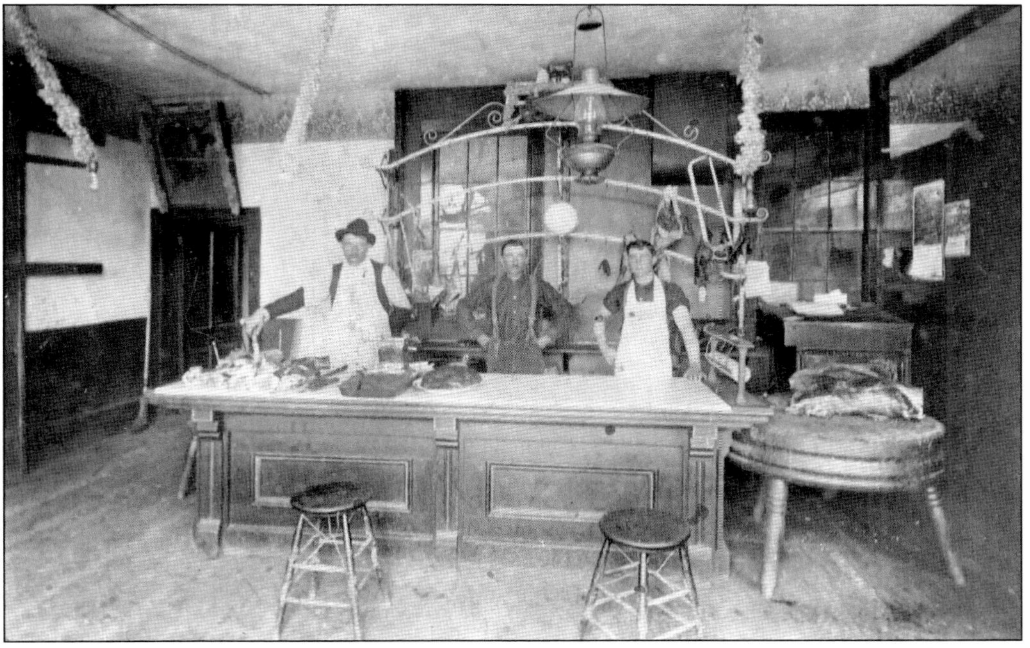

Leo Viox mans the counter at his Viox Meat Market with (in no particular order) Charley Steen and Charles Viox around 1900. Originally established in a tent in the railroad town of Bryan, the market operated under various owners until 1953. Reflecting the standards of the time, there was no refrigeration. Consumers could watch their meat order prepared on the cutting block to the right. (Courtesy of Sweetwater County Historical Museum.)

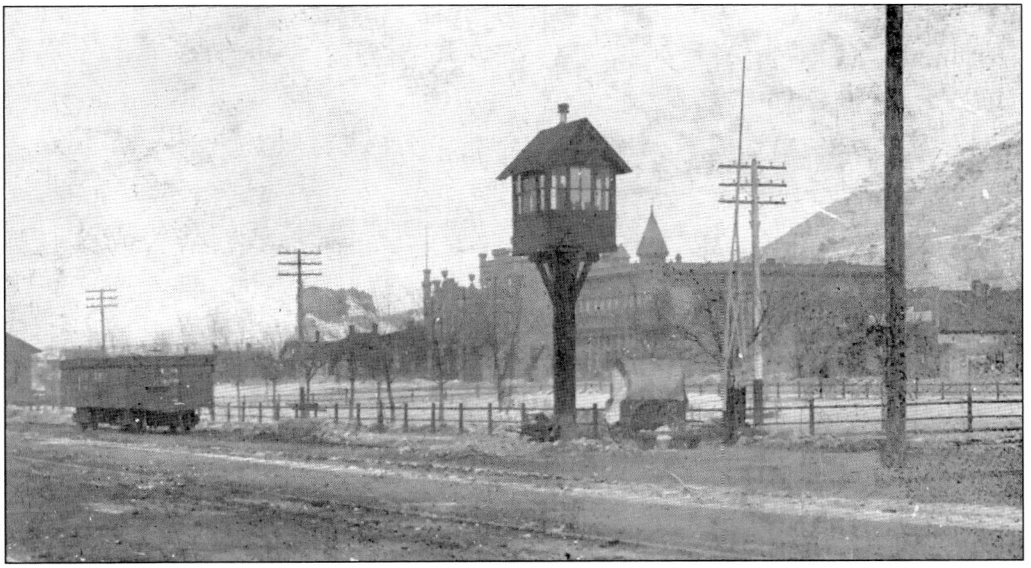

Green River's business district was bisected by the large rail yard, making the at-grade-level crossing an important link in the chain of commerce. In order to prevent traffic from colliding with the trains, a guard was stationed in the elevated structure. His job was to watch for oncoming trains and lower or raise the gate to regulate the traffic. (Courtesy of Sweetwater County Historical Museum.)

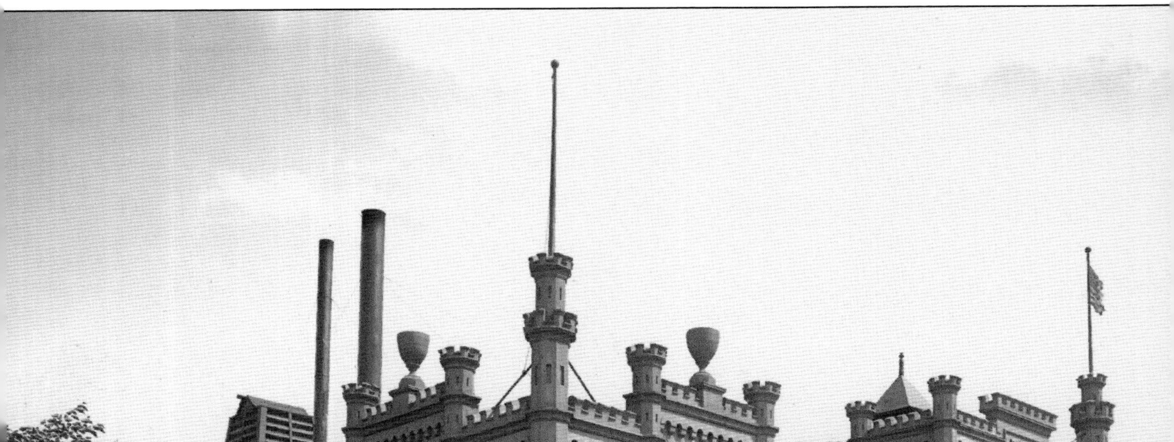

The most architecturally distinctive building in Green River, the Sweetwater Brewing Company, was built in 1900 of stone quarried from a nearby canyon. Owner and brewmaster Hugo Gaensslen came to Green River from the Chicago area in 1895. He constructed the unusual building in memory of the castles in his native Rhineland and of the Chicago Water Tower, a landmark located near the Gaensslen family's first American home in Chicago. Associated with the brewery complex were two icehouses and a bottling shed. Ice was harvested from the Green River during the winter months and was stored in the large insulated icehouse buildings to chill the beer during the warmer months. The beer produced here took awards at the Columbian Exposition in Saint Louis (1904) and the Lewis and Clark Centennial Exposition in Portland (1905). (Courtesy of Sweetwater County Historical Museum.)

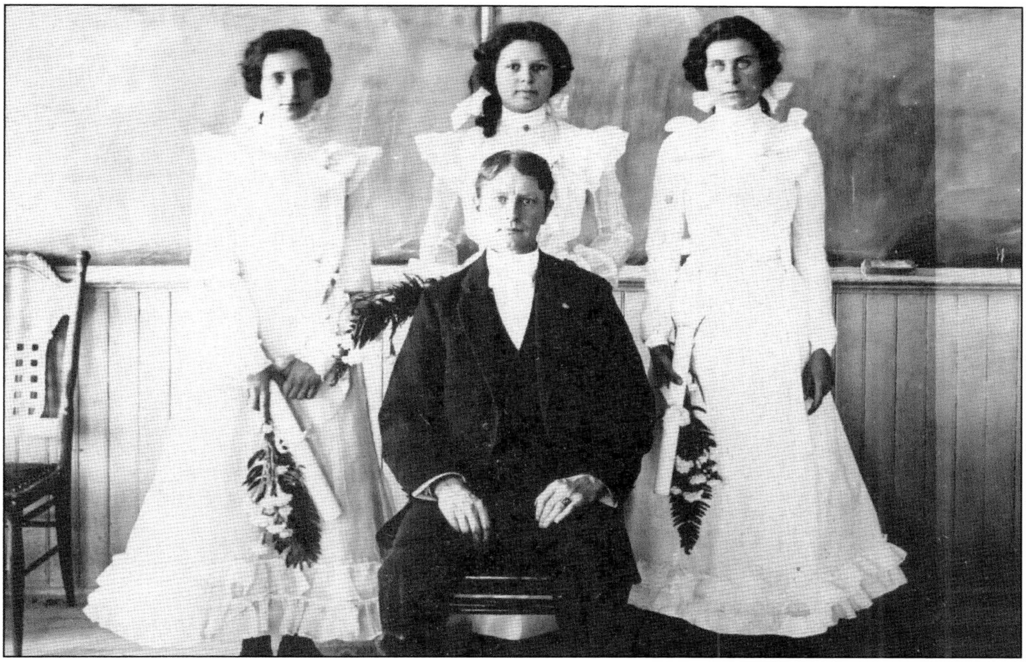

This 1902 image depicts the first class in Green River to celebrate commencement exercises. Standing are, from left to right, Maude Rumble Peters, Nellie Dankowski Bishopp Elder, and Ida Viox Nolan. Professor H. J. Wendt sits in the middle. (Courtesy of Sweetwater County Historical Museum.)

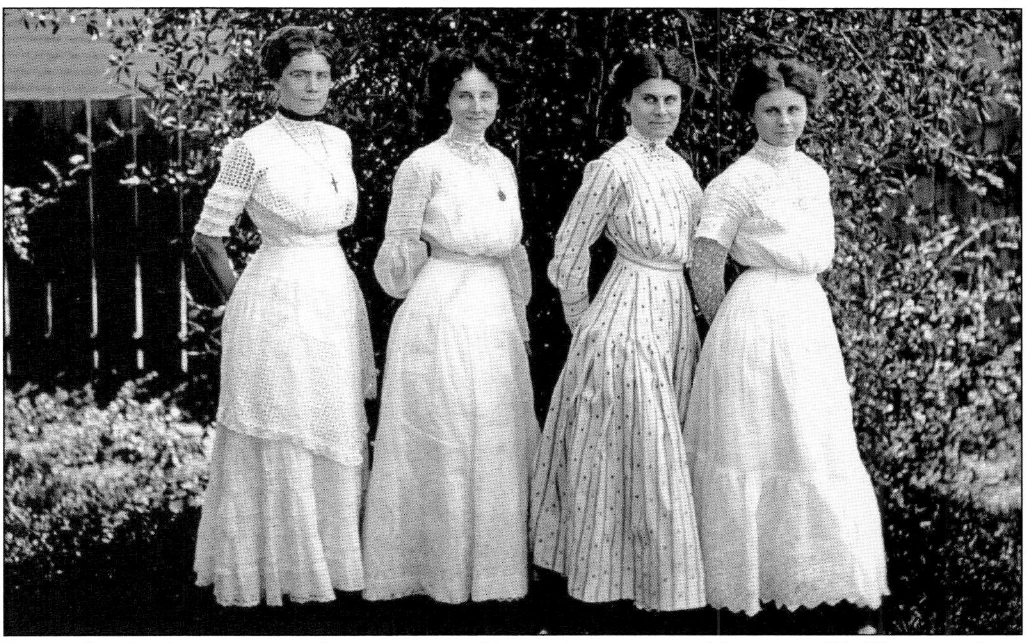

Reputed to be the prettiest girls in town, the Viox girls are pictured here in 1902. They are, from left to right, Marie "Mayme", Eleanor, Ida, and Louise. The Viox family ran a successful butcher shop in Green River in the early 20th century. Marie died at the age of 101 in 1981, having lived in Green River until 1971. (Courtesy of Sweetwater County Historical Museum.)

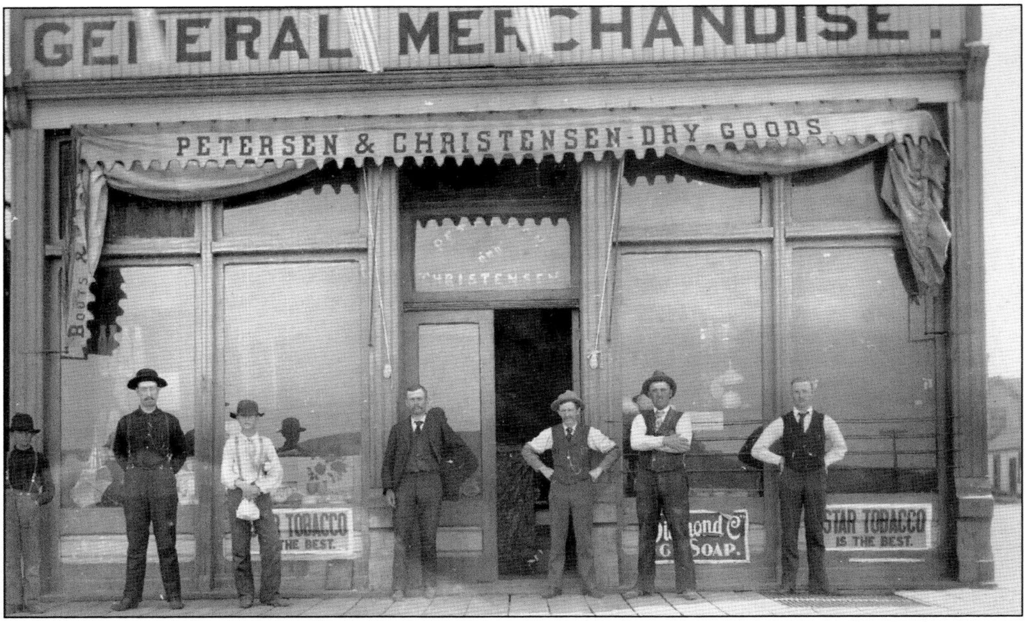

A crowd gathers in front of the Petersen and Christensen mercantile on the Fourth of July in 1902 or 1903. Proprietor Peter Christensen stands in the open doorway with his hands on his hips. The building is thought to have been built around 1880, and the store was in business by 1895, though exact details are not known. In 1916, the business, then owned solely by P. O. Christensen, moved to the north side of town. (Courtesy of Sweetwater County Historical Museum.)

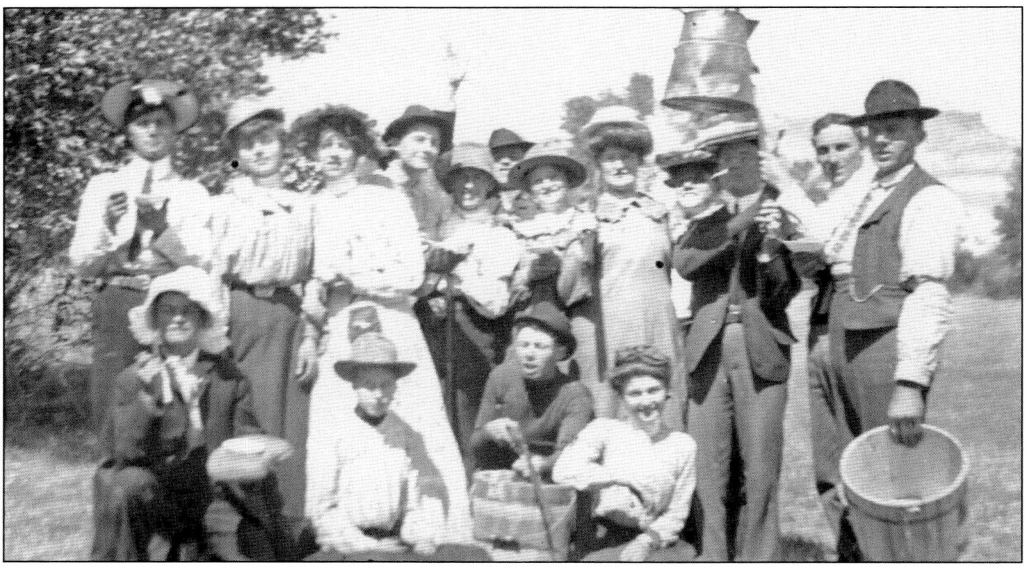

A favorite outdoor activity in Green River was picnicking. In this 1903 image, some of the picnickers are clowning for the camera by switching headgear. Pictured are, from left to right, the following: (first row) Pete Gras, Celia ?, Ted Bishopp, and unidentified; (second row) Charles Viox, Alida Peters, Nellie Peters, unidentified, Nellie Dankowski Bishopp, Mattie Mundt, three unidentified people, Joseph Gras, unidentified, and James Thomsen. (Courtesy of Sweetwater County Historical Museum.)

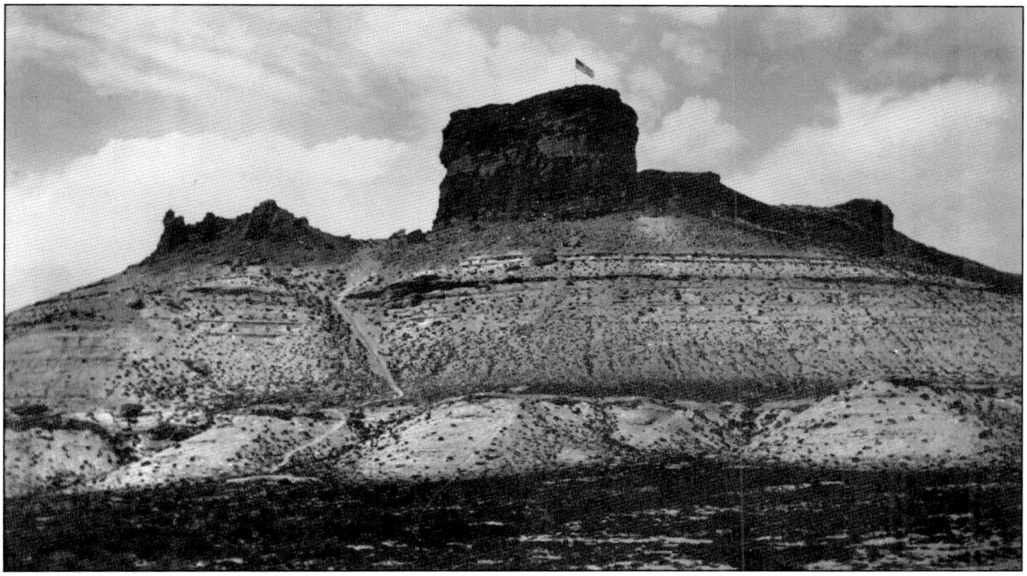

"The first thing to greet the eyes of those early risers was the large American flag streaming from Castle Rock, 600 feet above us," wrote the *Green River Star* on July 5, 1904. The placement of a new pole and a larger flag was accomplished that year by Emil Gaensslen and William Hutton and coincided with the annual Fourth of July celebration. This image dates to the 1920s. (Courtesy of Sweetwater County Historical Museum.)

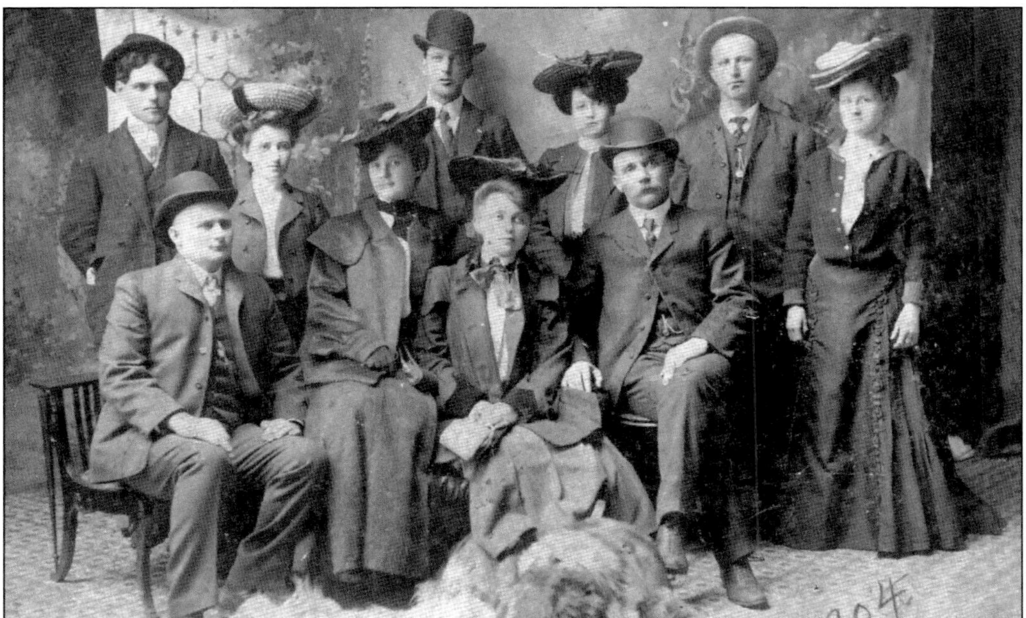

In this 1904 image, the cast of a play is assembled. All of the men were employed by the Union Pacific Railroad. Pictured are, from left to right, the following: (first row) Bob Fosdick, May Fosdick, Alida Peters, and Bill Peters; (second row) Jess Fairchild, Elizabeth Mockler Fairchild, Jock Corvin, Kate Corvin, Art Unsler, and Nora Unsler. The dog is not named. Elizabeth Mockler Fairchild was one of the early librarians for the town. (Courtesy of Sweetwater County Historical Museum.)

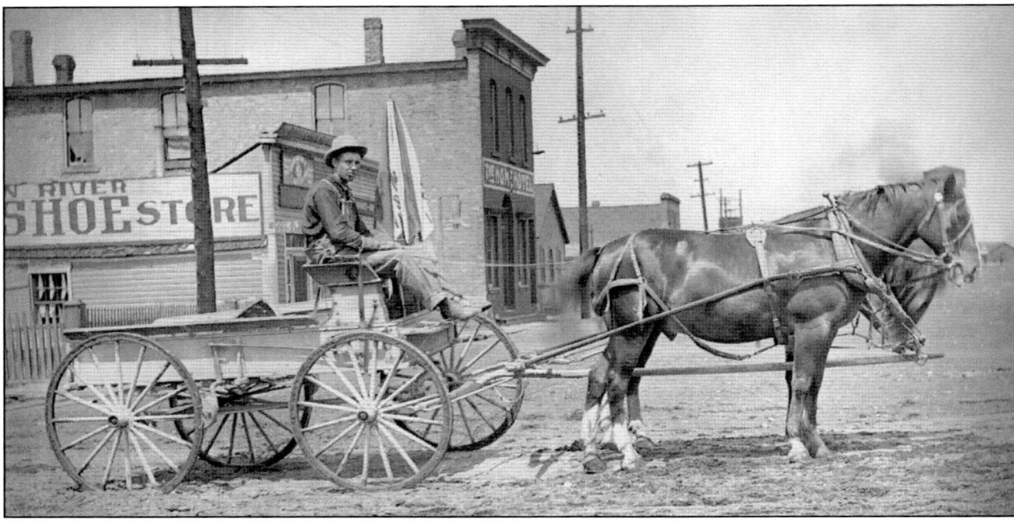

This 1905 image shows Chris Jessen, who later became Sweetwater County sheriff, driving the P. O. Christensen Mercantile wagon. The shoe store pictured here was operated by Charles Eggs from 1886 to 1916. The adjacent building served as a billiards hall, hotel, and bar for decades under the names of Billiard and Liquor Saloon (1878), Hotel Castle Rock (1891), Home Hotel (c. 1900), and the Castle Rock Bar (1910). (Courtesy of Sweetwater County Historical Museum.)

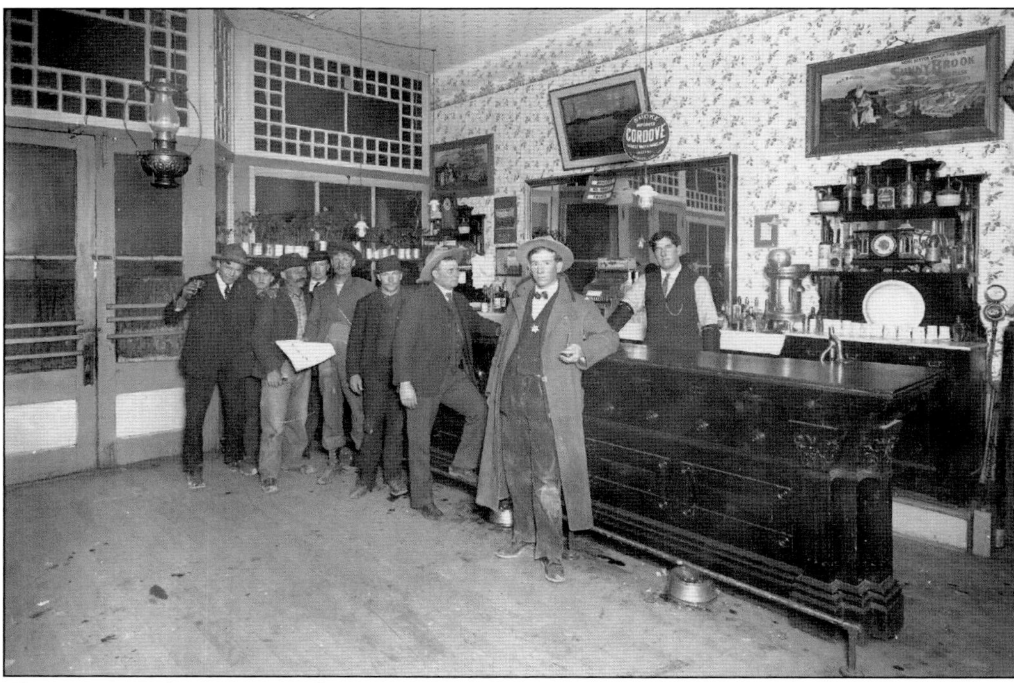

This is a typical Green River bar scene of 1900–1915 period. Frank Kidd (second from the right) was the chief of police in Green River from 1901 to 1902 and from 1912 to 1914. To his left sits Charles Young, who served as Sweetwater County sheriff from 1903 to 1904. The bar is tended by Les Fogel. (Courtesy of Sweetwater County Historical Museum.)

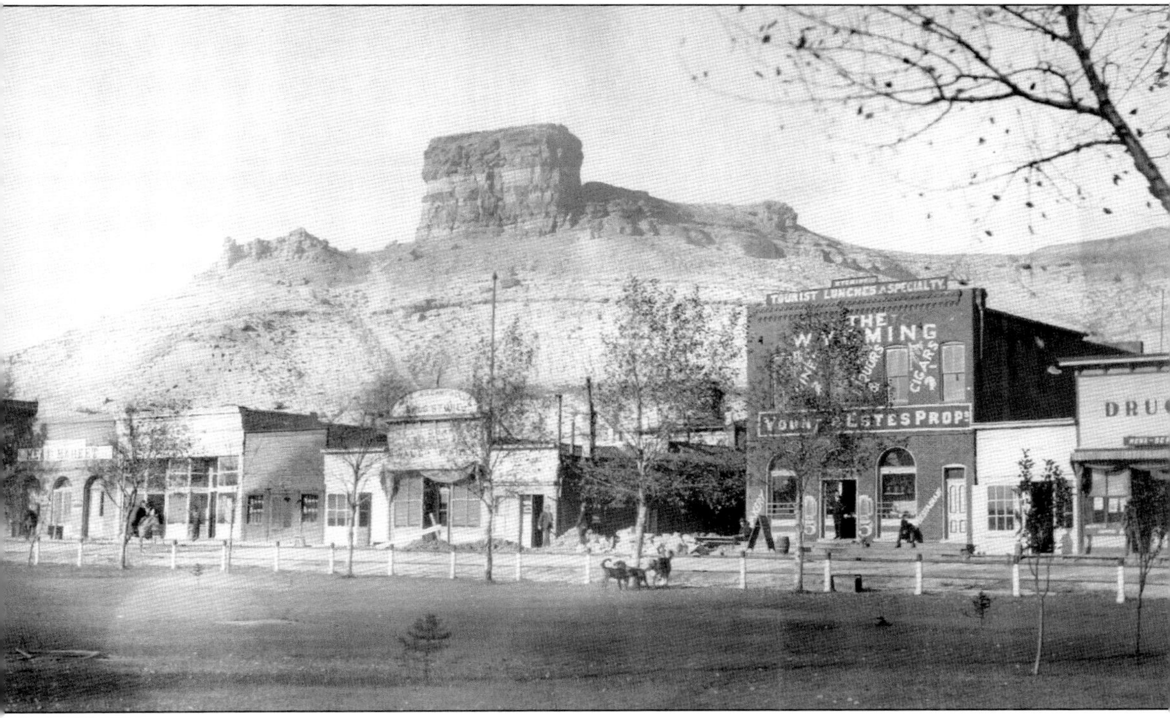

In this 1906 image, the north-side business district has grown to include the amenities of gracious living. Greenery gave a respite from the desert surrounding the town, and various businesses provided luxury items for local shoppers. These businesses included the Viox Meat Market, the Crocker Jewelry Store, a "game room," the Mrs. H. H. Campbell Drug Store, the Wyoming Saloon, a restaurant, a bakery, and the Chrisman Drug Store. (Courtesy of United States Geological Survey.)

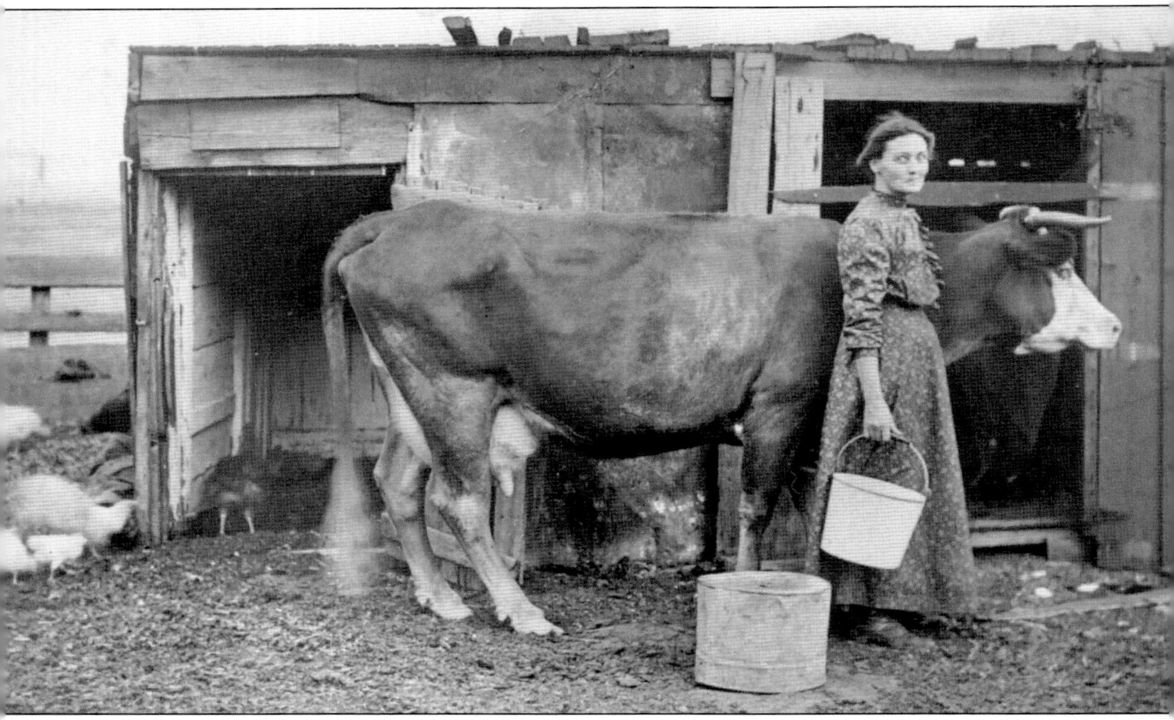

Maggie Theresa Riley and her four-legged companion supplied dairy products to residents of Green River. Riley lived in Green River for roughly 60 years, passing away in 1943. After the 1903 death of her husband, she supported herself and two sons by selling dairy and poultry products. This image from the early 20th century suggests that livestock were allowed to roam the streets freely. (Courtesy of Sweetwater County Historical Museum.)

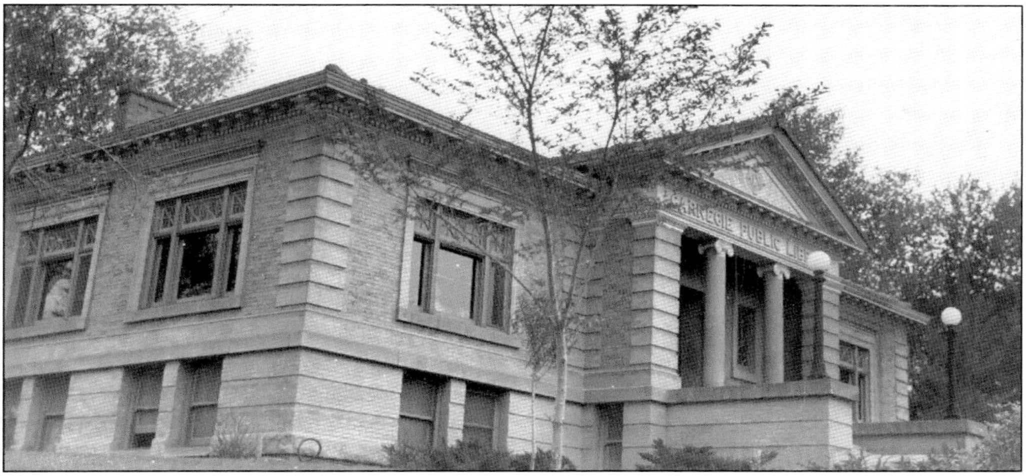

The Green River Public Library, completed in 1907, was financed with a $20,000 grant from the Carnegie Foundation. A promoter of literacy, steel magnate and philanthropist Andrew Carnegie funded the construction of libraries for small towns. A tax levy was assessed to operate the library, which closed in 1980 and was replaced by the Sweetwater County Library. The library building was then used as a courthouse. (Courtesy of Sweetwater County Historical Museum.)

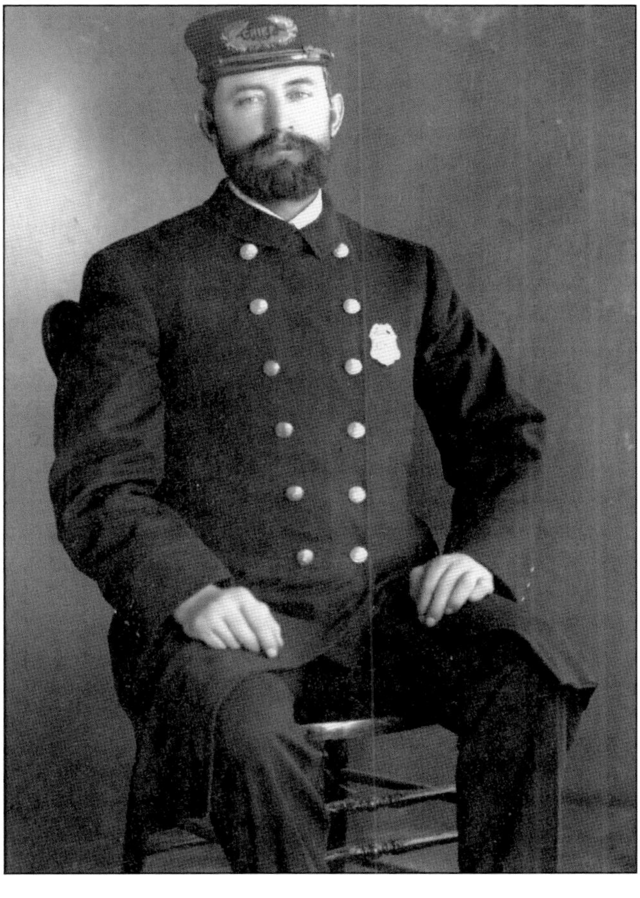

James "Jack" Moriarty served as a deputy for the Rock Springs Police Department at the time of the Chinese Massacre in 1885. He then served as deputy sheriff under Charles Young from 1903 to 1904. After moving to Green River, Moriarty served jointly as town marshal, street commissioner, and fire warden from 1905 to 1921. He also served periodically as a sheriff's deputy under Matt McCourt from 1909 to 1916. (Courtesy of Sweetwater County Historical Museum.)

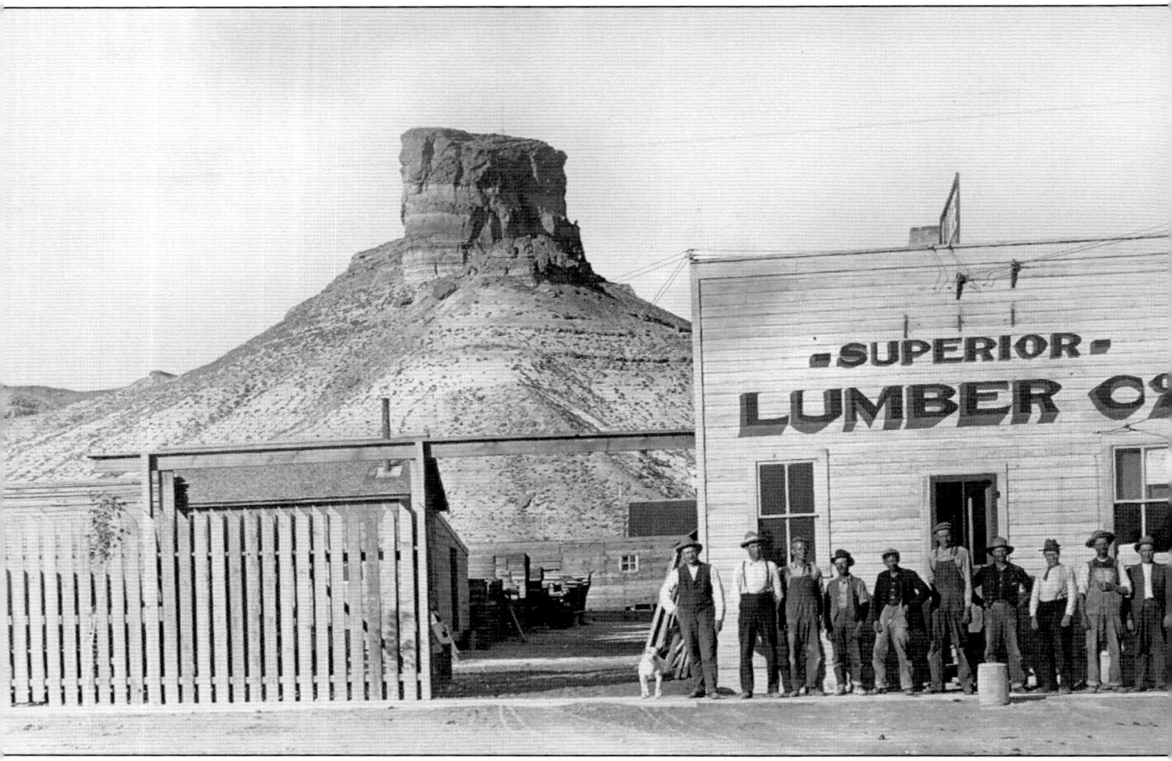

The Green River branch of the Superior Lumber Company of Rock Springs opened in 1908. It continued under the same ownership until 1913, when it was purchased by William and Jack Evers, who changed the name to the Green River Lumber Company. In 1916, the Weber Lumber Company of Ogden, Utah, took over the lumber and coal businesses of both the Green River Lumber Company and E. E. Peters Lumber. (Courtesy of Sweetwater County Historical Museum.)

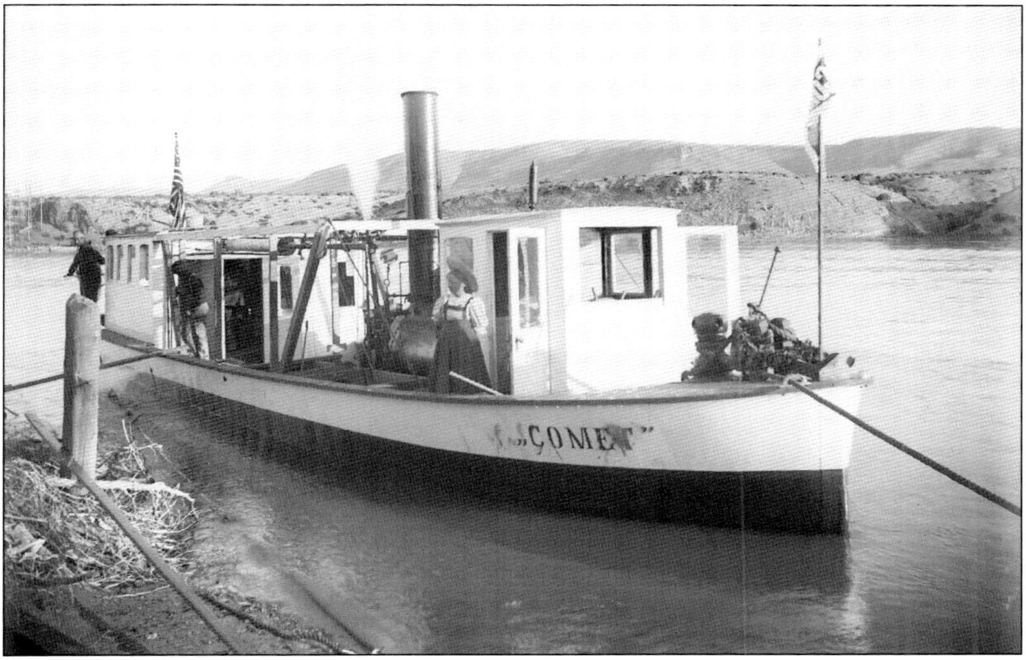

The *Comet*, a 60-foot stern-wheeler steamboat, was christened in July 1908 by the Green River Navigation Company. It was designed to carry goods to Linwood, Utah, located 50 miles downstream. The downstream trip took eight hours, while the return trip took 33 hours, with frequent stops for refueling. That year, the Green River was recognized as being impractical for navigation. Shortly thereafter, the *Comet* was scrapped and sunk. (Courtesy of Sweetwater County Historical Museum.)

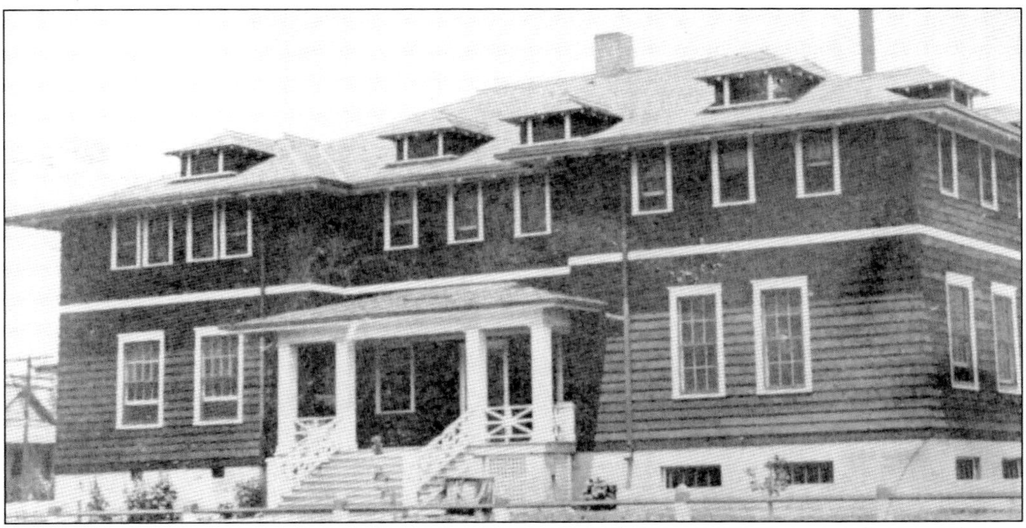

The Union Pacific Railroad Clubhouse was constructed in 1909 to accommodate employees who had layovers in Green River. The clubhouse was equipped with pool tables, reading rooms, a library, bathrooms, and numerous sleeping apartments. An addition was built in 1937. By 1969, this building was declared obsolete, and a new cement-slab clubhouse was built. (Courtesy of Sweetwater County Historical Museum.)

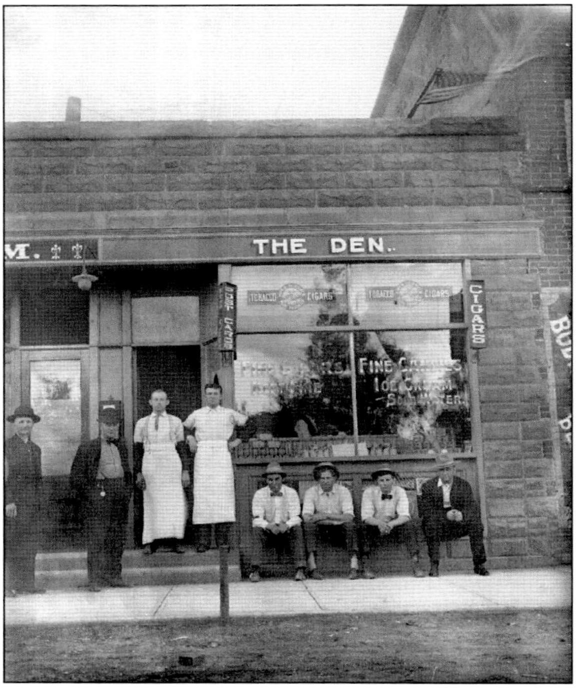

The Den, shown here around 1909, was constructed in 1872 as the Family Grocery Store. The building housed many businesses over the years, including the Lewis General Merchandise Store (roughly 1880–1900), the Jensen Meat Market (1900–1907), the City Meat Market (1908–1913), the Green River Market (1913–1919), and the Golden Rule Store (1919–1920), among others. Assembled on the steps in no particular order are Johnny Harris, Ira Bishopp, Jack Logan, Thomas Cottle, and Heriot Riddle. Matt McCourt is second from the left. (Courtesy of Sweetwater County Historical Museum.)

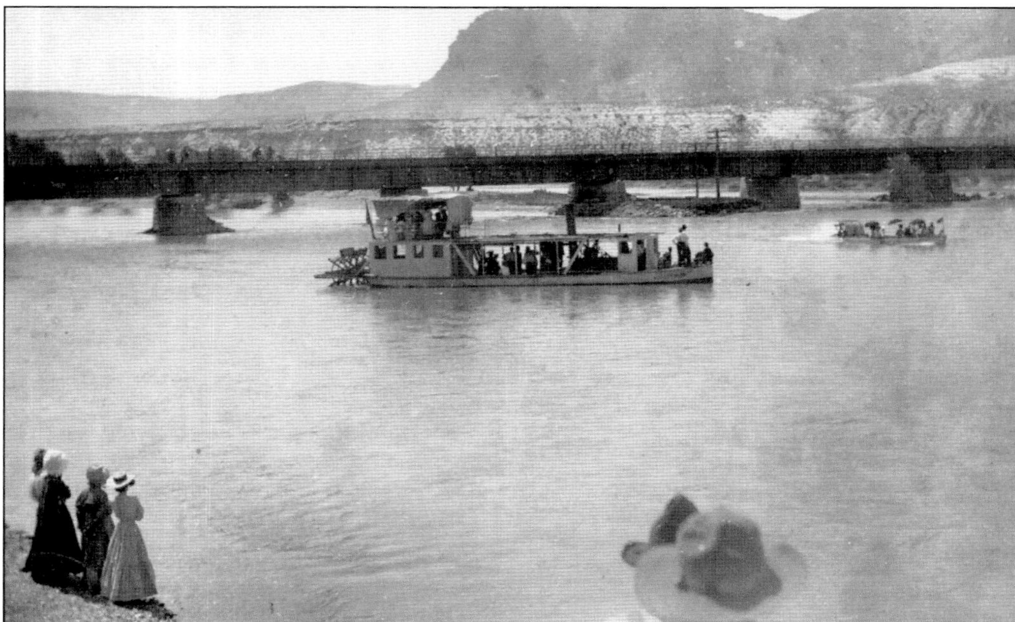

The Green River armada patrols the waterfront around 1910. The larger boat, the *Comet*, was built as a commercial venture. The smaller vessel, the *Sunbeam*, was an attraction at the amusement park on Island Park. This stern-wheeled gasoline launch, along with its twin, the *Teddy R.*, piloted excursions north to Big Piney and south to Buckboard Crossing. The park included a dance pavilion, a dock, a carousel, and a refreshment stand. (Courtesy of Sweetwater County Historical Museum.)

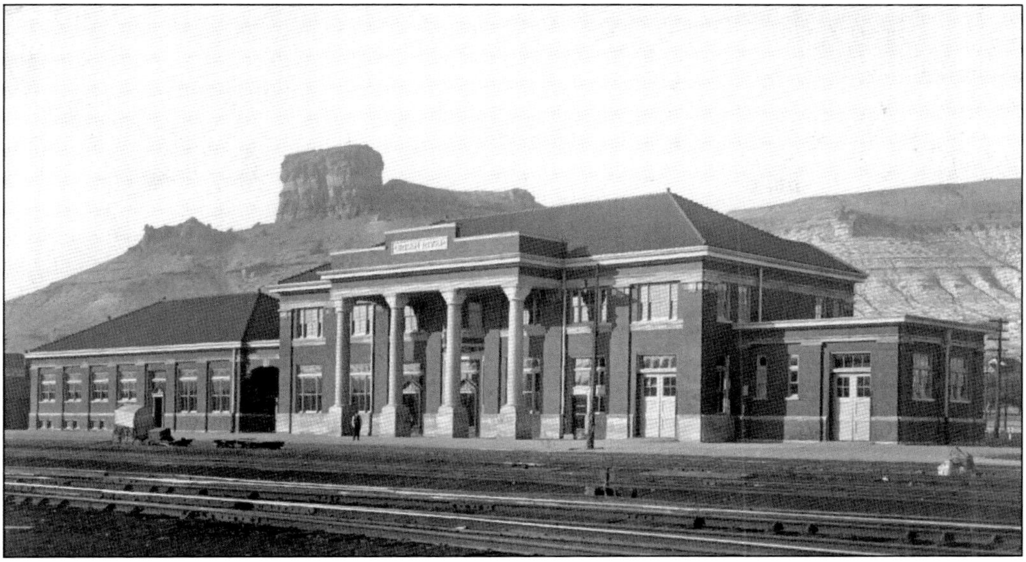

This 1910 postcard image of the Green River Union Pacific Railroad Depot shows a newly built structure that is a classic example of depots in the early 20th century. Once bustling with passengers boarding trains, the depot is more subdued now. The structure is currently being used for office space by the railroad, as passenger trains no longer come through the area. (Courtesy of Sweetwater County Historical Museum.)

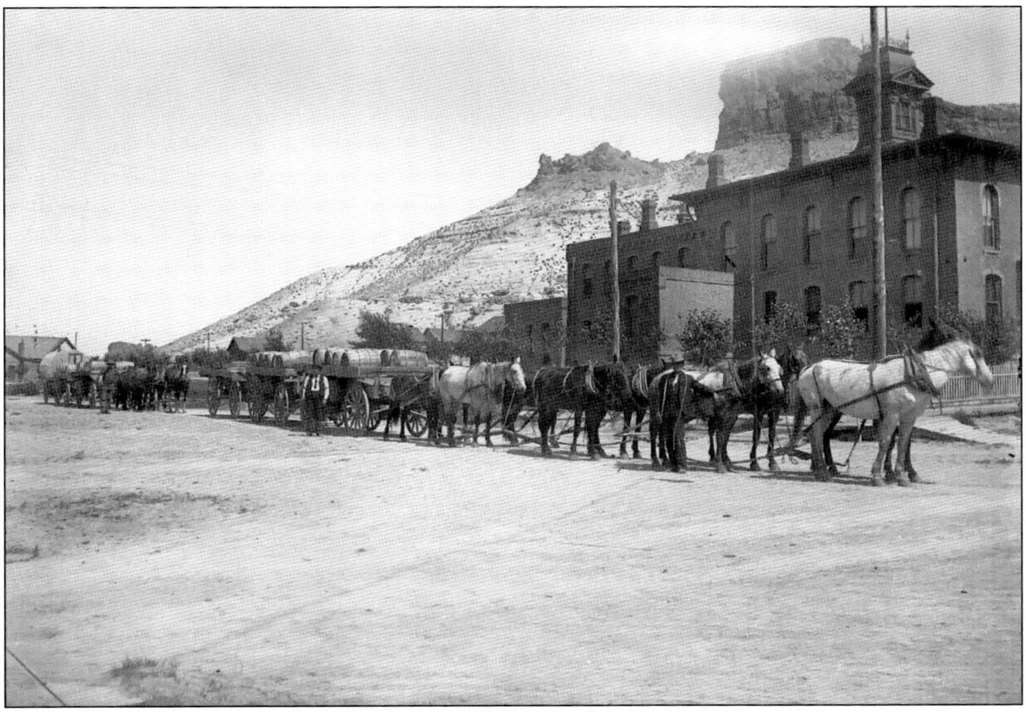

Harvey and Stowe Freighters prepare to haul off 36 barrels of beer produced at Sweetwater Brewing Company. This 1910 image shows how small cargoes were transported to and from the rail yard and for short hauls into the interior. (Courtesy of Sweetwater County Historical Museum.)

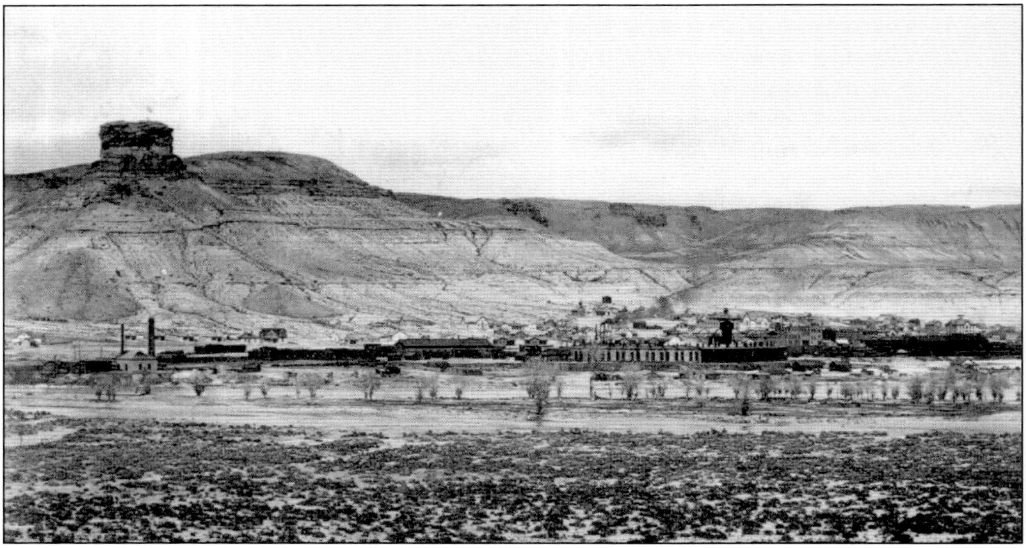

This postcard image of Green River dates to the second decade of the 20th century. The unusual view of the community apparently was shot from the western side of town, south of the river. The image shows the busy Union Pacific Roundhouse, the brewery, the courthouse, the Episcopal church, and Castle Rock (sporting a flag). (Courtesy of Sweetwater County Historical Museum.)

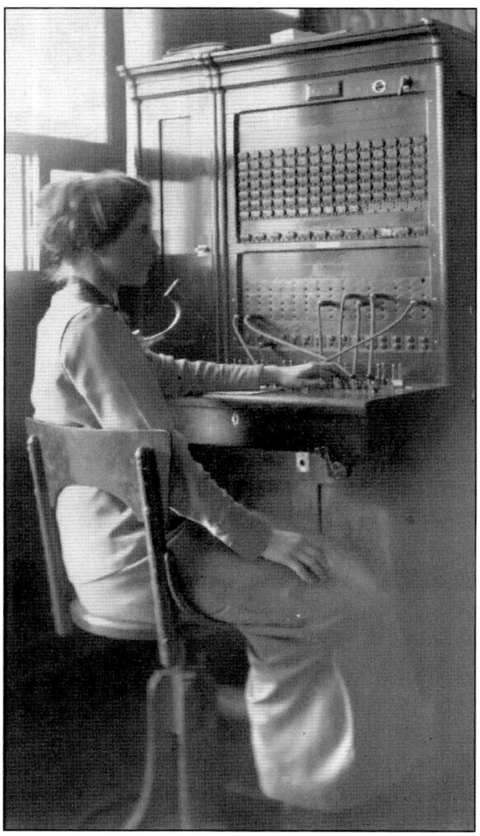

Mary "May" Moriarty, pictured here in 1913 at the age of 23, was the daughter of James and Julia Moriarty of Green River. May, who worked as switchboard operator, married Charles Viox in 1914. She was an active community member and was involved with the Altar and Rosary Society, the Parent Teacher Association, the Woman's Club, the Democratic Party, and the American Legion Auxiliary. She was also a 74-year member of the Royal Neighbors of America. (Courtesy of Sweetwater County Historical Museum.)

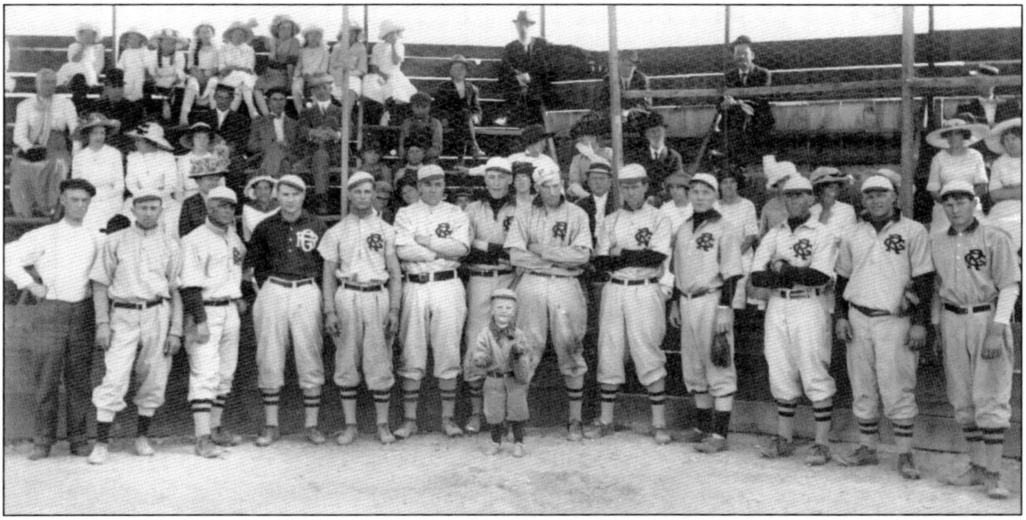

The 1913 Green River Civic League baseball team was one of the better teams in the region. The team helped to finance itself with a popular charity dance. Pictured here are, from left to right, manager William Upton, Weller Bishopp, Herbert and W. Herbst, ? Hensley (or Henley), ? Sharp, Emery Mulica, Carl Gaensslen, Ray Black, team captain "Doc" Gaston, Emil Droege, Jimmie Maher, unidentified, and Lawrence E. Curry. (Courtesy of Sweetwater County Historical Museum.)

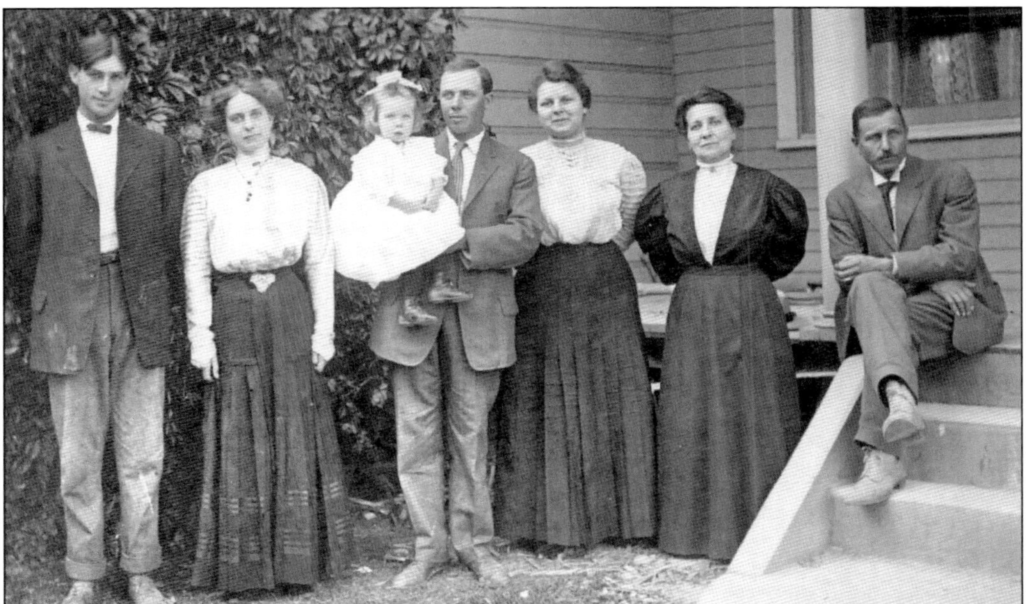

The family of Stanislaw Dankowski, a Green River barber, poses in 1913 or 1914 . In 1917, at the age of 58 or 59, Stanislaw enlisted in the U.S. Navy, becoming one of the oldest men in active duty during World War I. He served through the end of the war. Pictured are, from left to right, Anthony Jeffers, Jean Dankowski Jeffers, E. T. Bishopp, Jean Flora Bishopp, Nellie Dankowski Bishopp, Anna Dankowski, and Stanislaw Dankowski. (Courtesy of Sweetwater County Historical Museum.)

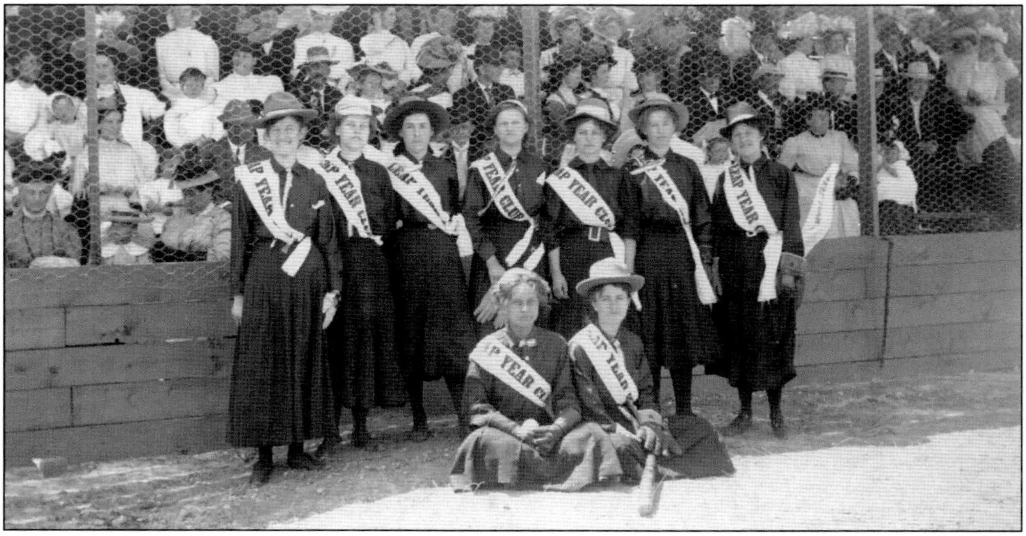

The Leap Year Club of Green River formed a baseball team, shown here in 1915. Established in 1904, which was a leap year, the club was an association of women originally formed to take advantage of the tradition that, during a leap year, a girl could ask a man to a social event without stigma. The club existed for several leap years, with frequent mentions in the social pages. (Courtesy of Sweetwater County Historical Museum.)

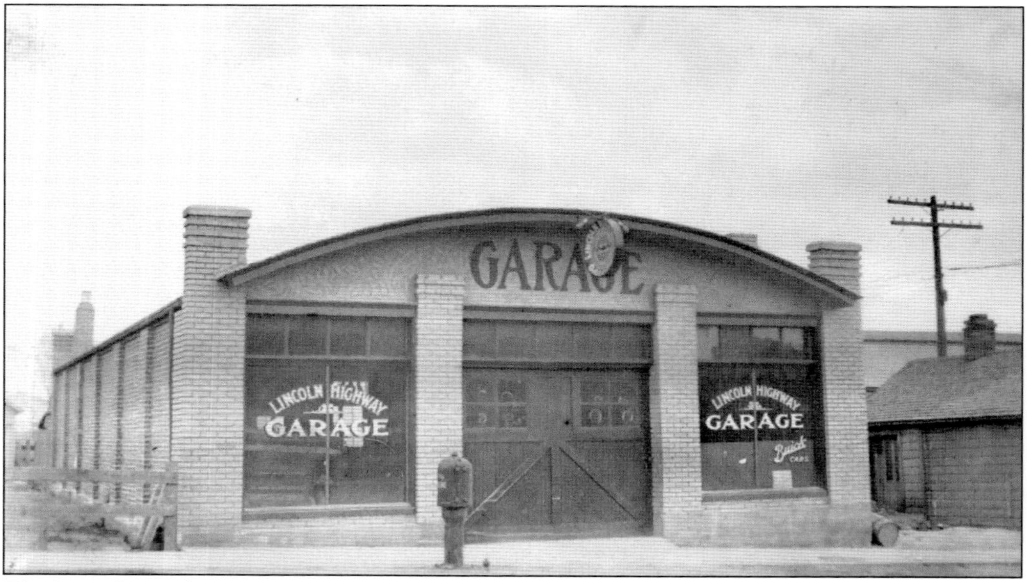

The Lincoln Highway Garage was built in 1915, only to be demolished in 1919 to make way for the Tomahawk Hotel. A new garage was built around the corner in 1921 and is still in use today. The Lincoln Highway was designated in 1913 and went through the business district of Green River well into the 1940s, bringing important commerce into the city. (Courtesy of Sweetwater County Historical Museum.)

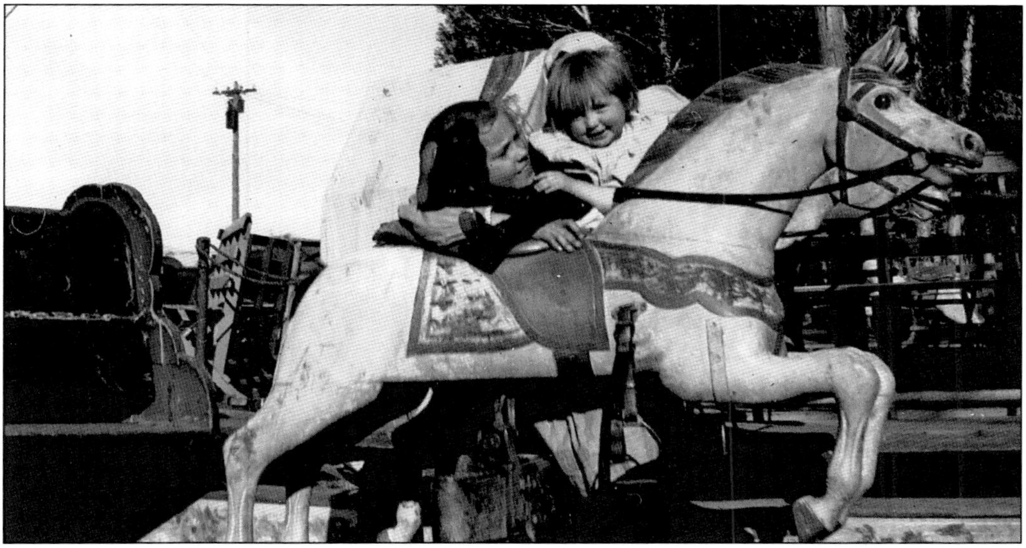

Children enjoy a carousel ride in this *c.* 1915 image. This carnival ride was located at Island Park, which was a popular summer entertainment spot. The park attracted city residents as well as visitors from Rock Springs and other towns in the area. Today Island Park is known as Expedition Island, and it remains a center for summer recreation. (Courtesy of Sweetwater County Historical Museum.)

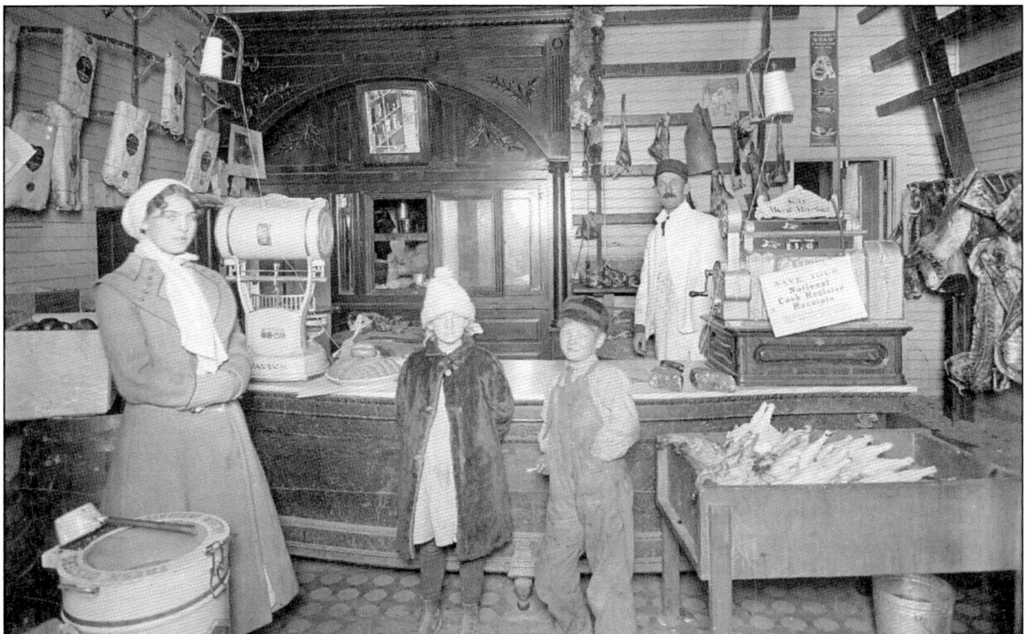

This image shows the interior of the City Meat Market around 1915. Noted for its cleanliness, the City Meat Market, owned by George Harris Jr., kept its displayed inventory of meat and oysters uncovered and without refrigeration. The customers pictured here are, from left to right, Clara Christensen, Mabel Lowe, and Francis "Shorty" Fye. (Courtesy of Sweetwater County Historical Museum.)

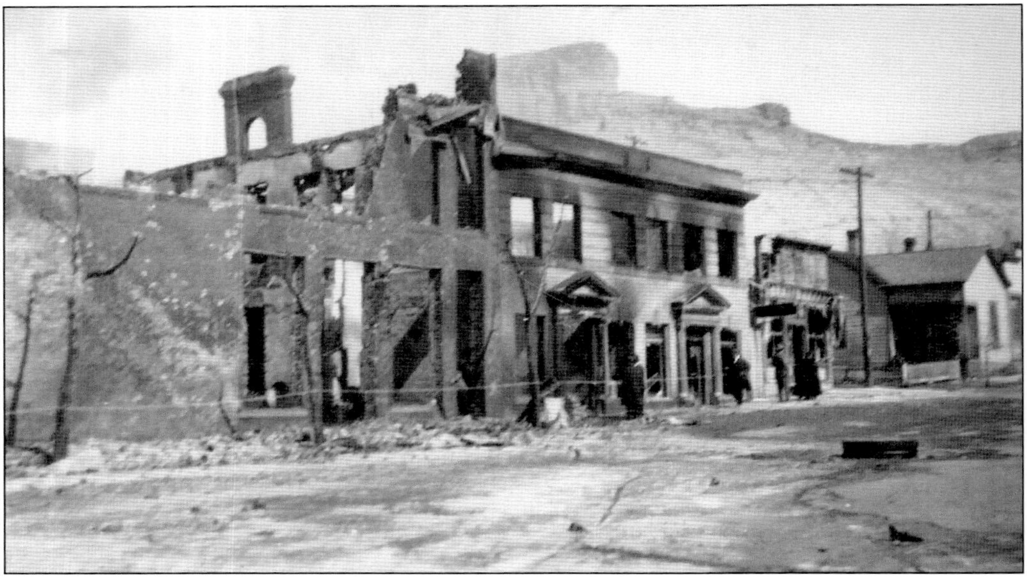

On March 25, 1917, the Green River Mercantile and its associated businesses were burned down as the result of a defective furnace. The fire spread rapidly, and high winds put large sections of the business district in jeopardy. The losses to the mercantile, bank, and post office were complete. The site was the former location of the Morris Mercantile and Morris State Bank. The Green River Mercantile continues to operate and is one of the oldest businesses in Wyoming. (Courtesy of Sweetwater County Historical Museum.)

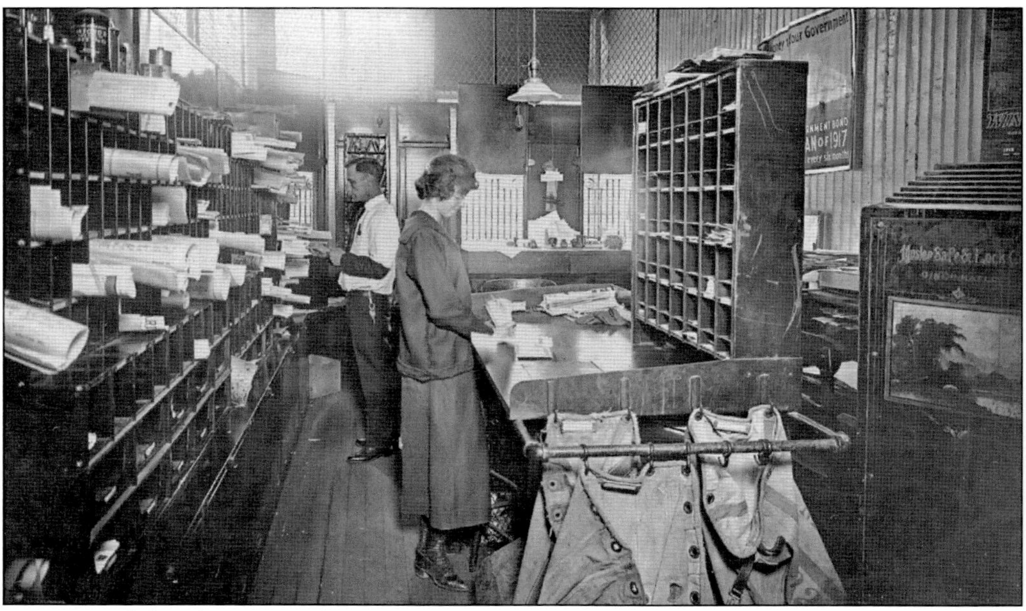

Sorting and distributing mail in this 1918 photograph are Postmaster W. A. Johnson and an unidentified assistant. In 1917, a fire destroyed the post office, which was housed in the Green River Mercantile block. Subsequently, the post office was located in various businesses and houses. At the time of this photograph, the post office was within the new location of the Green River Mercantile. (Courtesy of Sweetwater County Historical Museum.)

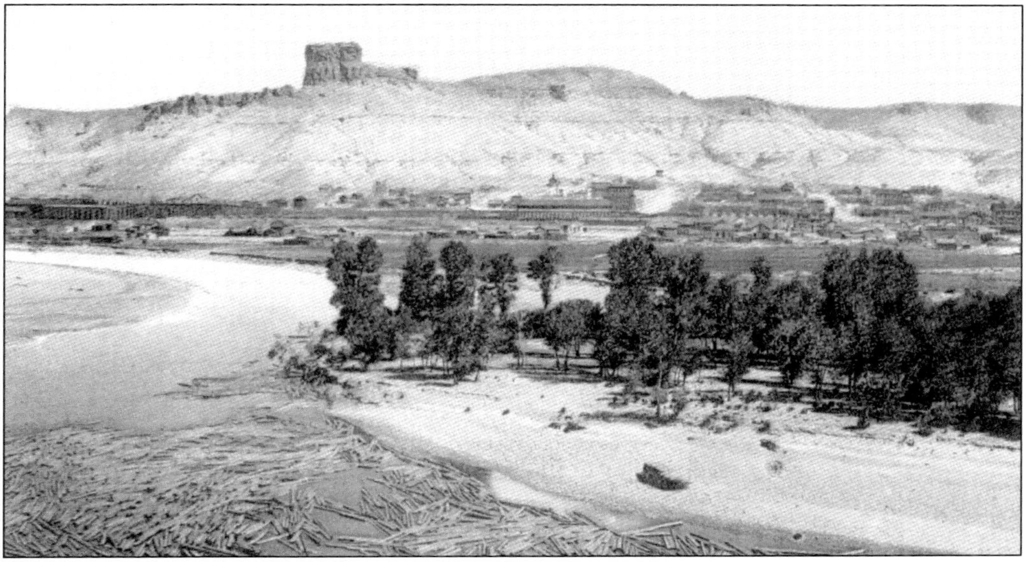

This postcard image of Green River in 1918 shows the Green River choked with railroad ties, which were kept from proceeding downstream by a large boom. Between 1868 and 1941, trees were cut upstream, and the rough ties were floated to Green River. The ties were then gathered and shipped to Laramie for processing into railroad ties. (Courtesy of Sweetwater County Historical Museum.)

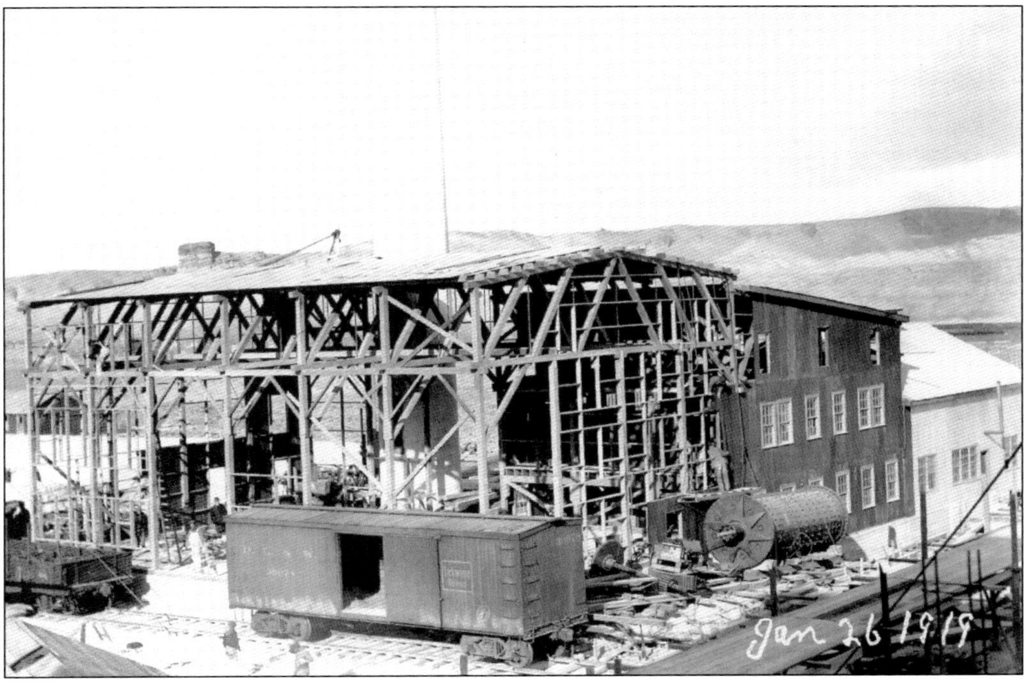

In 1916, the United States began looking for domestic substitutes for materials imported from Germany. Potash was one such product. In 1918, the Liberty Potash Company incorporated and built a plant on the south side of the Green River. The plant had just begun production when the war ended. With cheaper foreign potash flooding the market, the plant was defunct by the mid-1920s. (Courtesy of Sweetwater County Historical Museum.)

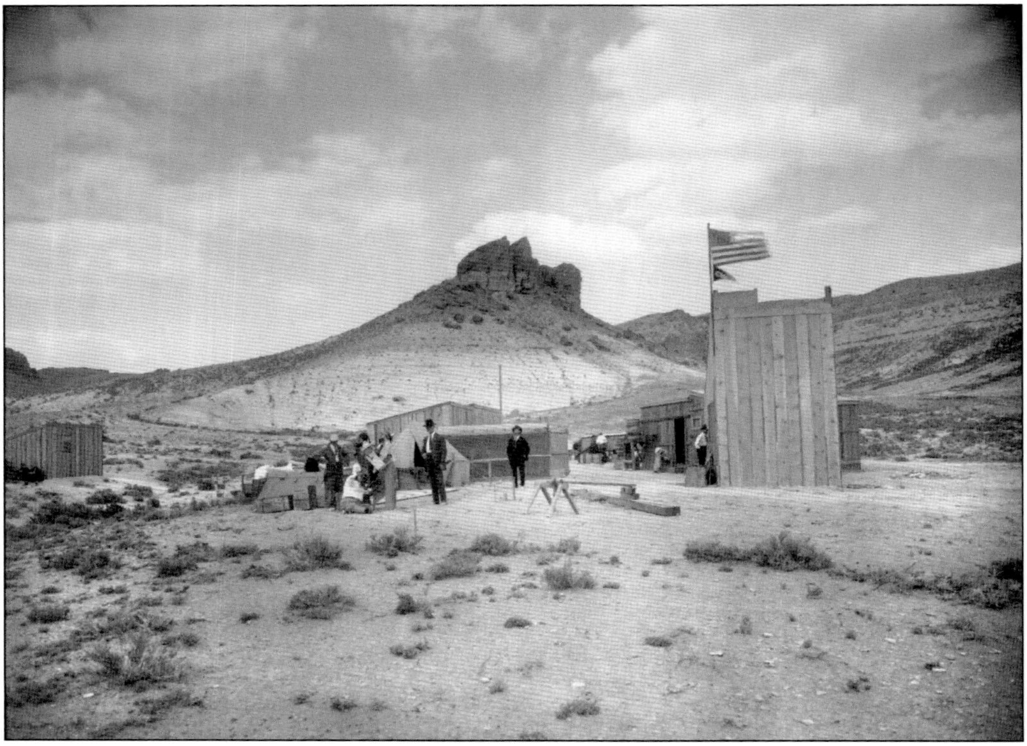

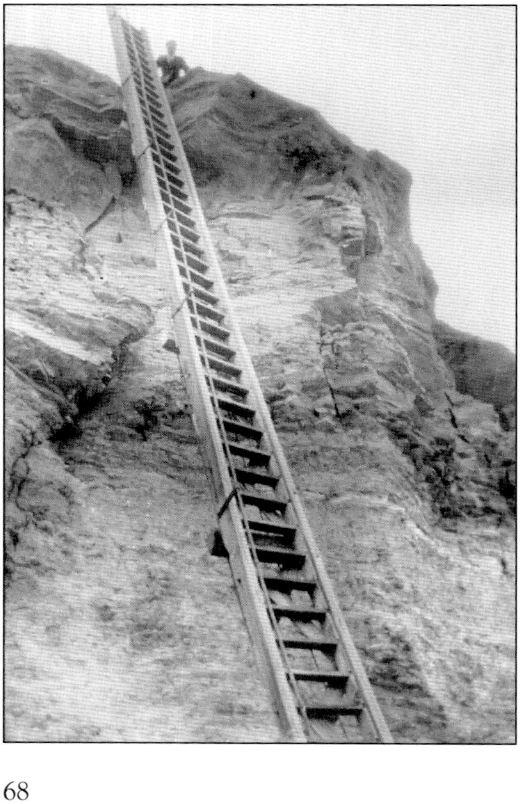

For a brief period in the early summer of 1918, when a total eclipse occurred, Green River was a center for the study of astronomy. The town was host to several groups, including one from the University of Chicago's Yerkes Observatory. Green River was located in a place where the total eclipse could be seen and was chosen as an observation site because of the prevalence of clear weather. Ironically, the observations made during the eclipse on June 8 were hampered by a light cloud cover, but the local paper reported the discovery of a new star. The Yerkes team was in the area for about a month preparing for the event. Note the man in the white shirt setting up a piece of equipment near the hastily constructed observatory buildings. The camp was located on the outskirts of Green River. The flag from the steamship *Comet* was flown by the researchers and appears below the American flag. The team placed a ladder that ascended to the top of Castle Rock. The ladder was removed some years later, as it had become a hazard. (Courtesy of Sweetwater County Historical Museum.)

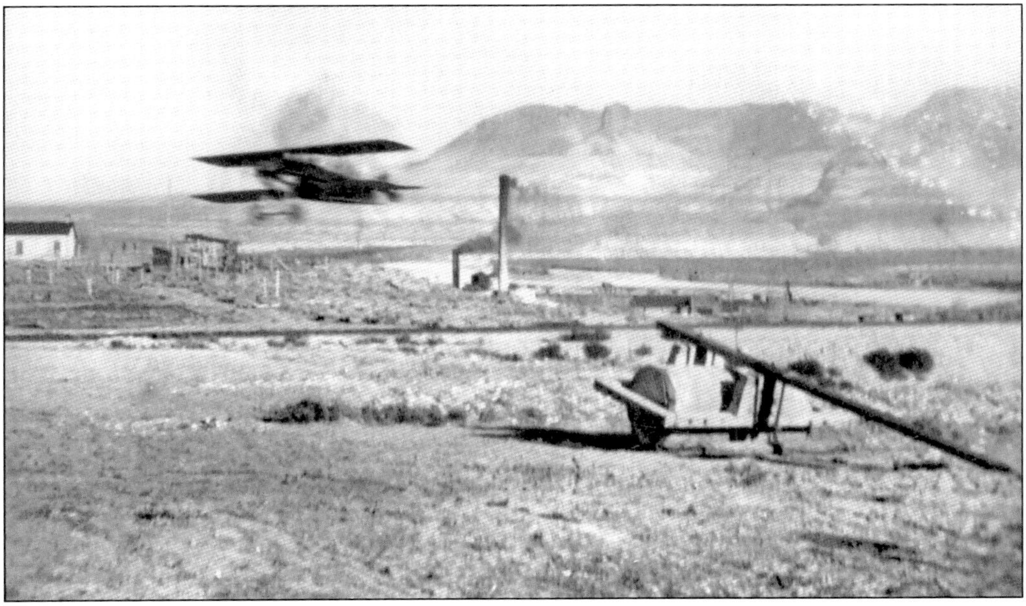

Soaring into a clear Wyoming sky, a participant in the 1918 air race takes off from the Hutton Heights airfield. In the background on the left, the Hutton family farm is visible. William Hutton and his wife ran a small farming operation on the bench above the river. The area still bears the name Hutton Heights. (Courtesy of Sweetwater County Historical Museum.)

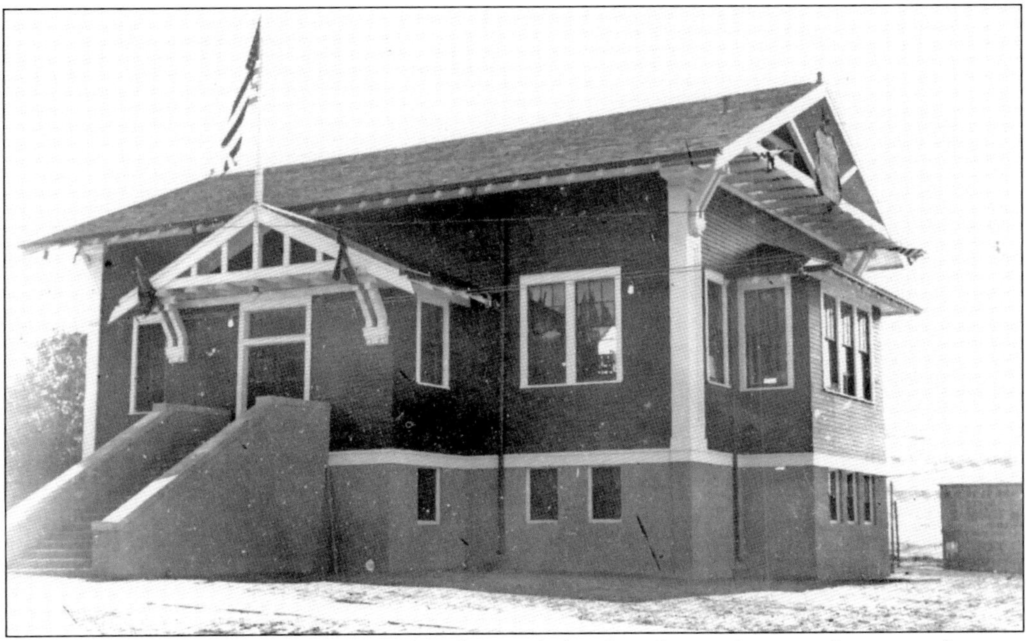

Built in 1918, the Union Pacific Social Hall provided a place for employees to have social events and meetings. The hall was used for classrooms until 1942, and in the late 1950s and early 1960s it served as a dance studio. The Lions and the Cub Scouts of America also used the structure. The Eagles later purchased and demolished it to make space for a parking lot. (Courtesy of Sweetwater County Historical Museum.)

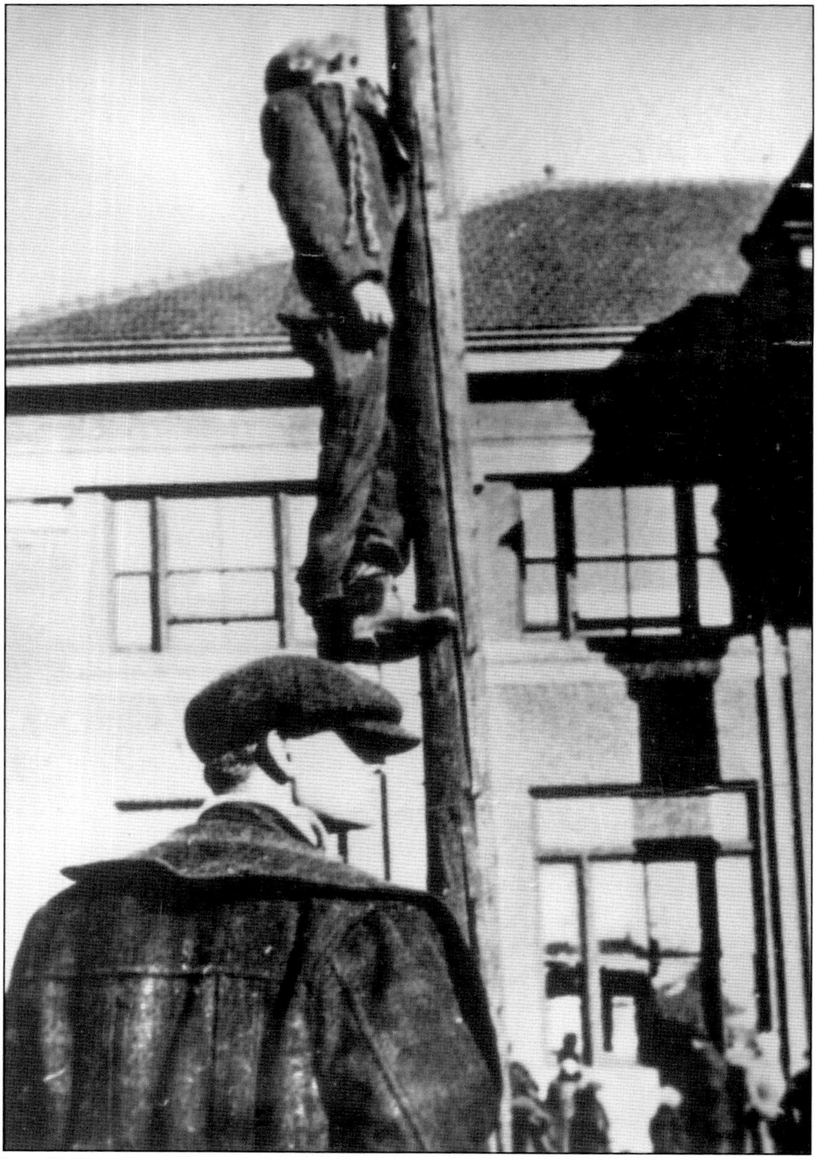

In December 1918, an interracial dispute led to the lynching of Joel Woodson, a black man who worked as a janitor in the social hall. Woodson became angry at the lunch counter's waitress after she brought him dried mush instead of sausage. The waitress threw salt shakers at Woodson when he called her a "damned liar." Two men at the counter, recorded only as Miller and Curtis, threw Woodson out of the lunch counter. A short time later, Woodson returned and shot Miller through the heart and Curtis in the wrist, shouting, "You will never lay a hand on me again!" Woodson fled after shooting the men, but he was soon was captured. Miller was dead, and Curtis was sent away for medical attention. When locals learned of the killing, a mob gathered and removed Woodson from jail. Ignoring the pleas for reason and justice from local attorney T. S. Taliaferro, the howling mob hung Woodson from a pole in front of the depot. The corpse hung on the pole within sight of passing trains. The authorities turned a blind eye to the lynching, and no one was tried for Woodson's murder. (Courtesy of Sweetwater County Historical Museum.)

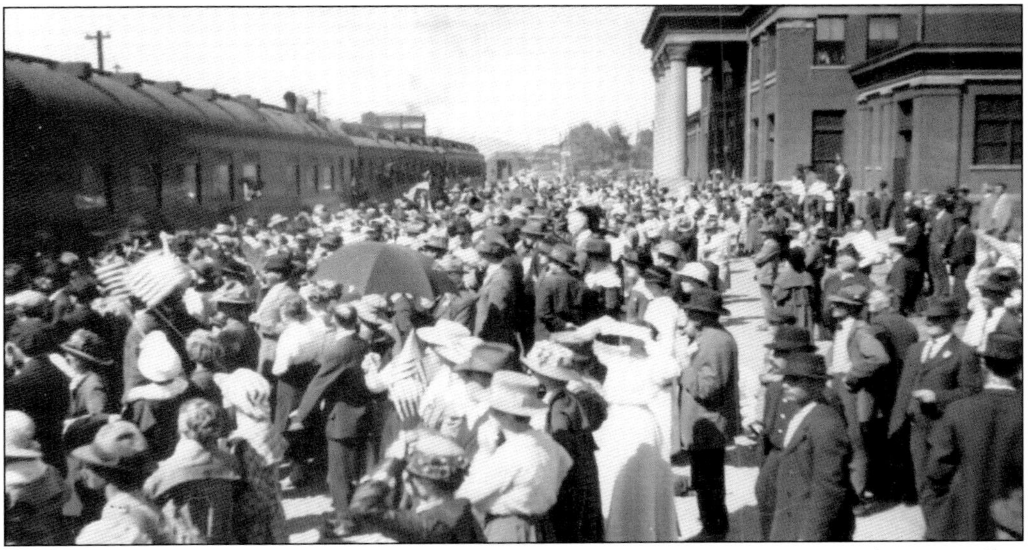

This photograph, taken around 1917, shows the citizens of Green River seeing volunteers off to serve "over there" during World War I. Similar scenes were played out across the nation as the United States mobilized soldiers by the hundreds of thousands to join "the war to end all wars." (Courtesy of Sweetwater County Historical Museum.)

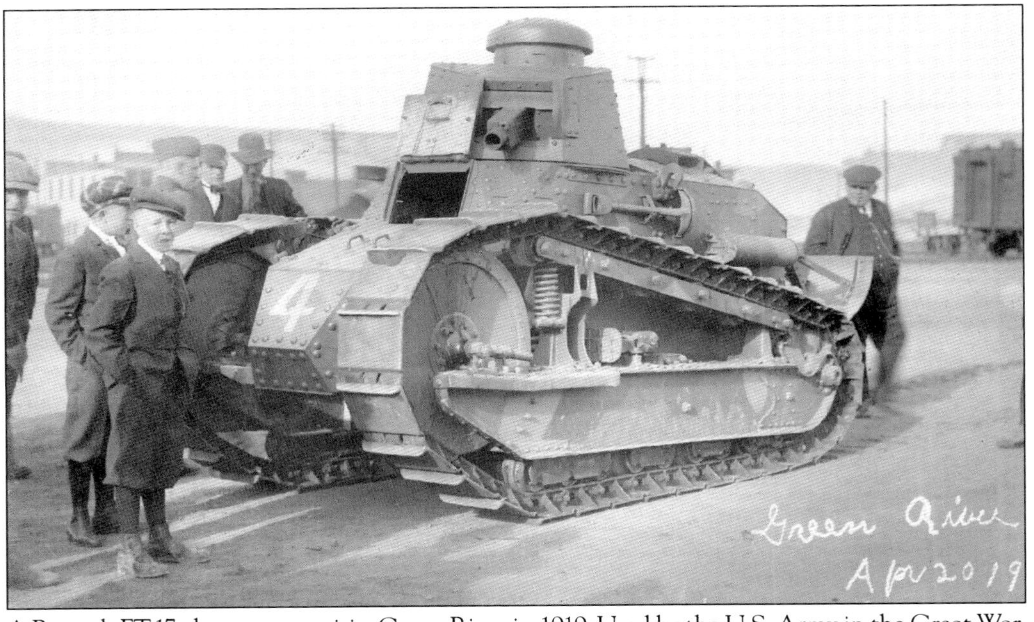

A Renault FT-17 char cannon visits Green River in 1919. Used by the U.S. Army in the Great War, the lightly armored Renaults could reach a speed of eight miles per hour. They were used as breakout weapons once the trench lines were breached. These nimble tanks, affectionately called Whippets by the troops, spread chaos in the areas behind the enemy trenches, making it more difficult for the enemy to launch counterattacks. (Courtesy of Sweetwater County Historical Museum.)

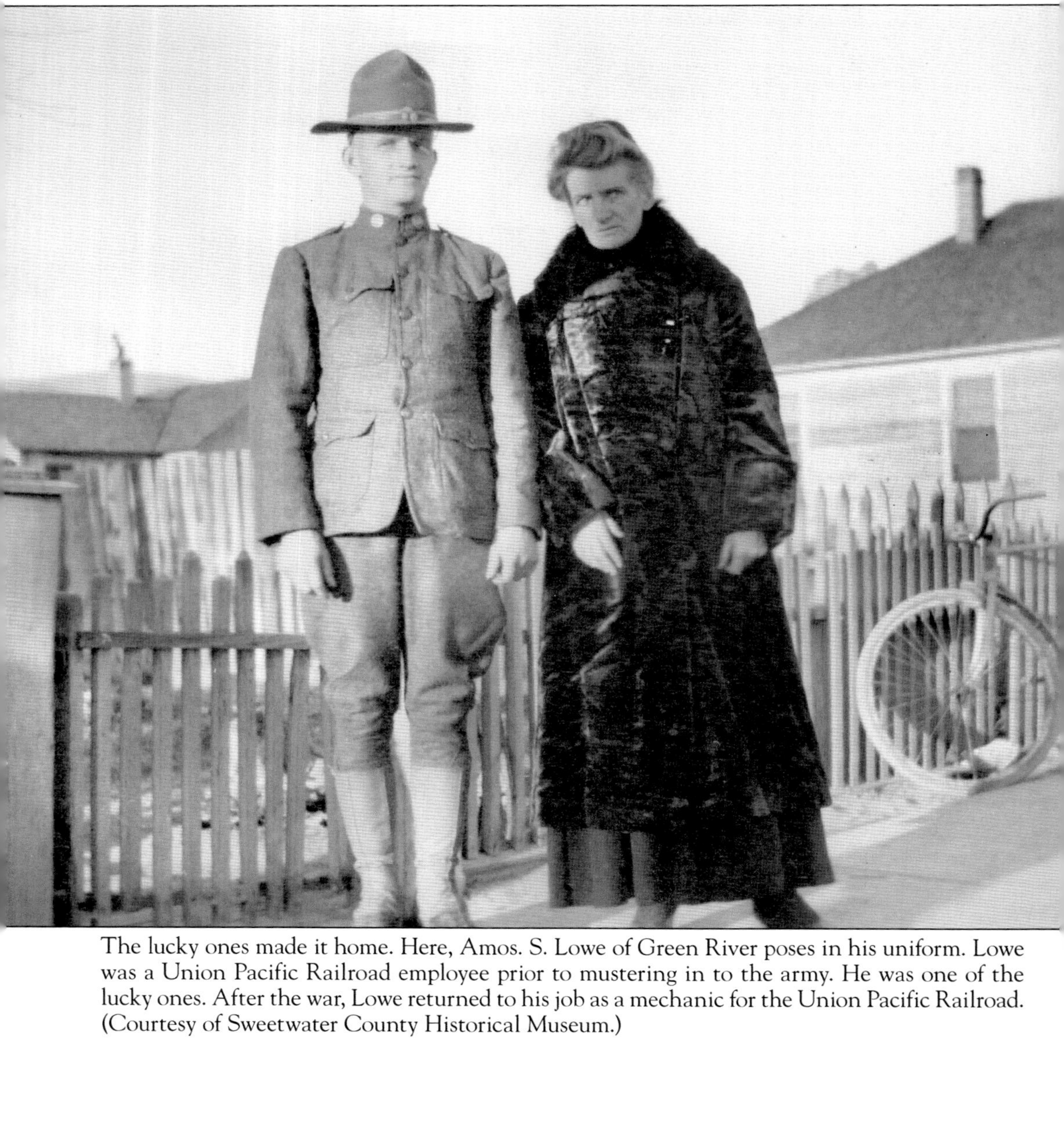

The lucky ones made it home. Here, Amos. S. Lowe of Green River poses in his uniform. Lowe was a Union Pacific Railroad employee prior to mustering in to the army. He was one of the lucky ones. After the war, Lowe returned to his job as a mechanic for the Union Pacific Railroad. (Courtesy of Sweetwater County Historical Museum.)

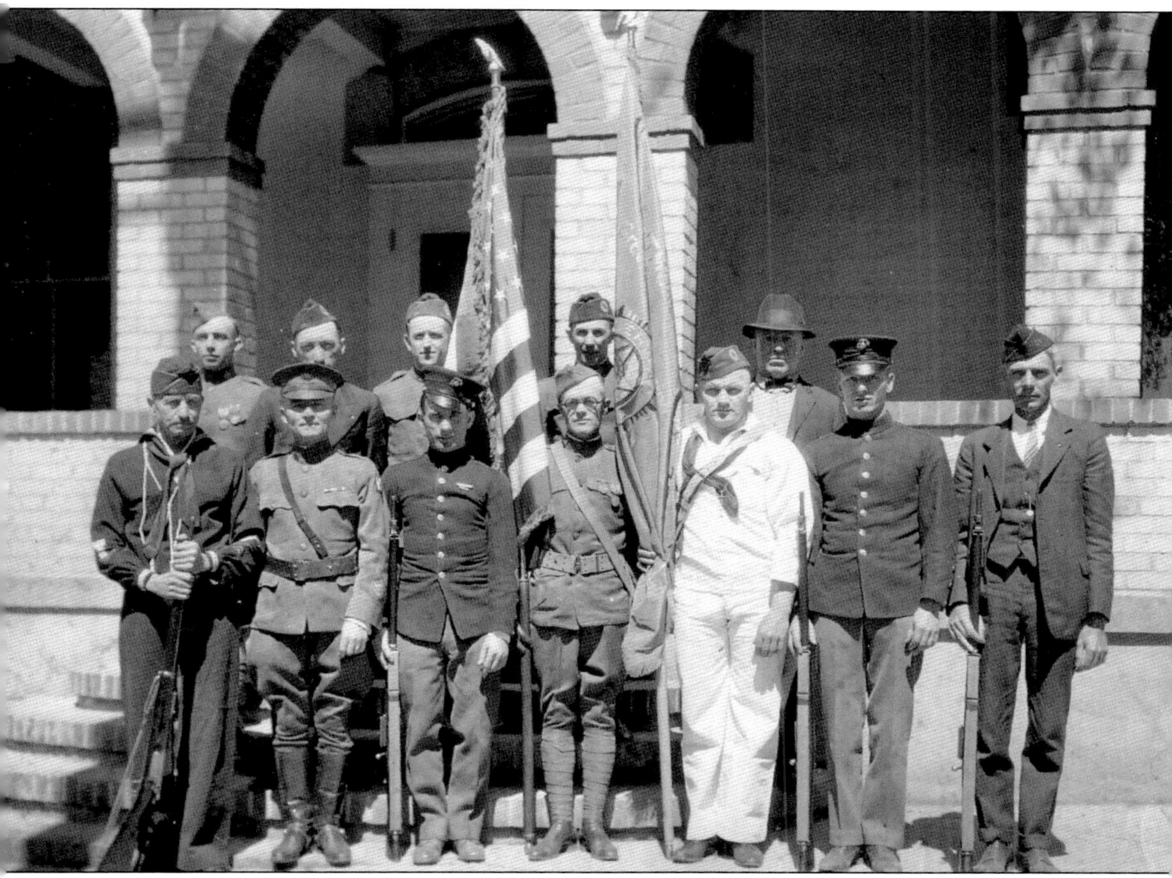

World War I veterans from Sweetwater County pose for a postwar image. Pictured are, from left to right, the following: (first row) Stanislaw Dankowski, Floyd Hirsch, Herbert Cooley, Robert "Doc" Hoover, unidentified, Francis Fye, and E. Sedlacek; (second row) unidentified, Cliff Reagan, Leslie Dunham, Edgar Fleetwood Waggener, and Matt McCourt. (Courtesy of Sweetwater County Historical Museum.)

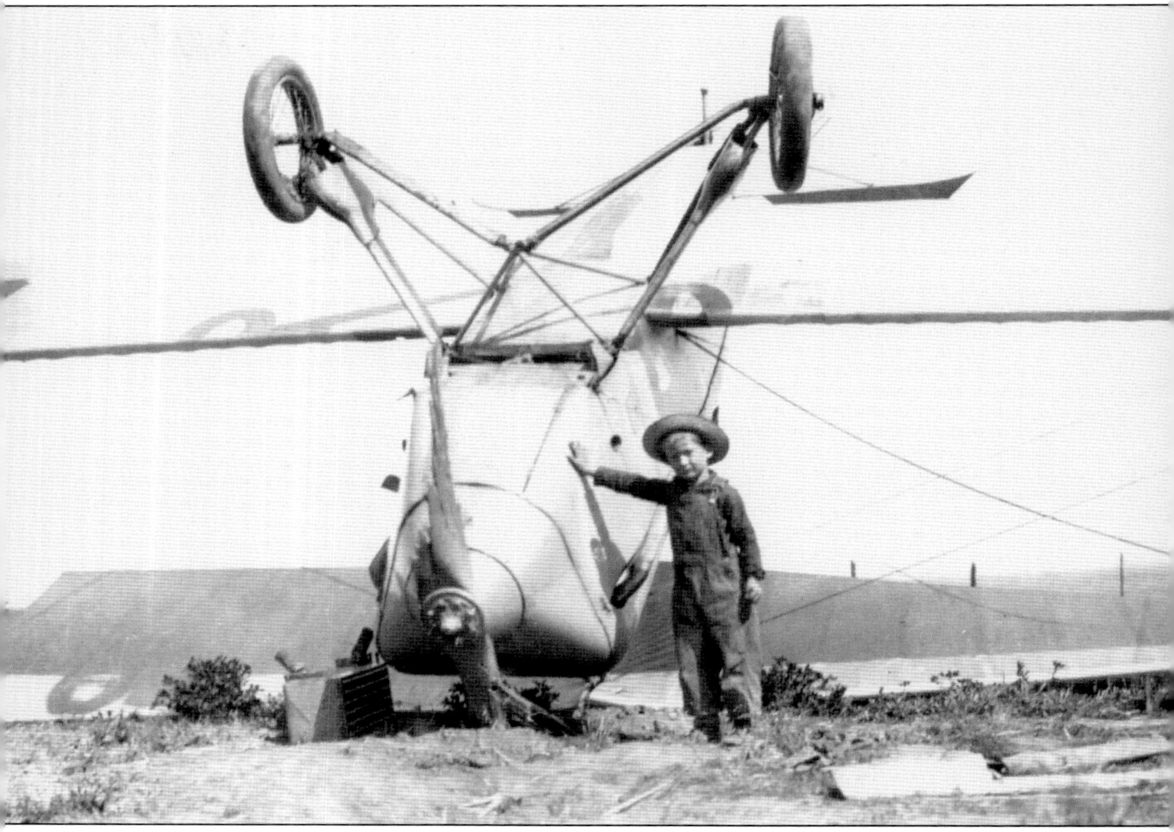

A boy poses by a De Havilland DH-4 biplane that flipped while attempting a landing at the Hutton Heights airfield. As a promotion for the U.S. Army Air Corps, the air race of 1919 stopped in Green River, where the planes were guarded overnight by Boy Scouts. Boy Scout Troop No. 1 was awarded the broken propeller blade, which is now on display at the Sweetwater County Historical Museum. (Courtesy of Sweetwater County Historical Museum.)

Four

PROHIBITION, DEPRESSION, AND WAR 1919–1945

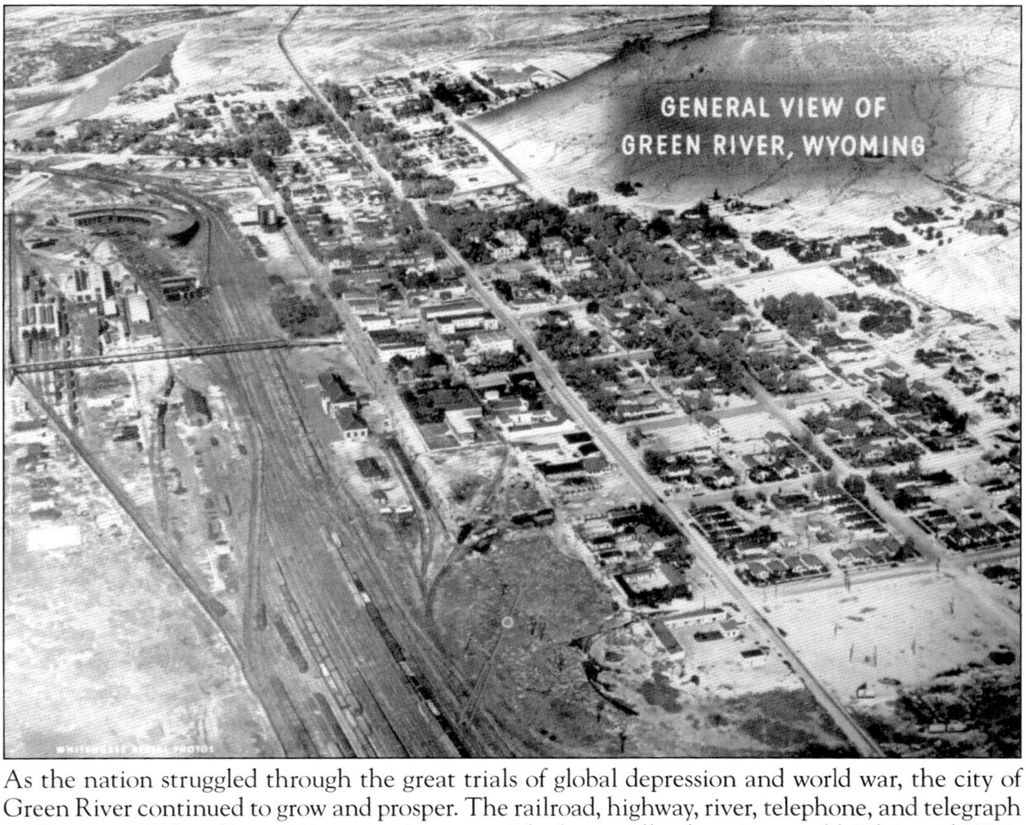

As the nation struggled through the great trials of global depression and world war, the city of Green River continued to grow and prosper. The railroad, highway, river, telephone, and telegraph traffic assured that Green River was in tune with the rapidly changing world. This mid-1930s aerial photograph of Green River shows U.S. Highway 30 and the Union Pacific mainline, which cut straight through town. The 28-stall roundhouse, the water towers, and the coaling chutes are all long-gone, though they were major landmarks during the heyday of railroad travel. (Courtesy of Sweetwater County Historical Museum.)

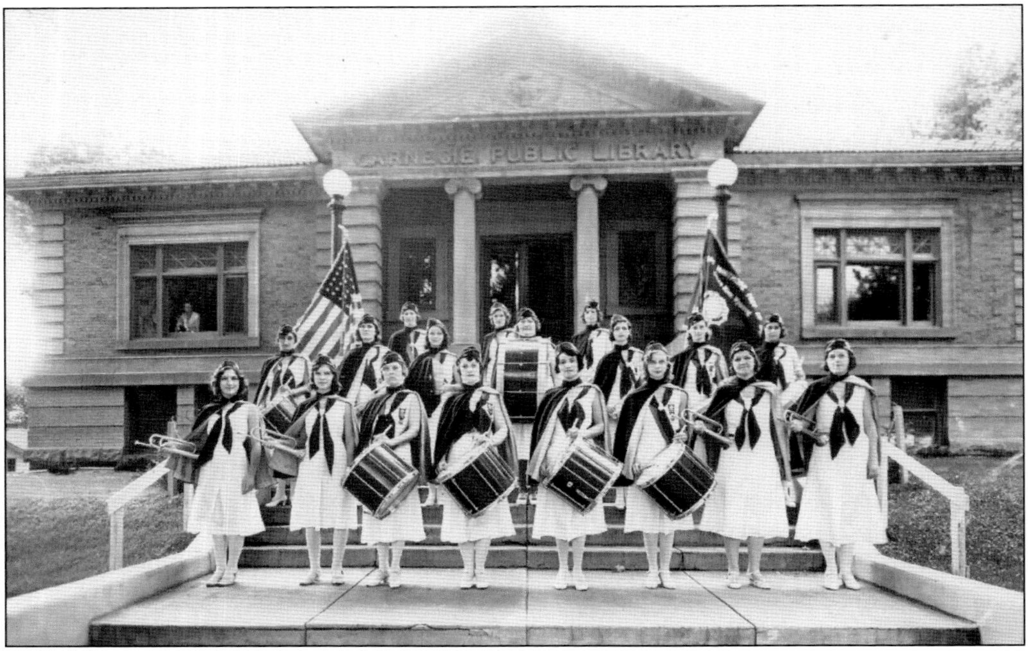

The Green River Drum and Bugle Corps, pictured here in 1920, was featured at parades and community events. By the late 1930s, it was known as one of the finest in the intermountain states. Two members are identified in this image: Lilly Deyarmond (first row, third from left) and Harline Hutton (first row, far right). (Courtesy of Sweetwater County Historical Museum.)

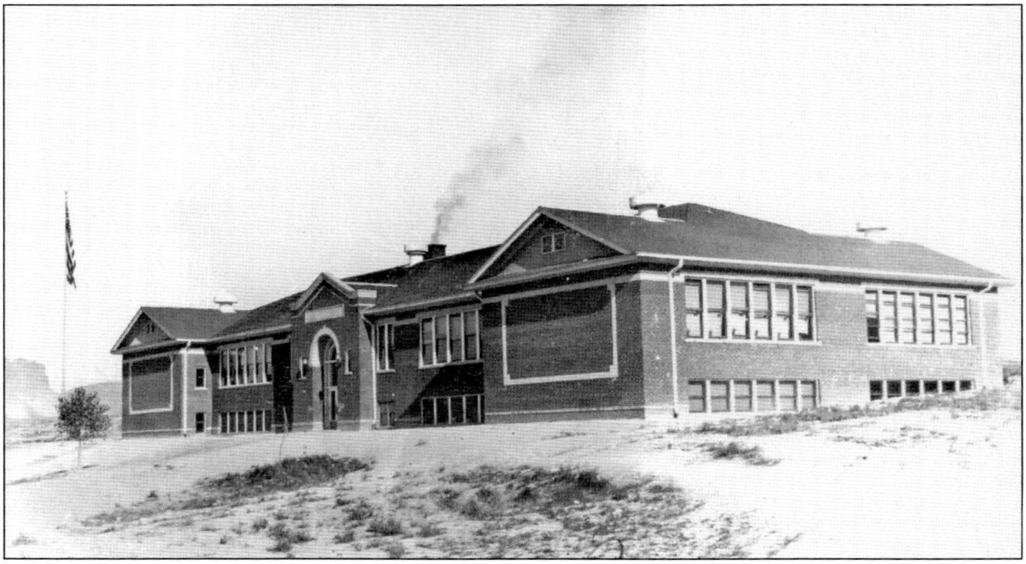

The Lincoln High School was built by Evers Brothers Construction in 1920 for $95,000. Additions were constructed in 1921 and 1925, and a gymnasium with a balcony was attached to the auditorium in 1930. The structure burned in 1940, and only the gymnasium survived. Classes were moved to the Jefferson Elementary School after the fire. The high school was reconstructed from 1941 to 1942 for $220,000. A fire in 2006 prompted demolition of the building in 2007. (Courtesy of Sweetwater County Historical Museum.)

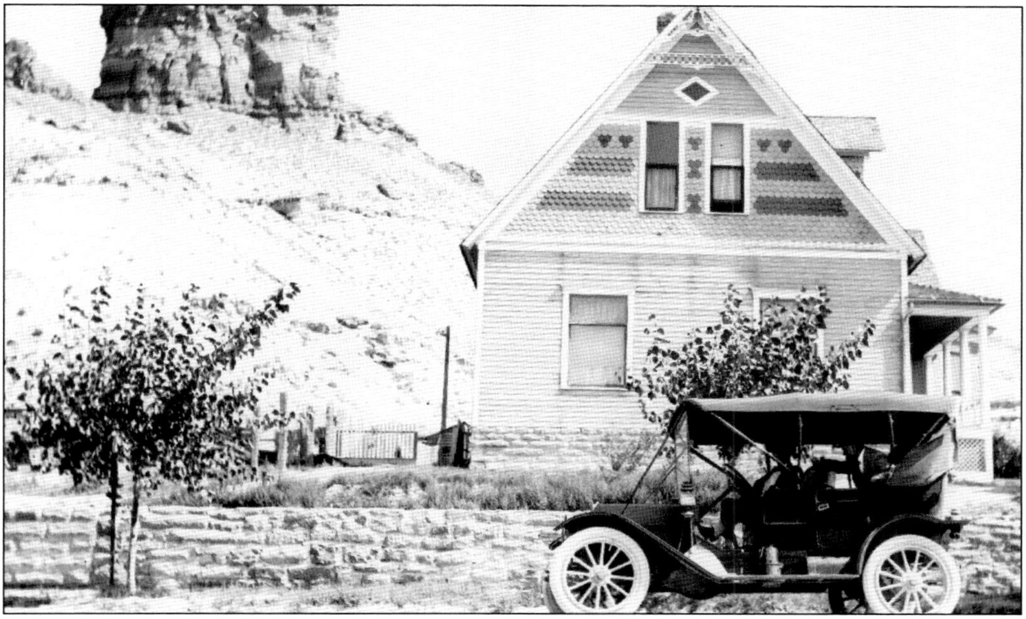

The Rolfe House, depicted in this 1920 image, was built in 1890. Over the next 14 years, it was owned by John Gilligan, W. R. Malonek, and Charles L. Young before being acquired by the Chrisman family. James Chrisman was the owner at the time of this photograph. (Courtesy of Sweetwater County Historical Museum.)

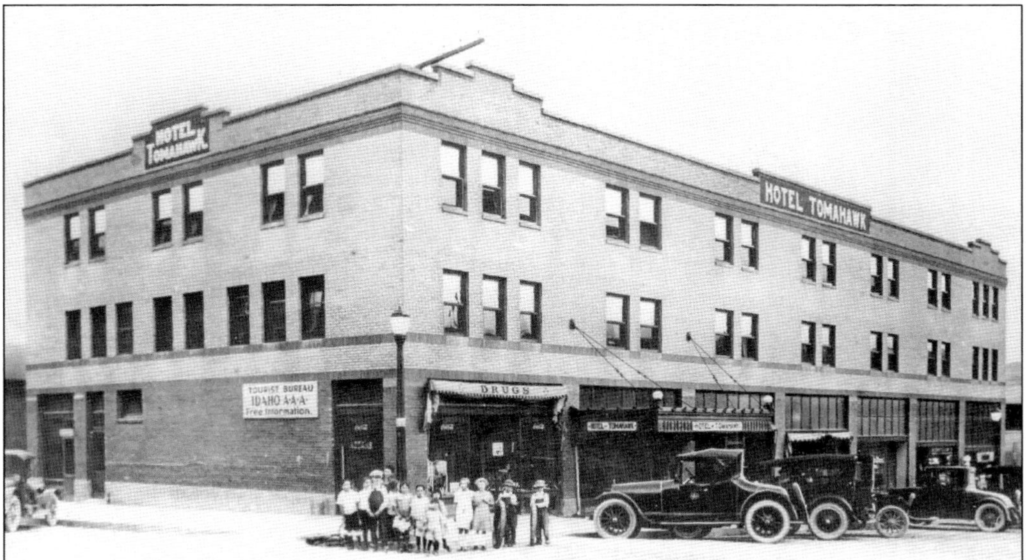

Named for primary investors Tom Welsh and Dr. Jacob Hawk, the Hotel Tomahawk was constructed in 1921 along the route of the Lincoln Highway. The six storefronts held various businesses, including a drugstore, a JC Penney, a bank, and offices of Allied Chemical (a soda ash company). The hotel remained in operation until 1982. The building continues to serve as a location for small businesses. (Courtesy of Sweetwater County Historical Museum.)

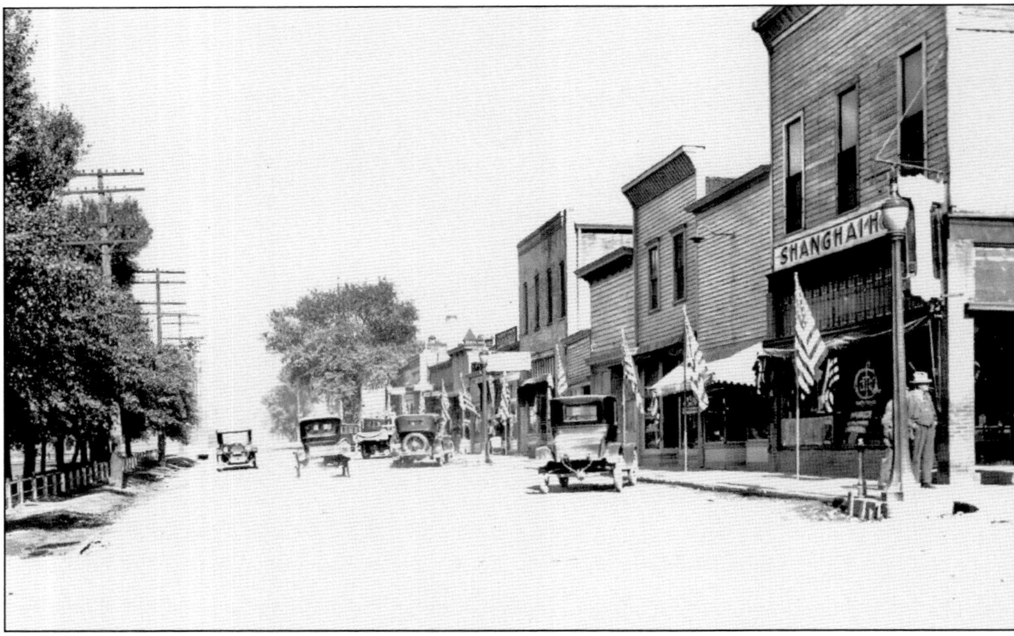

This 1920s street view of Green River prominently features the Shanghai, a restaurant and rooming house. The Shanghai originally occupied only a portion of the property, but it took over the second floor in 1921. The restaurant was popular with Union Pacific workers. (Courtesy of Sweetwater County Historical Museum.)

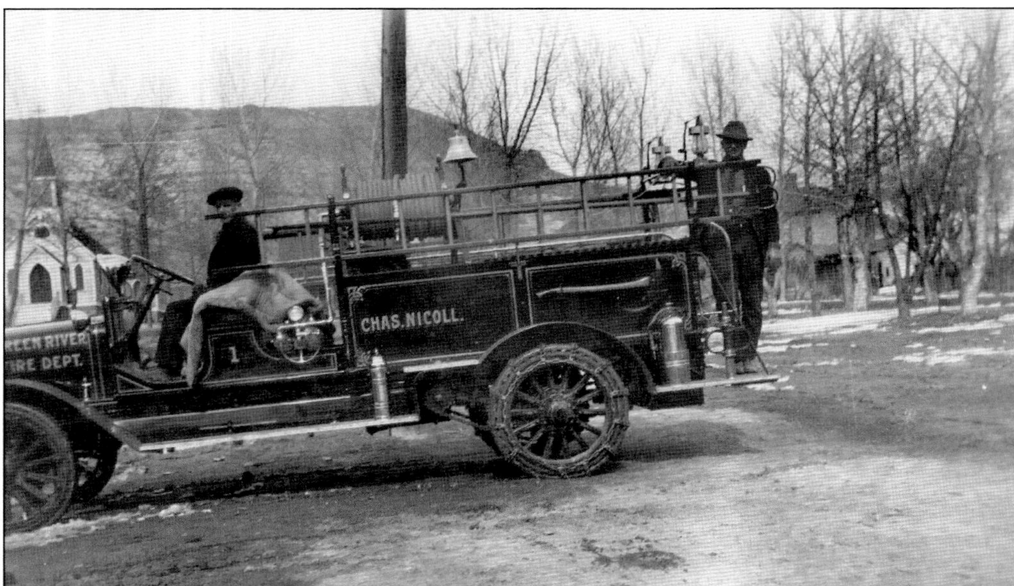

William Hutton and Chris Jessen pose with Green River's newest fire truck. Purchased in 1921, this American La France truck was state-of-the-art in the early 1920s. The engine was designated "C. Nicoll Truck No. 1" in honor of the mayor. The vehicle cost $5,200, much of which was obtained through fund-raising events. Major contributors, such as the Union Pacific Railroad, also helped with the purchase. (Courtesy of Sweetwater County Historical Museum.)

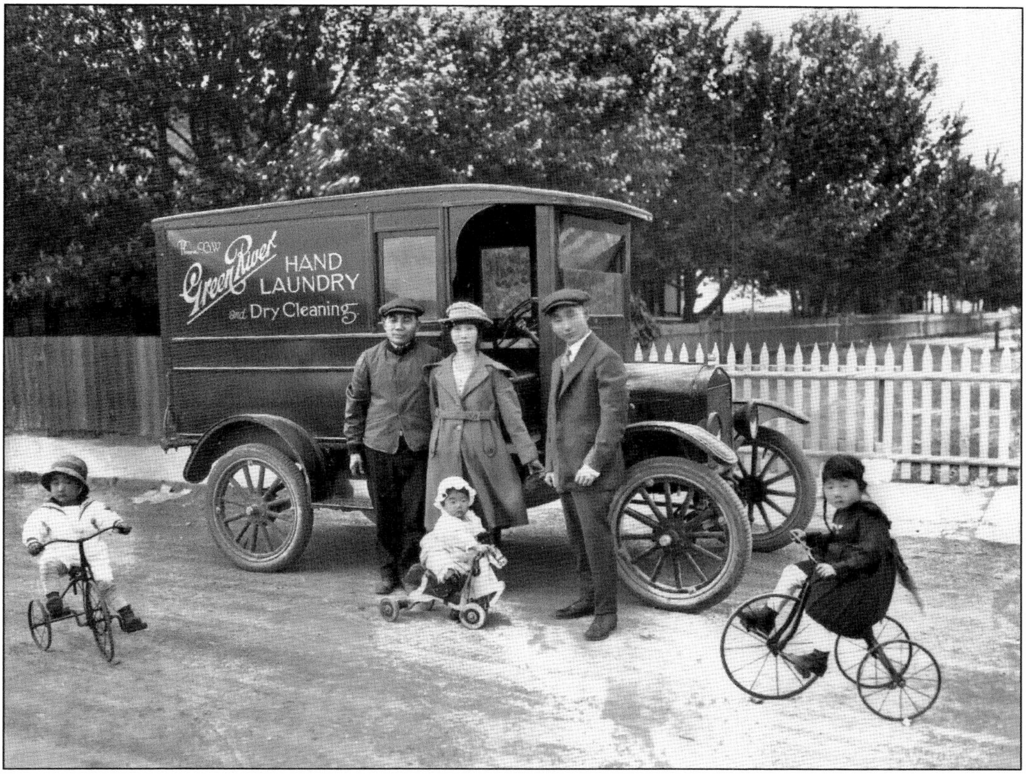

The Sunada family, one of Green River's earliest Japanese American families, owned and operated the Green River Hand Laundry from 1920 to 1938. This image dates to about 1923. The family eventually grew to include nine children. During the anti-Japanese hysteria of World War II, the Sunada family avoided incarceration in an internment camp with help from city officials and neighbors. (Courtesy of Sweetwater County Historical Museum.)

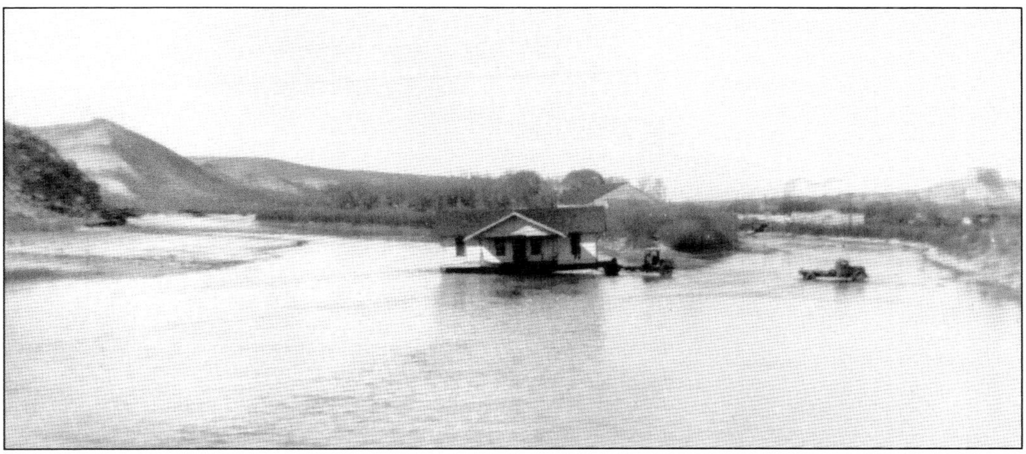

This 1920s image shows a house being removed from land acquired by the potash plant. It is a long-standing tradition in Wyoming to move structures to new locations rather than demolishing them. Even demolished buildings often found new life when the pieces were reassembled into a new building. (Courtesy of Sweetwater County Historical Museum.)

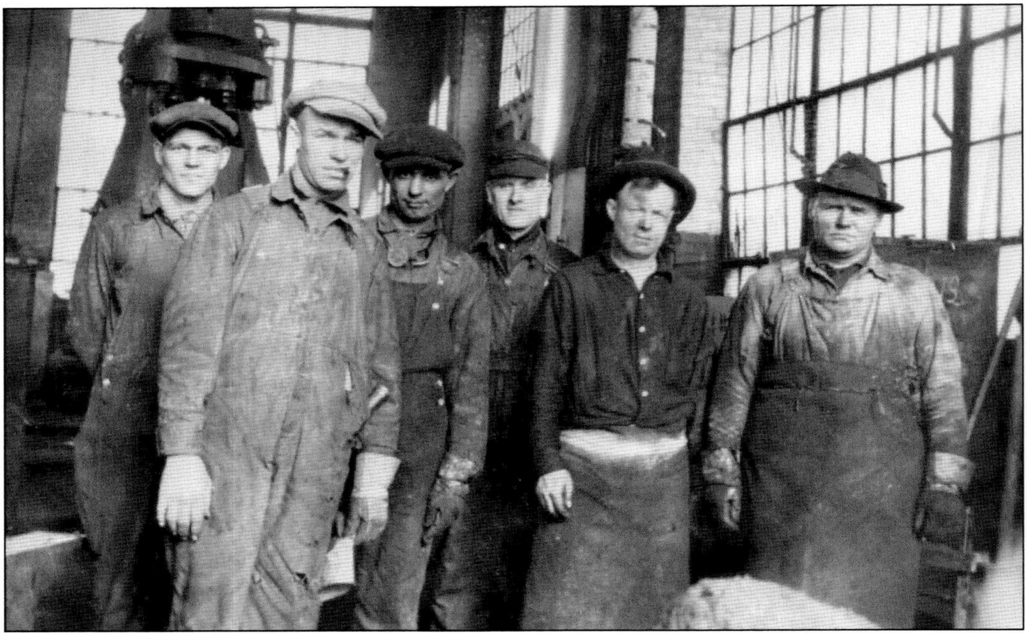

The Union Pacific Railroad continued to be a major employer during the Great Depression. The variety of skilled laborers employed by the railroad is evidenced by the crew of steamfitter and under-sheriff Bob Coomes. The crew members (left to right) were boilermaker George Langdon, metalworker Joe Wilson, electrician and crane operator Clifton "Sparky" Suggs, blacksmith Frank "Blackie" Morgan, and blacksmith Hardy Rollins. (Courtesy of Sweetwater County Historical Museum.)

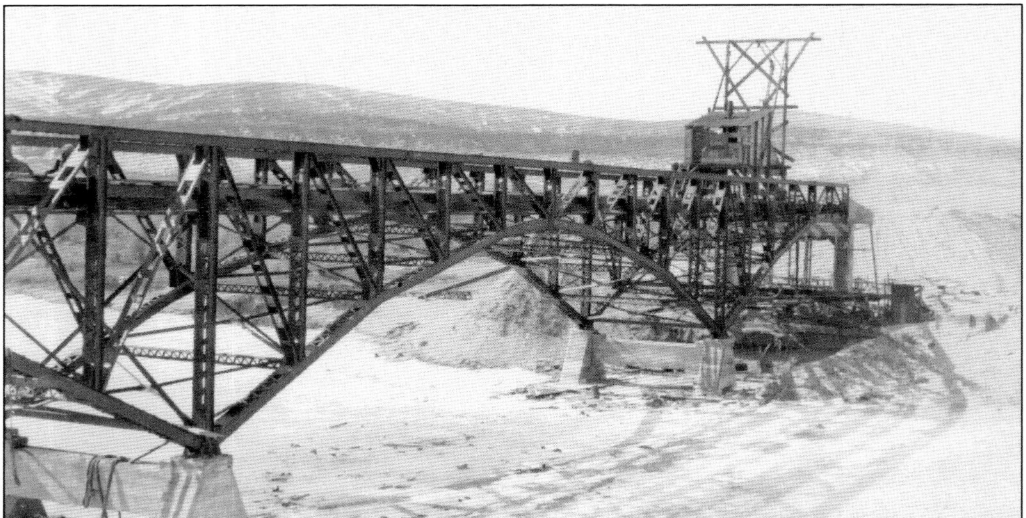

The Lincoln Highway bridge, crossing the Green River three miles west of the city, opened the area to interstate automobile traffic. In 1924, the year of this image, the Lincoln Highway route near Green River was changed, and the route through Telephone Canyon was abandoned in favor of going through Jamestown to the west. The new route was roughly the same as that taken by Interstate 80 today. (Courtesy of Sweetwater County Historical Museum.)

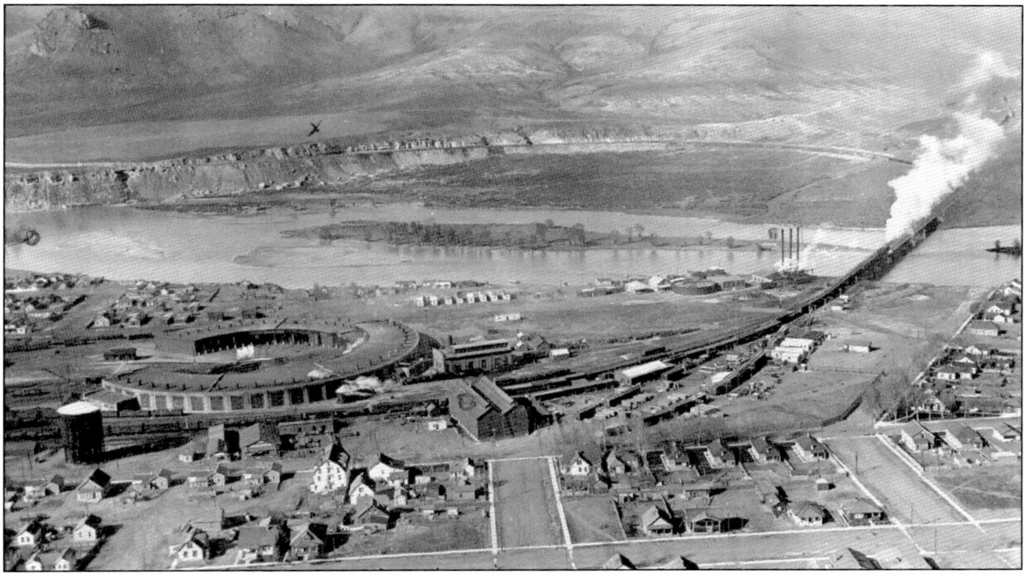

Built in 1872 as a 15-stall roundhouse, the Green River roundhouse had grown to 46 stalls surrounding a 138-foot turntable by the 1920s. It was large enough to handle the Big Boys, the largest steam engines ever made. One of these great machines is shown here crossing the river bridge. (Courtesy of Sweetwater County Historical Museum.)

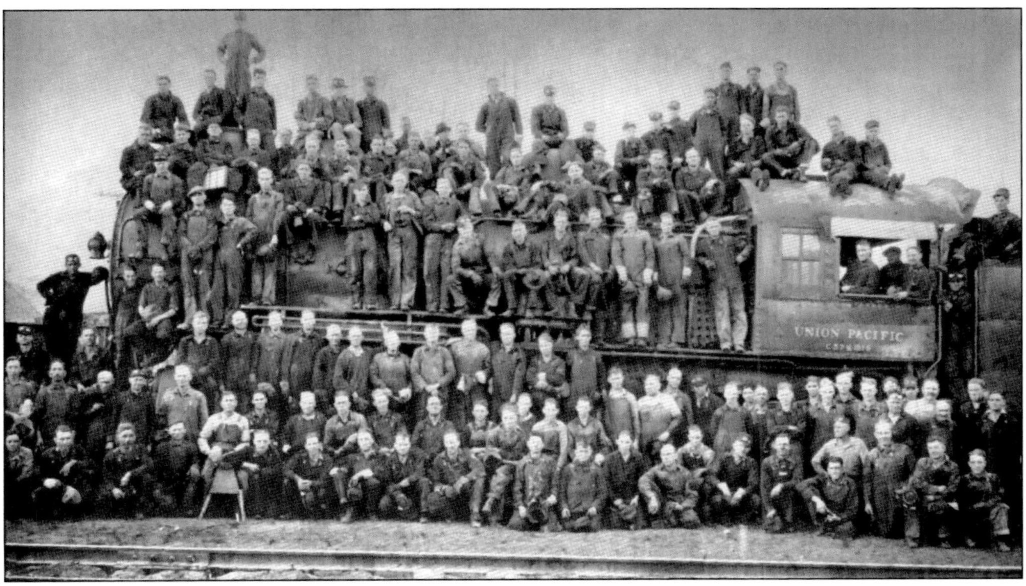

This 1927 image of the Green River roundhouse shows rail yard workers posing on an engine. The roundhouse allowed engines to be turned and repaired. The original roundhouse was moved from Bryan in 1872 and was expanded in 1919 to 46 stalls. By 1965, there were only three stalls remaining. The roundhouse operated until its demolition in 1977. (Courtesy of Sweetwater County Historical Museum.)

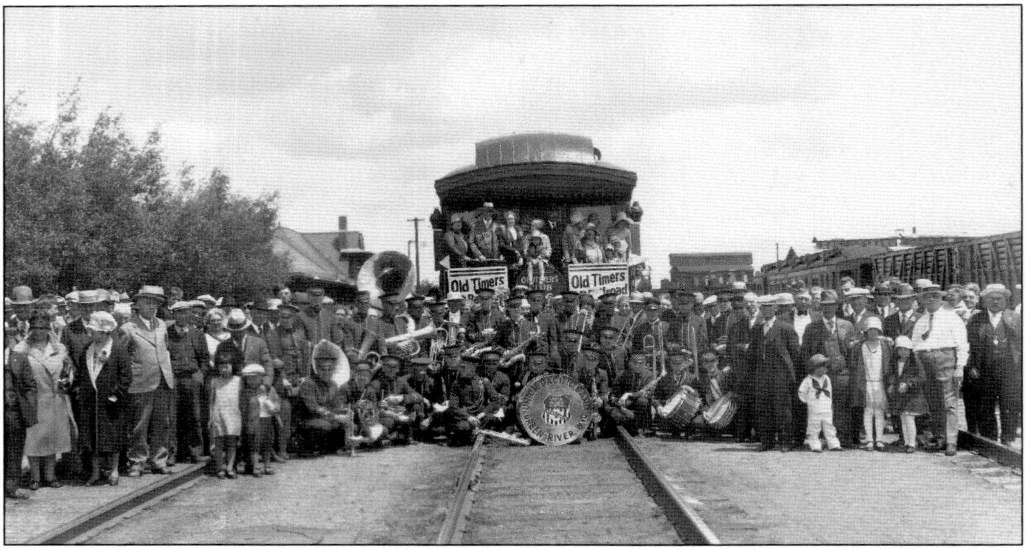

Shown here in the mid-1920s, Green River's Union Pacific Band plays at a gathering of the Old Timers Club, an organization dedicated to retired Union Pacific Railroad workers. The image appears to have been taken at another railroad station, possibly Rock Springs. In the crowd to the left of the band are Edith, George, and Manijyo Sunada. (Courtesy of Sweetwater County Historical Museum.)

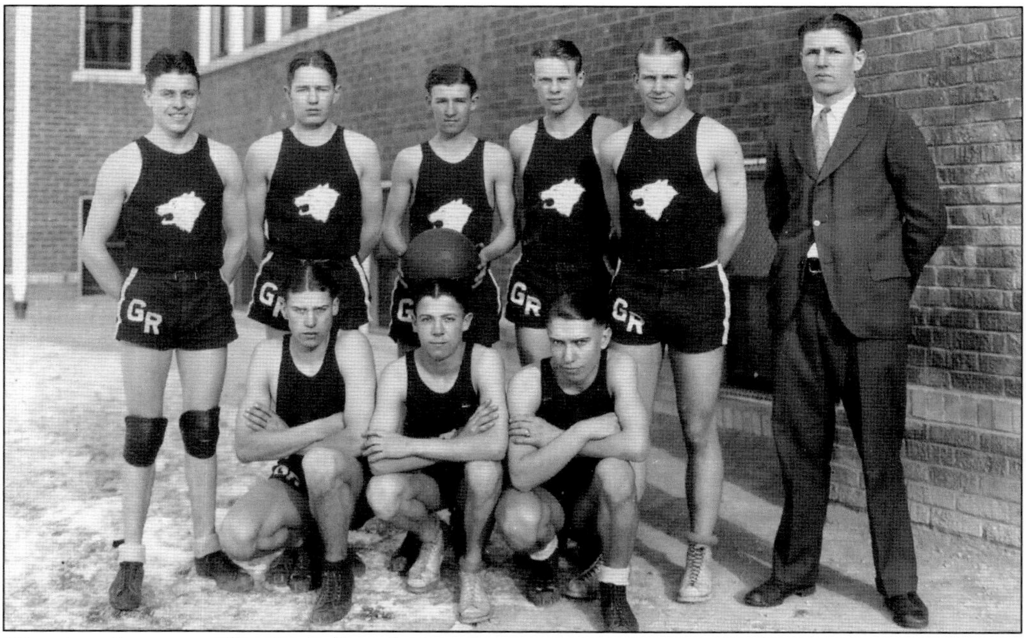

"Our fourth season of Basketball in the Southwestern Conference was the best that Green River High School has ever had," proclaimed the 1925–1926 *Rendezvous*, the school yearbook. Led by Coach Milam, the team won 6 out of 18 games. Pictured here are, from left to right, the following: (first row) Herman Petersen, Weldon Davis, and Dean Darius; (second row) Vincent Simonin, James Crosson, Burnell Chapman, Ross Davis, Paul Cooley, and coach G. M. Milam. (Courtesy of Sweetwater County Historical Museum.)

William Evers was the mayor of Green River from 1925 to 1935. Under his administration, the Green River Ordinance was passed in 1931. Evers arrived in Green River in 1909 and worked as a carpenter. In 1918, he and a partner established the Superior Lumber Company of Rock Springs and opened a branch in Green River. That same year, Evers started the Evers Brothers construction company. (Courtesy of Sweetwater County Historical Museum.)

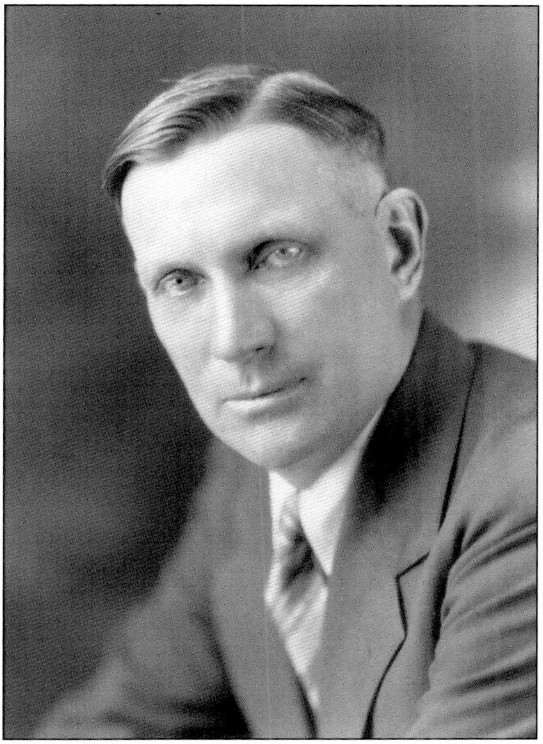

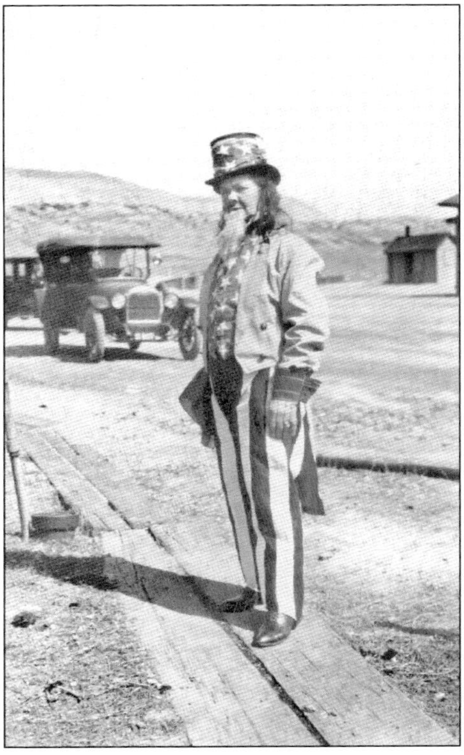

Pictured here in the mid-1920s is Flora Bishopp in the guise of Uncle Sam for the Fourth of July holiday in Green River. Independence Day was a festive event in Green River during this era. People of all ages competed in events, which included a ladies' nail-driving race, potato-sack and egg races for the children, and even a fat man's race. The evening brought traditional fireworks. (Courtesy of Sweetwater County Historical Museum.)

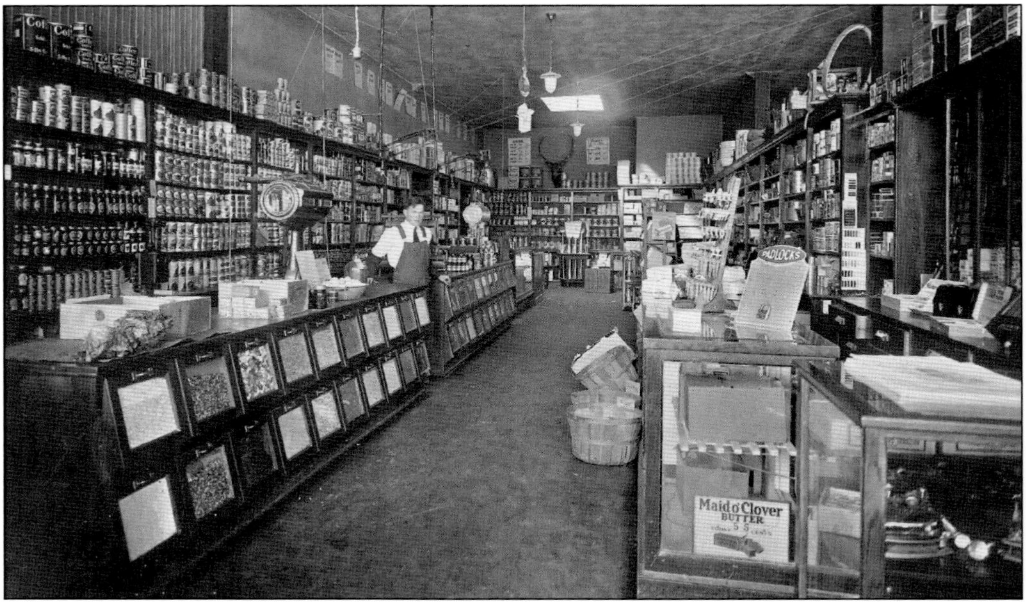

The Green River Mercantile holds one of the oldest business licenses in Wyoming. It has been in business since 1910, when it took over the Lawrence and Hoadley General Store. The mercantile has provided a variety of services, including general merchandise sales, automobile sales, and even embalming. The Green River Mercantile is still in business under the Taliaferro family's management. (Courtesy of Sweetwater County Historical Museum.)

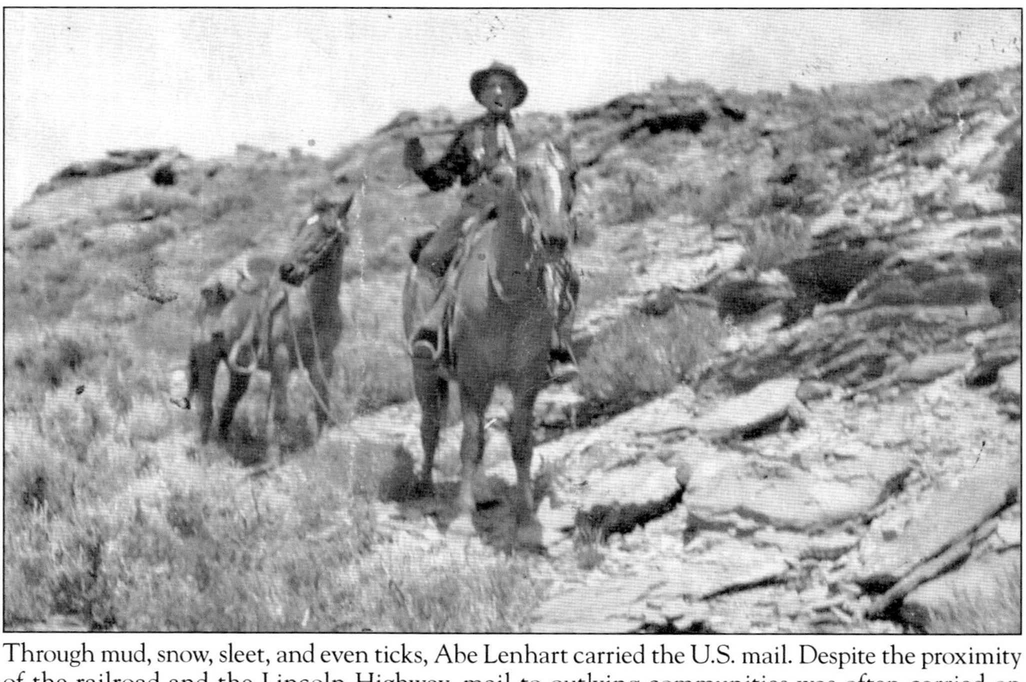

Through mud, snow, sleet, and even ticks, Abe Lenhart carried the U.S. mail. Despite the proximity of the railroad and the Lincoln Highway, mail to outlying communities was often carried on horseback. A rider could shave a few miles off the trip by departing from the wagon roads and taking a more direct route. (Courtesy of Sweetwater County Historical Museum.)

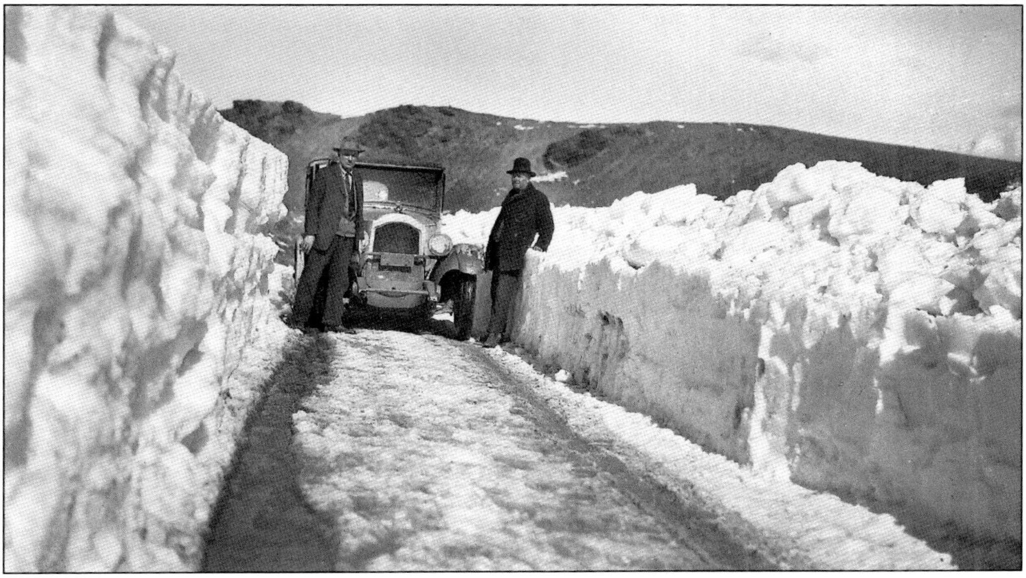

The year 1926 was not a record snow year, but keeping the streets clear without modern machinery was always a challenge. From this image, it is evident that the hills above Green River had been blown almost clean of snow, while the people occupying the lowlands were tasked with digging out through drifts that were several feet deep in places. (Courtesy of Sweetwater County Historical Museum.)

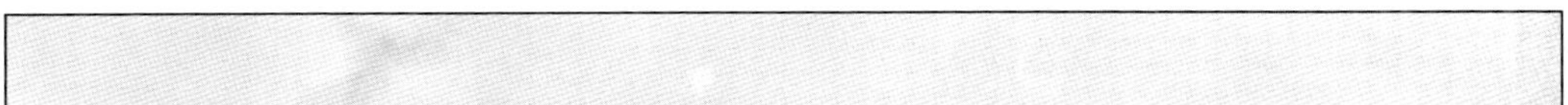

These 1927 football players pose on the field at Lincoln High School. Many of the sons of prominent Green River families are pictured here, including Donald Nicoll (first row, far right), Norman Nolan (first row, far left), Ross Davis (second row, fourth from right), and Carl Gaensslen (second row, sixth from right). (Courtesy of Sweetwater County Historical Museum.)

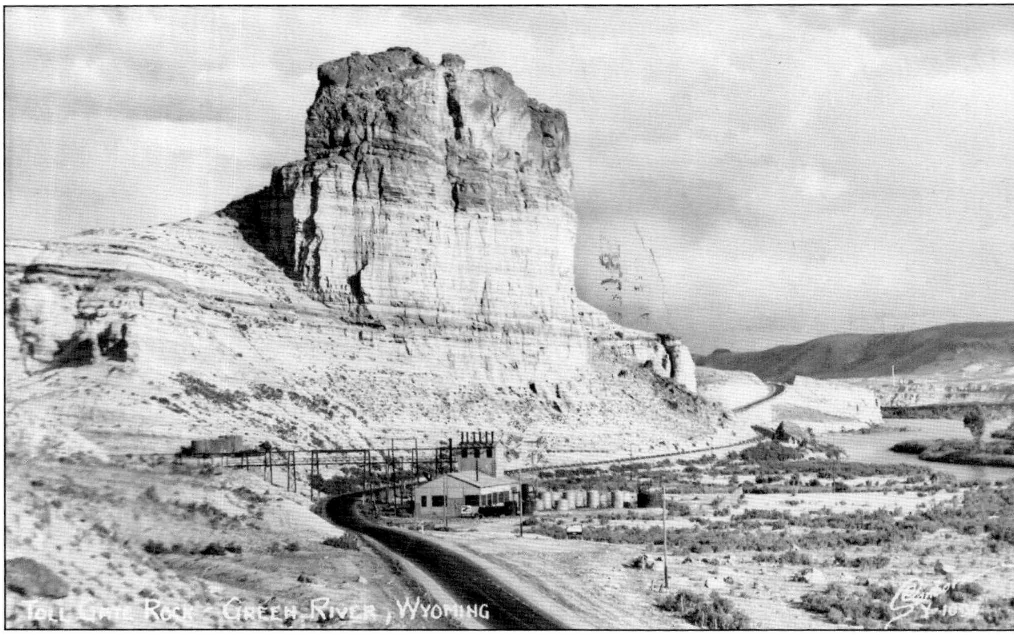

The Wyoming Oil Products Oil Shale Refinery was constructed in the shadow of Toll Gate Rock by entrepreneur J. E. Hines in 1928. Since 1921, it had been believed that the Green River area contained large overlooked supplies of oil within its shale deposits. The refinery does not appear to have been successful; the building was taken over by the district court in 1935. (Courtesy of Sweetwater County Historical Museum.)

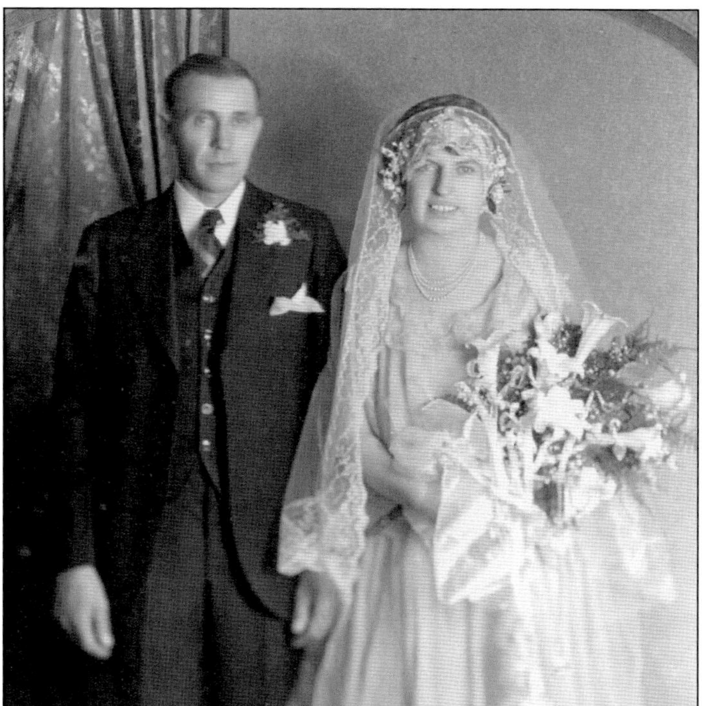

Louise Spinner and George Graf pose on their wedding day, June 24, 1930. Spinner was the daughter of Karl Spinner and Therese Weber, who wed in Germany and then immigrated to Green River, where Louise was born in 1904. Her father ran the Spinner Meat Market. Graf was a native of Colorado who came to the Green River area to work for the local power company. (Courtesy of Sweetwater County Historical Museum.)

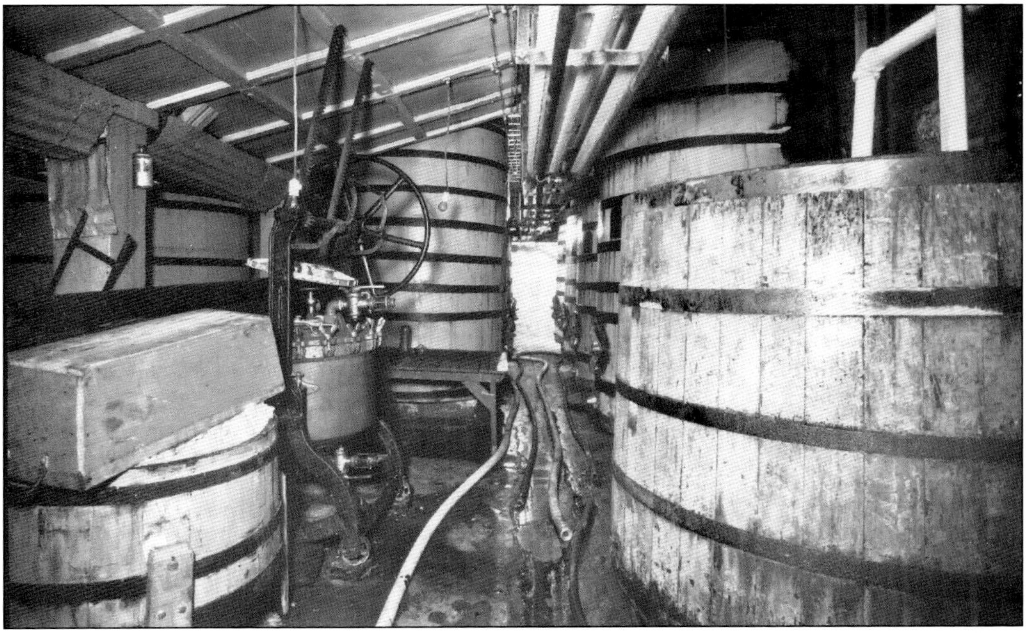

This early 1930s image shows the fermentation vats at the Sweetwater Brewing Company, which produced award-winning beer. Established in 1872, the brewery switched to soft drinks and "near beer" in 1920 with the institution of Prohibition. Following the repeal of Prohibition, the brewing of beer began again. (Courtesy of Sweetwater County Historical Museum.)

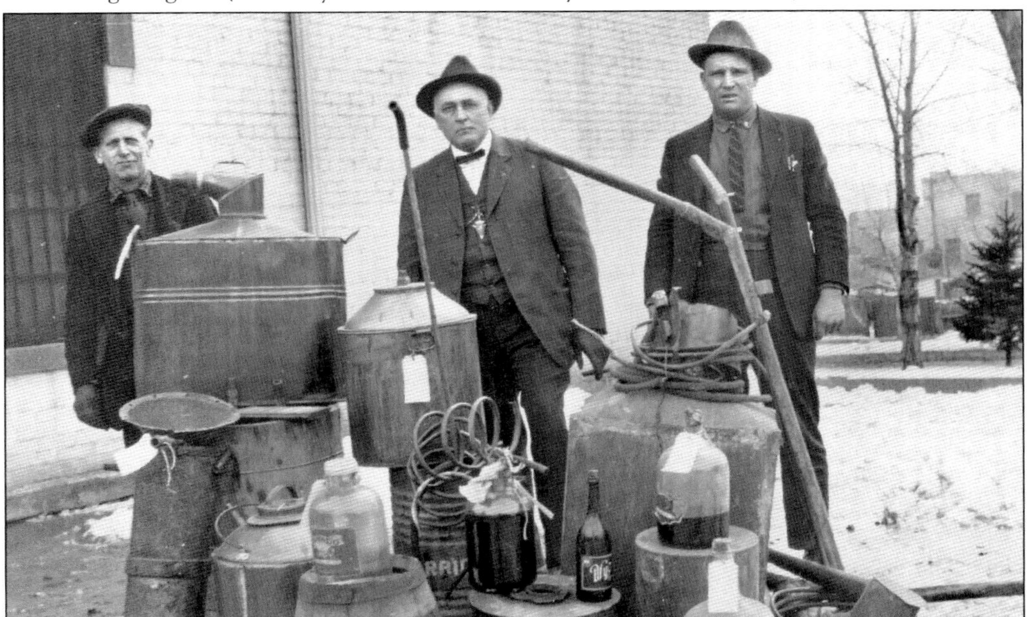

Pictured here in front of the Sweetwater County Courthouse with confiscated stills and other paraphernalia are, from left to right, Chief of Police Mike Maher, Sheriff Al Morton, and Under Sheriff Chris Jessen. Still raids were common in the hills outside of Green River during Prohibition (1920–1933). (Courtesy of Sweetwater County Historical Museum.)

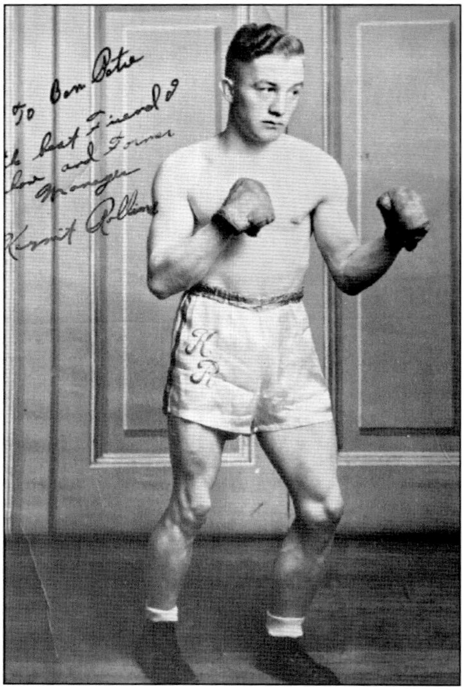

This 1931 postcard image of Kermit Rollins shows a young man, barely 17, who was crowned champion of the 112-pound class of the boxing division in the AAU tournament held in Salt Lake City. Local businessman Ben Petre acted as Rollins's manager in the tournament. Petre, Ed Dorsky, and Sheriff Chris Jessen, all from Green River, were there to witness Rollins's victory. (Courtesy of Sweetwater County Historical Museum.)

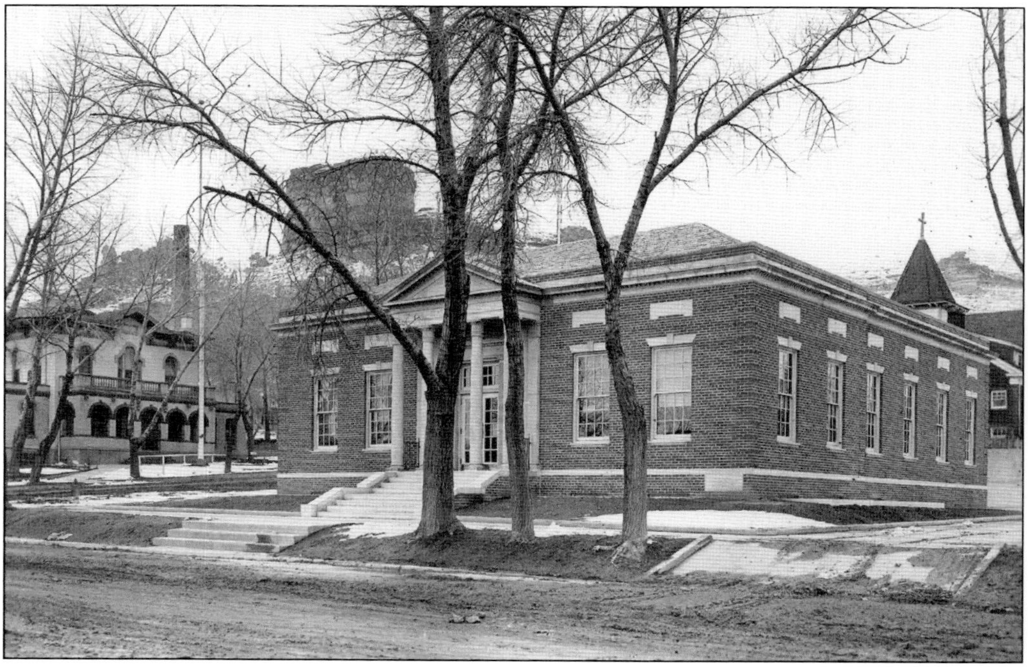

Built in 1931 and opened in 1932, this brick Greek Revival structure, featuring four stone pillars, was the first official federal building erected in Green River. Previously, the federal government had leased or rented the building that the post office occupied. This building was dedicated and opened on April 29, 1932. R. A. Hoover was postmaster, and Frank Kidd (who served as chief of police twice) was custodian of the new building. (Courtesy of Sweetwater County Historical Museum.)

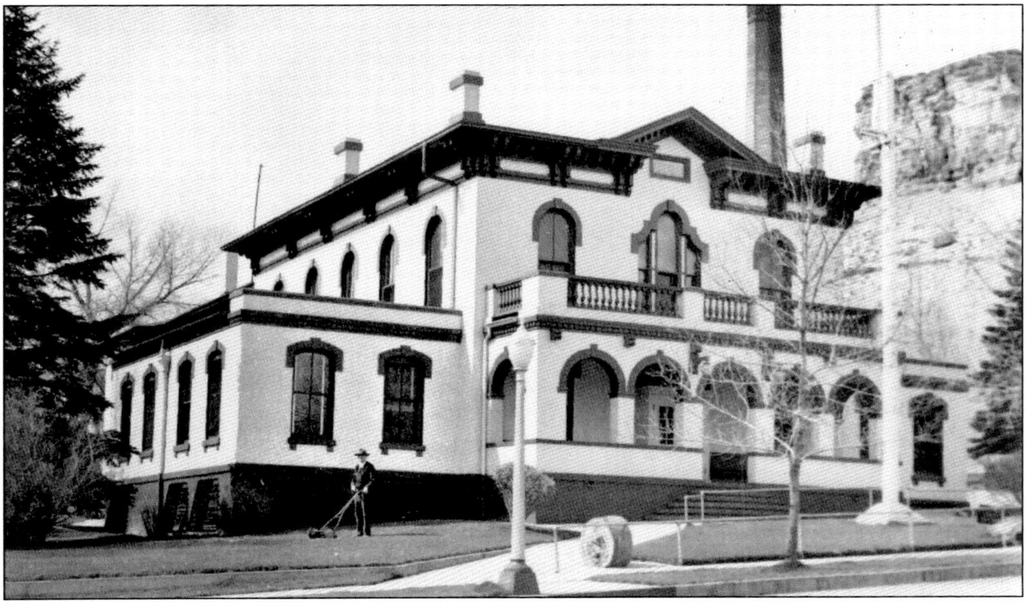

In 1929 and 1930, the Sweetwater County Courthouse was modified. Additions were put on the sides, the tower on the roof was removed, and the south wing and a heating plant were added. These changes were in response to the need for modernization and for more office space. In this 1950 image, custodian William Hutton mows the lawn in front of the courthouse. (Courtesy of Sweetwater County Historical Museum.)

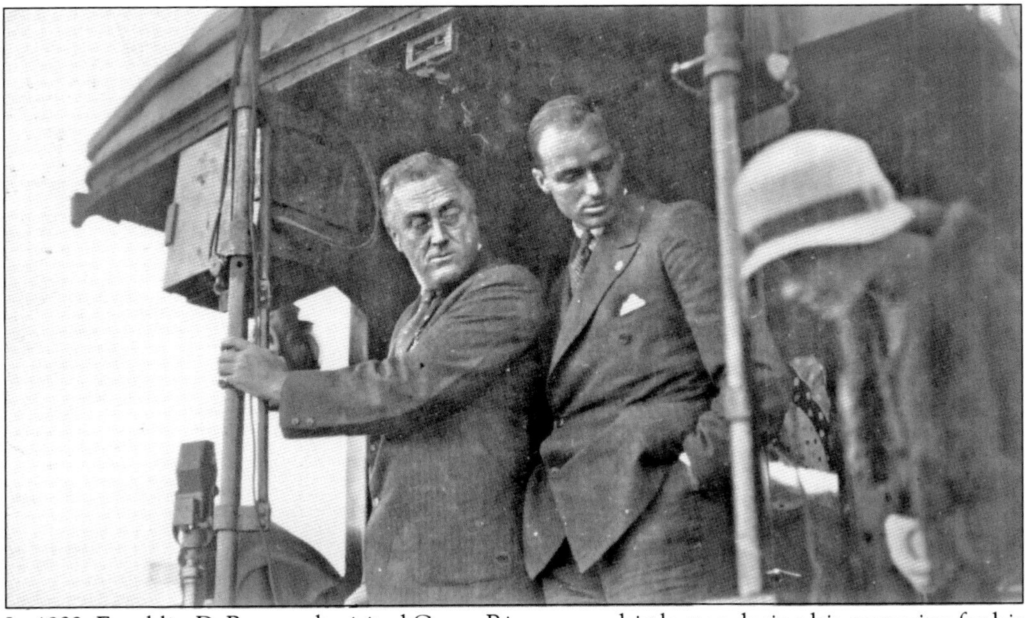

In 1932, Franklin D. Roosevelt visited Green River on a whistle stop during his campaign for his first presidential term. Greeted by a crowd of 900, Roosevelt was introduced by local Democrat Fred Johnson. Johnson's wife Rose is on the left. Roosevelt was entertained by the American Legion Auxiliary Drum Corps, from whom he requested several encores. (Courtesy of Sweetwater County Historical Museum.)

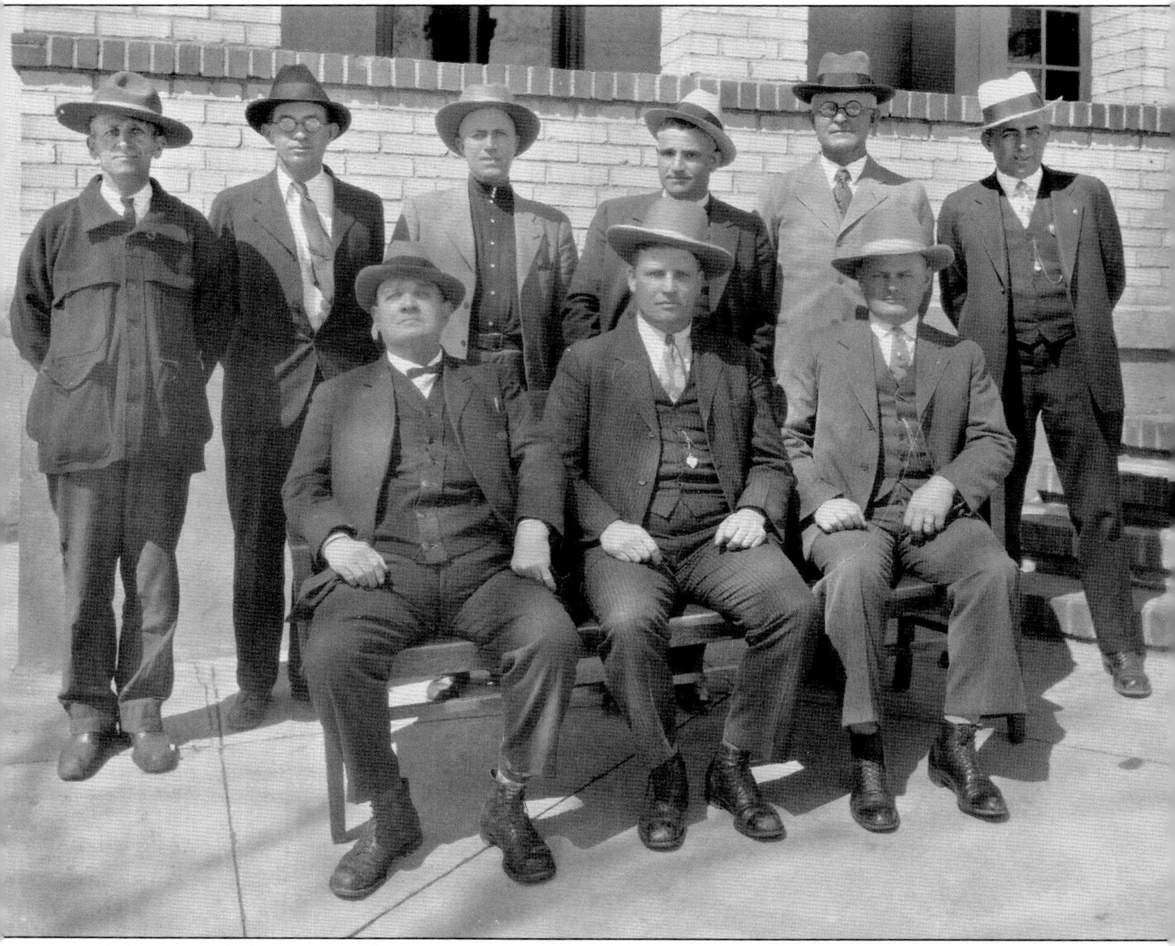

This is a 1931 portrait of southwestern Wyoming lawmen and friends. Pictured are, from left to right, the following: (first row) Chris Waechter (local merchant, bar owner, and vice president of the State Bank of Green River), Chris Jessen (county sheriff), and R. G. Johannsen (Green River under sheriff); (second row) William Hutton, Clarence Rador (Point of Rocks deputy), George Harris (Rock Springs deputy), Alphonse Bertagnolli (Superior deputy), John Hutton (former Green River chief of police), and Mike Maher (Green River chief of police). Policing Sweetwater County was difficult; it was one of the largest counties in the United States, with an area of nearly 10,500 square miles. The small number of paved roads and settled towns contributed to the "Wild West" feel of the county. During Prohibition, law enforcement aggressively attempted to put the bootleggers out of business. (Courtesy of Sweetwater County Historical Museum.)

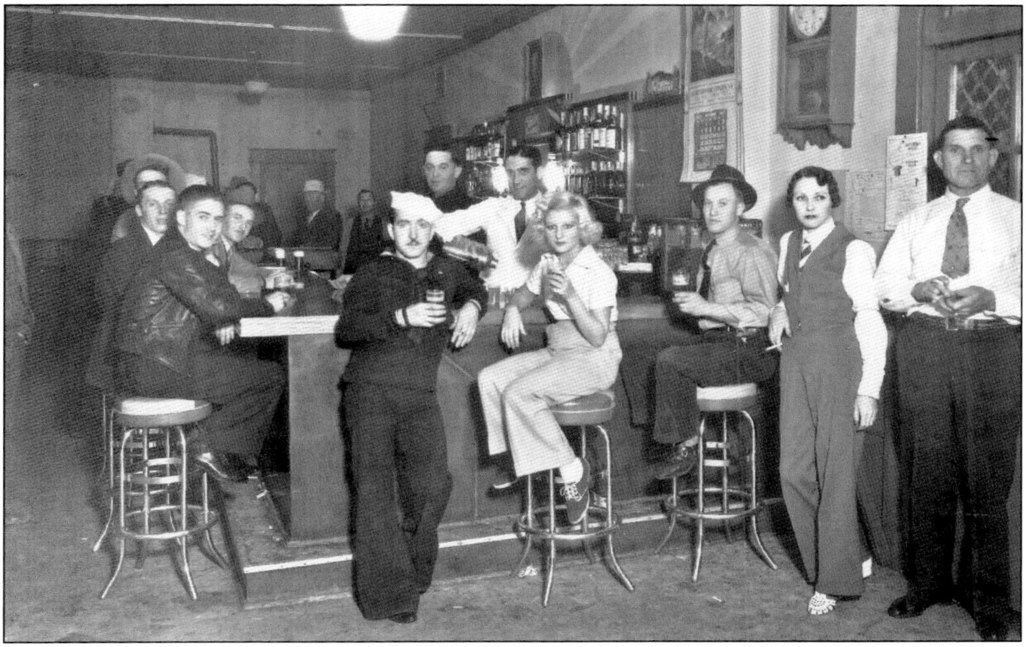

Though located in Green River's "red light district," the Oxford Club was known as a fairly respectable bar. Bartender Jimmy Passerelli (in the white coat), manager Henry Rizzi (behind the bar), and barmaid Mae Kizer (standing at the right) served customers. The Oxford, which allowed white people only, was built in 1919 by Isaiah "Cat Eye" Willis, a black man who also owned the nearby Owl's Club. (Courtesy of New Studio.)

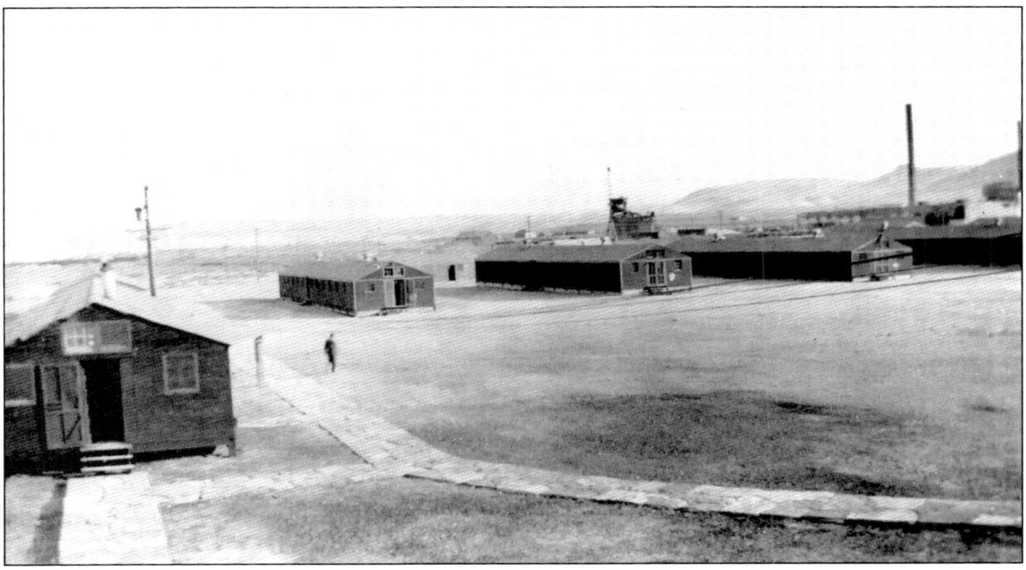

Established in 1933, the Civilian Conservation Corps (CCC) enlisted young men for six-month periods, with the potential to reenlist for two years. For their labor on various public projects, the men were paid $30 a month, $25 of which was sent to their families. Projects included erosion control, building roads, planting trees, trail and campground construction, and fighting fires. The Green River camp was closed in June 1942. (Courtesy of Sweetwater County Historical Museum.)

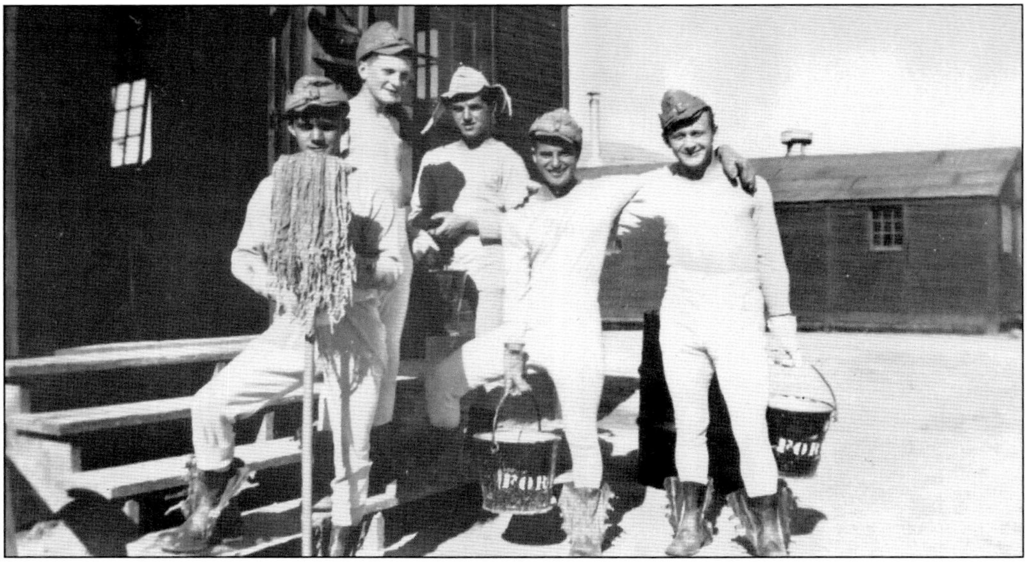

Clad in long underwear and galoshes, the CCC fire crew for Barracks No. 4 stands "ready" to fight the flames. The Green River CCC camp had four barracks that held 48 men apiece, as well as officer buildings, a bathhouse, toilets, a mess hall, a kitchen, a chapel, a clubhouse, an infirmary, and storage buildings. The camp was inhabited by men aged 17 through 20 who came primarily from the eastern United States. Youthful hijinks were common. (Courtesy of Sweetwater County Historical Museum.)

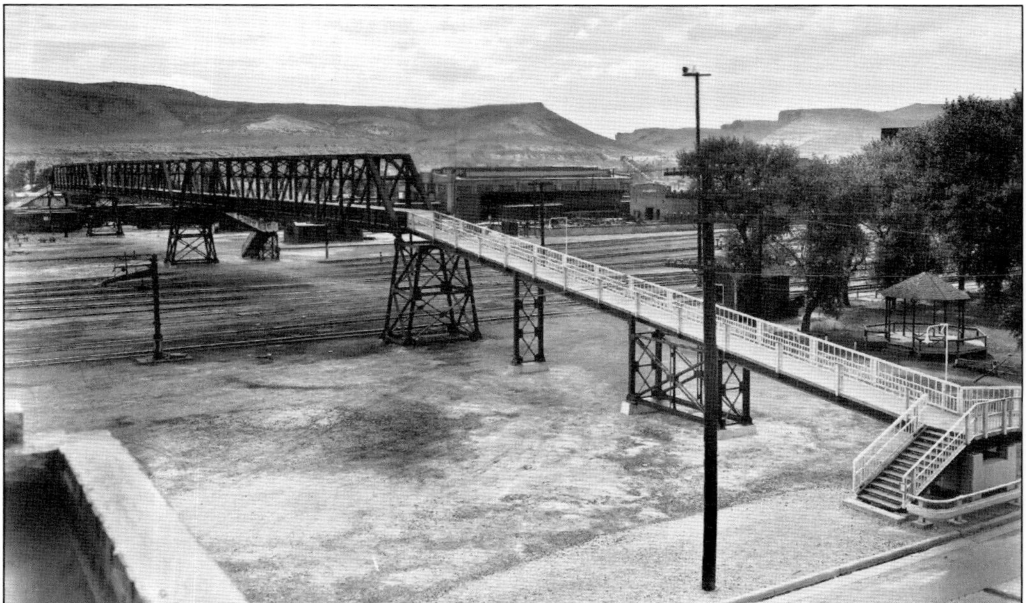

Built in 1938 as a response to federal efforts to close at-grade crossings of major railroads, the Green River pedestrian viaduct is a substantial metal structure that spans the rail yards. Part of the project was an automobile underpass located to the west of the structure. With schools located on the north side of the track, crossing was a worry for parents of children living on the south side. (Courtesy of Sweetwater County Historical Museum.)

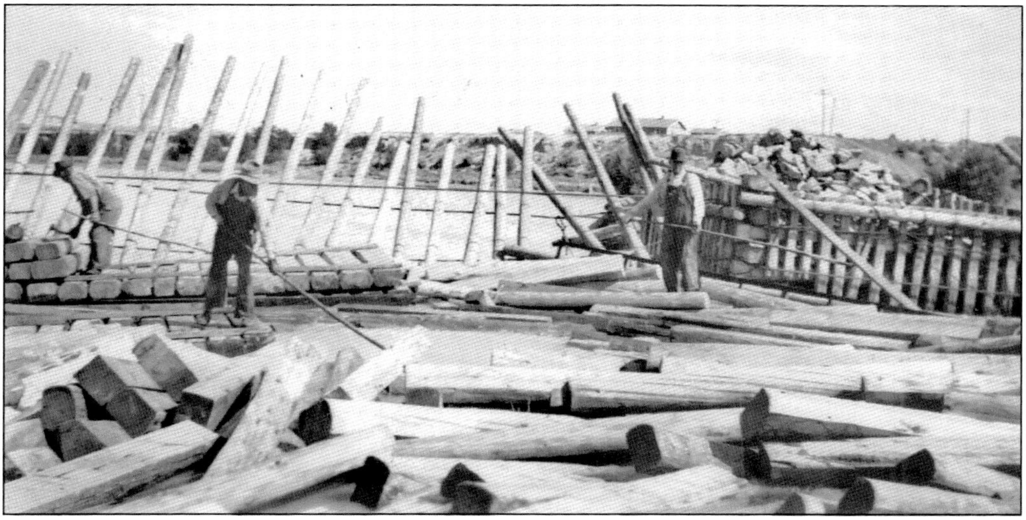

Ties, the wooden crosspieces on which the track was laid, were cut and shaped on the streams upriver and then floated down to Green River on the high waters during spring runoff. In town, they were caught by a boom that extended across the river. Roughly 300,000 ties came down the river each spring. The ties were pulled out of the water and loaded onto railcars for shipment to a plant in Laramie, where they were treated with creosote to prevent deterioration. Tie drives were held on the Green River annually from 1868 to 1945. Roughly 75 men, called tie hacks, were necessary to wrangle the ties. The men worked 10 hours a day for $5 in pay. The arrival of the ties at Green River meant the end of the drive and a great party for the tie hacks, fueled by liquor purchased from local establishments. (Courtesy of Sweetwater County Historical Museum.)

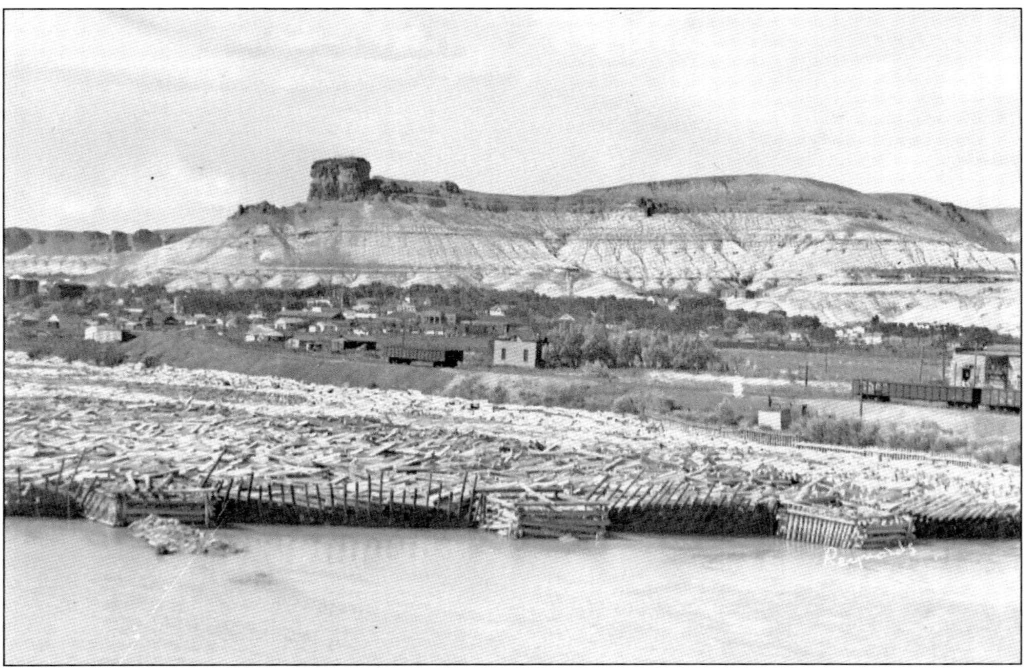

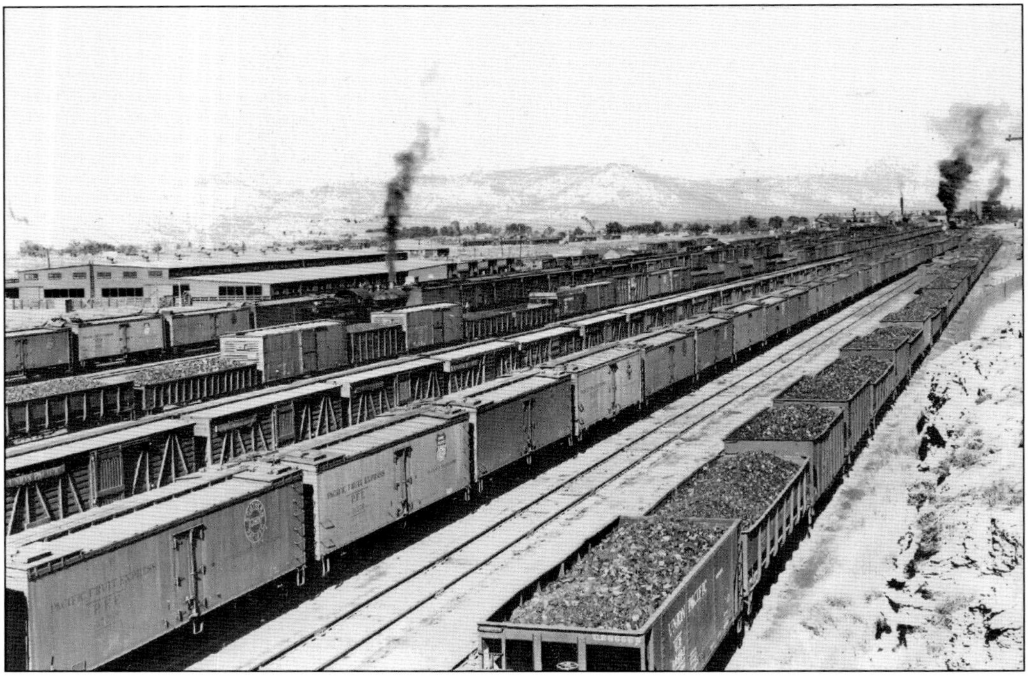

This 1939 image shows the wide variety of commodities handled by the railroad. Here the Green River yards are clogged with at least two coal trains, two fruit express trains, and a stock train. The Green River rail yard remains one of the busiest in North America today. (Courtesy of Sweetwater County Historical Museum.)

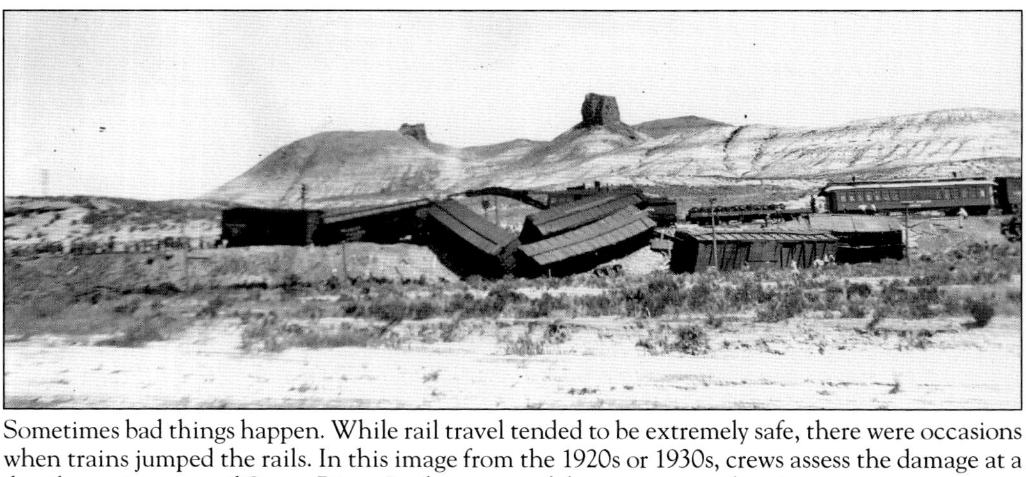

Sometimes bad things happen. While rail travel tended to be extremely safe, there were occasions when trains jumped the rails. In this image from the 1920s or 1930s, crews assess the damage at a derailment just east of Green River. In the center of the image, a car bearing a crane attempts to lift a fallen car from the embankment. (Courtesy of Sweetwater County Historical Museum.)

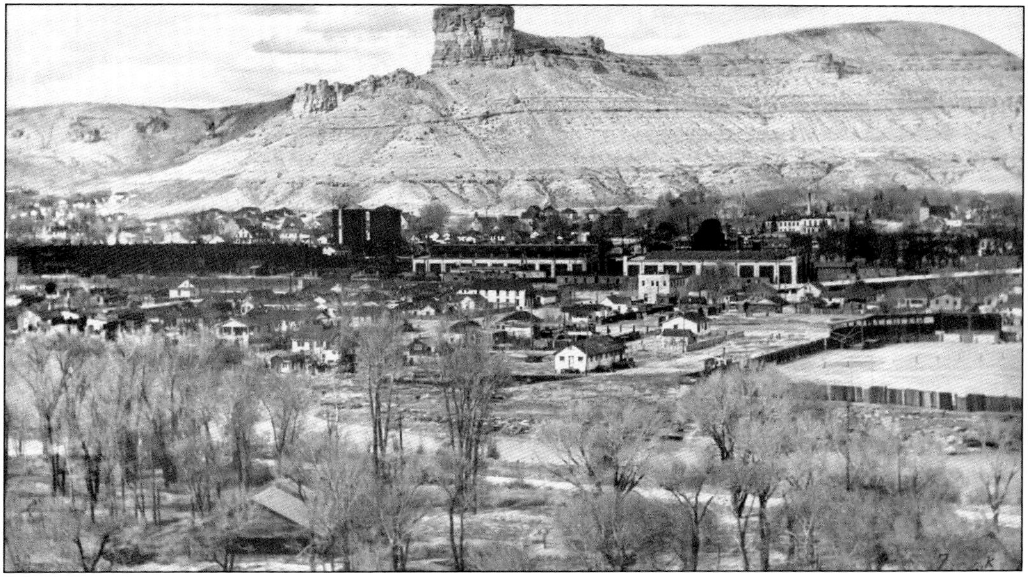

This is a 1939 image of Green River. Prominent in the right side of the image is the Evers' Ball Field diamond. New buildings are filling in available spaces north of the Green River. In the right foreground is the Expedition Island pavilion. Also prominent are the roundhouse, the coaling towers, the water towers, the pedestrian overpass, the Episcopal church, the Catholic church, and the Mormon church. (Courtesy of Sweetwater County Historical Museum.)

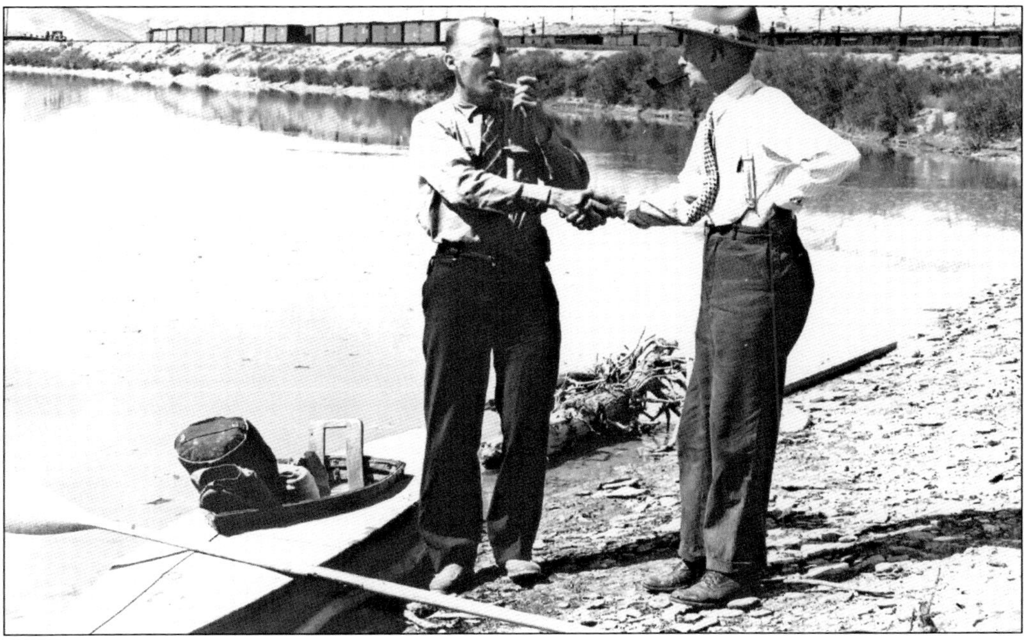

William Hutton (right) wishes bon voyage to Charles Mann (left) on September 11, 1939. Expedition Island was a favorite place for starting river journeys. Mann's watercraft was a folding kayak. The rocks in Lodore later damaged his boat when it was sucked under a ledge. Mann avoided drowning, but he lost his camera, pipes, gun, and some of his food supply. He made it to Lee's Ferry. (Courtesy of Sweetwater County Historical Museum.)

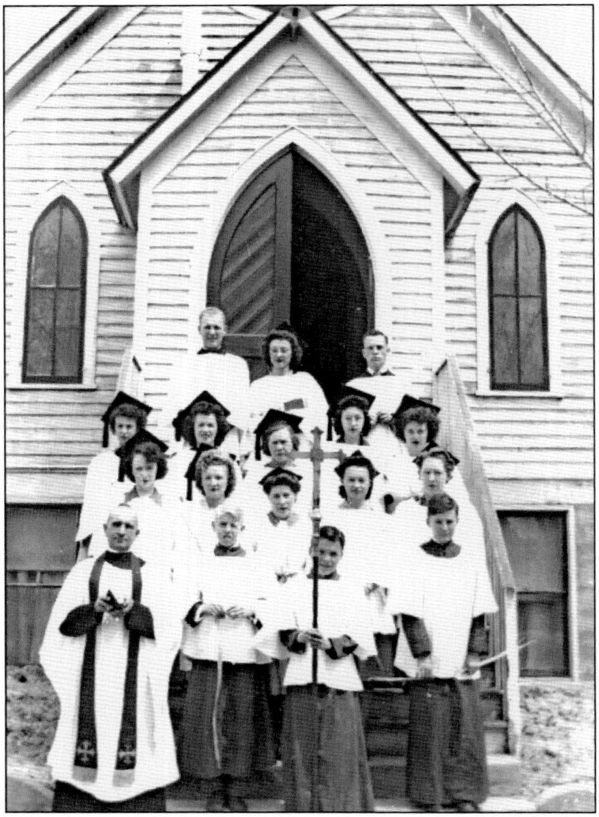

The St. John's Episcopal Church Choir was organized by Rev. R. E. Abraham prior to 1920. Due to the group members' outstanding performances of cantatas and choral arrangements, they were called upon to broadcast over the radio station in Laramie. Included in this picture taken in 1942 are Rev. C. L. Callahan, Herb Lewis, Jimmie Lowe, Lucille Snowden, Miss Jones, Clara Young, Ethel Hill Morris, Margaret Lenhart, Frieda Horton, Dale Morris, and Doug Johnson. (Courtesy of Sweetwater County Historical Museum.)

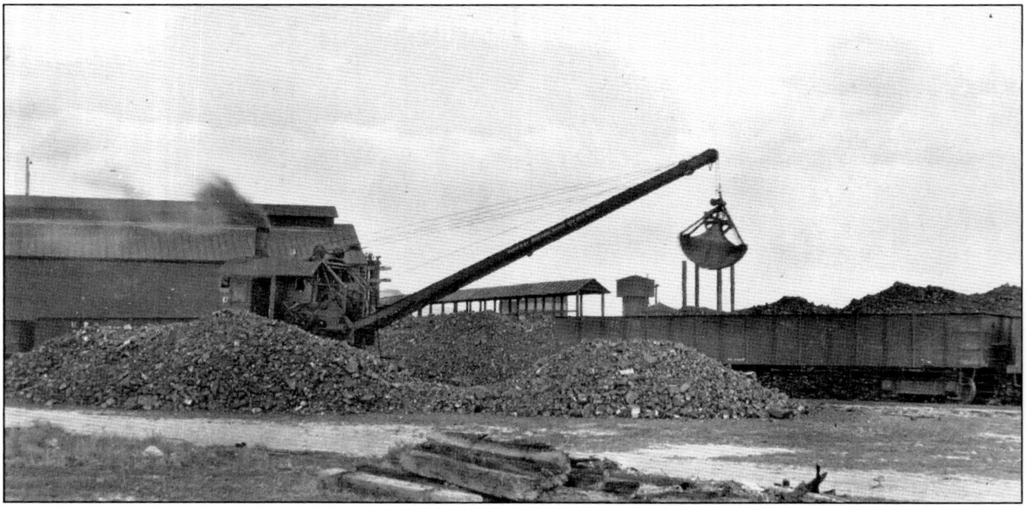

In this 1930s image, a steam shovel manufactured by Industrial Works of Bay City, Michigan, is stockpiling coal in Green River. The company was in business from 1873 to 1983 and was a major manufacturer of cranes. Coal was off-loaded from rail cars to provide fuel for locomotives and other heavy equipment, to heat buildings, and to provide electrical power. During World War II, coal stocks were crucial for keeping supplies moving along the rails. (Courtesy of Sweetwater County Historical Museum.)

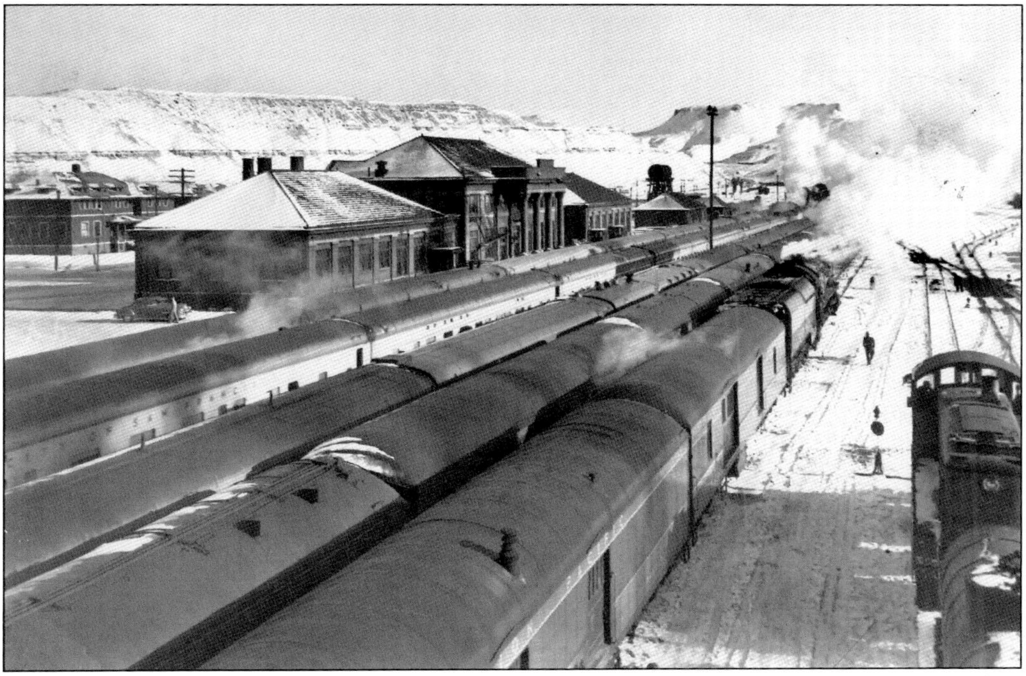

In the 1940s, diesel engines began to replace steam locomotives. While the steam engines were often more powerful and faster than diesel engines, the latter required less fuel, water, and maintenance. A diesel engine can be seen in the lower right portion of the image, while the other five trains appear to have steam engines. (Courtesy of Sweetwater County Historical Museum.)

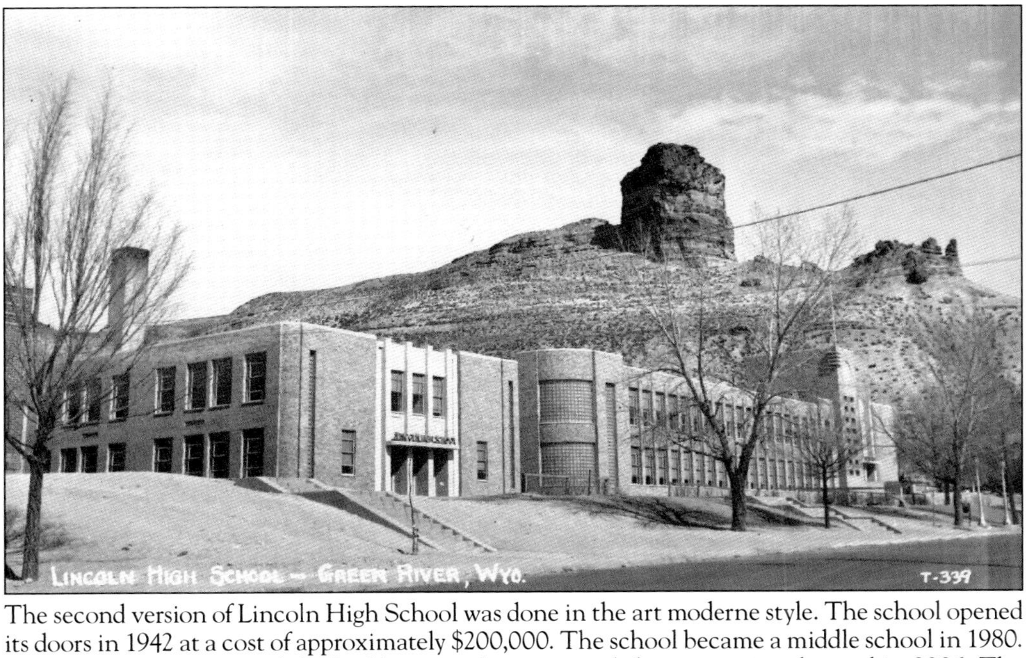

The second version of Lincoln High School was done in the art moderne style. The school opened its doors in 1942 at a cost of approximately $200,000. The school became a middle school in 1980. It was closed in 1998, and the building stood empty until the gymnasium burned in 2006. The school was demolished in 2007. (Courtesy of Sweetwater County Historical Museum.)

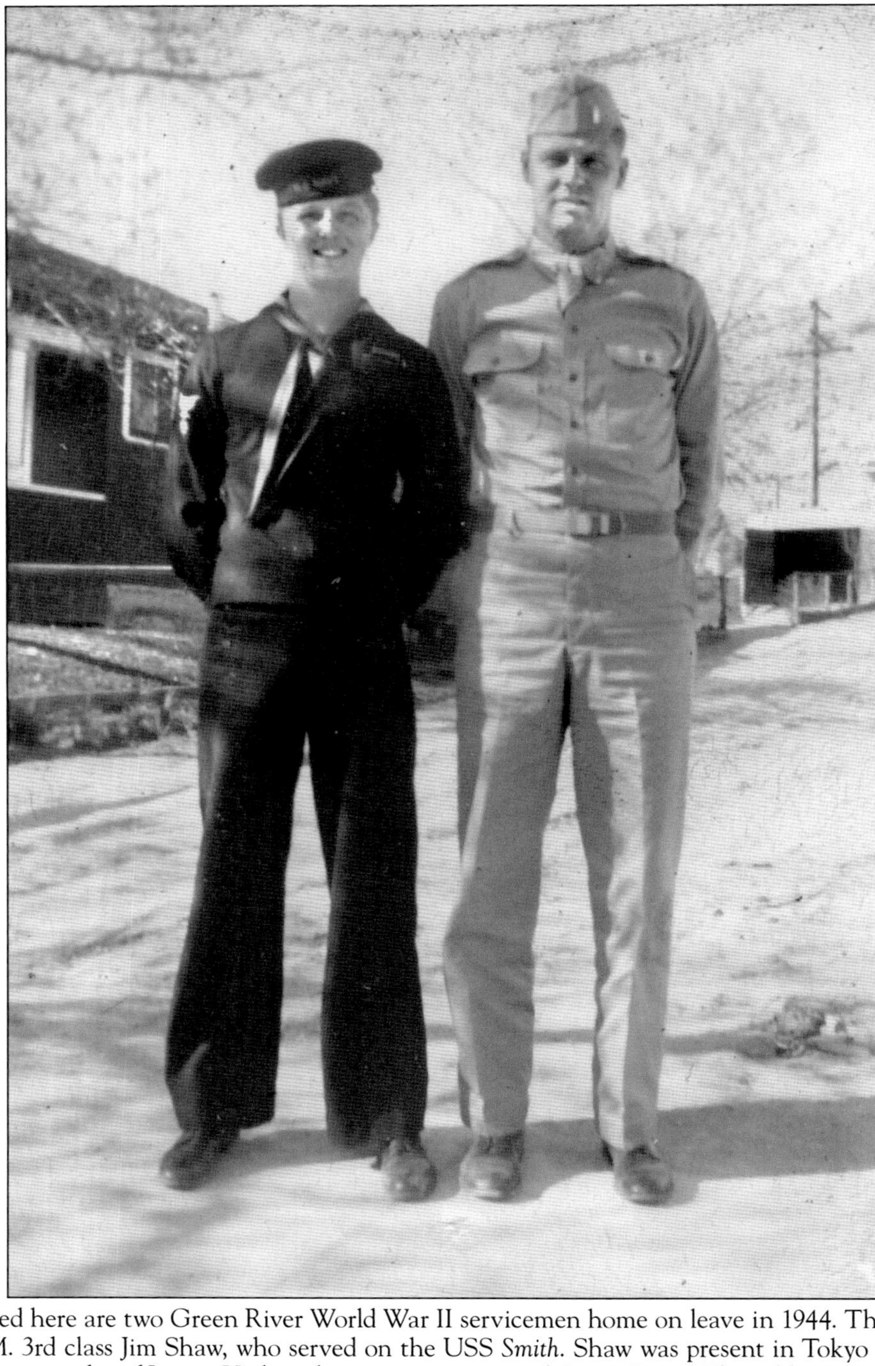

Pictured here are two Green River World War II servicemen home on leave in 1944. The sailor is Q.M. 3rd class Jim Shaw, who served on the USS *Smith*. Shaw was present in Tokyo Harbor for the surrender of Japan. He later became postmaster of Green River. The soldier is Jim Weir, who was an All-American basketball player for the University of Wyoming when it won the national championship in 1943. Weir was the third Cowboy chosen as an All-American. The championship team was coached by Ev Shelton and included famous Green River native Kurt Gowdy. (Courtesy of Jim Shaw)

Five

Work Hard, Play Harder 1946 and Beyond

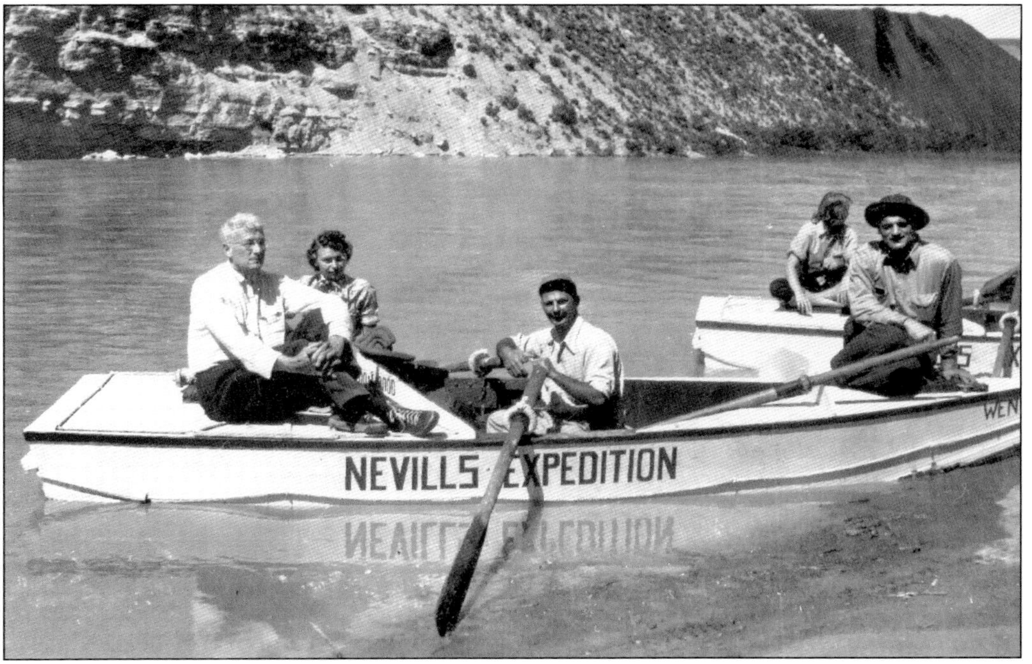

After World War II, the hard-working pace of Green River quickened because of new mining ventures, oil development, and natural gas expansion. A national recreational area and an interstate highway also brought increased tourism. The community placed great importance on the work to be done and the fun to be had. In this image, Norman D. Nevills of Mexican Hat, Utah, shoves off with a group of visitors on a 210-mile trip to Jensen, Utah. Nevills is seated in his flagship, the *Wen*. Known for roughly a decade as the world's number one fast-water man, Nevills had been a commercial river guide since 1938. He developed his own boat design, the cataract. (Courtesy of Sweetwater County Historical Museum.)

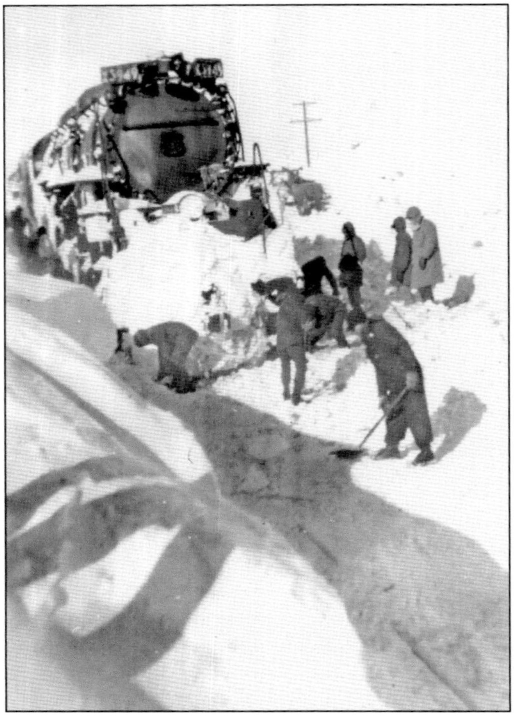

In January 1949, a series of blizzards hit southwest Wyoming and brought the rail industry to a halt. The dangerous storms marooned over 1,200 passengers in Green River. Snow drifts in excess of 30 feet, hurricane-force winds, and temperatures dropping to 51 degrees below zero made snow removal almost impossible. Community efforts assured the stranded travelers some comfort and entertainment. (Courtesy of Sweetwater County Historical Museum.)

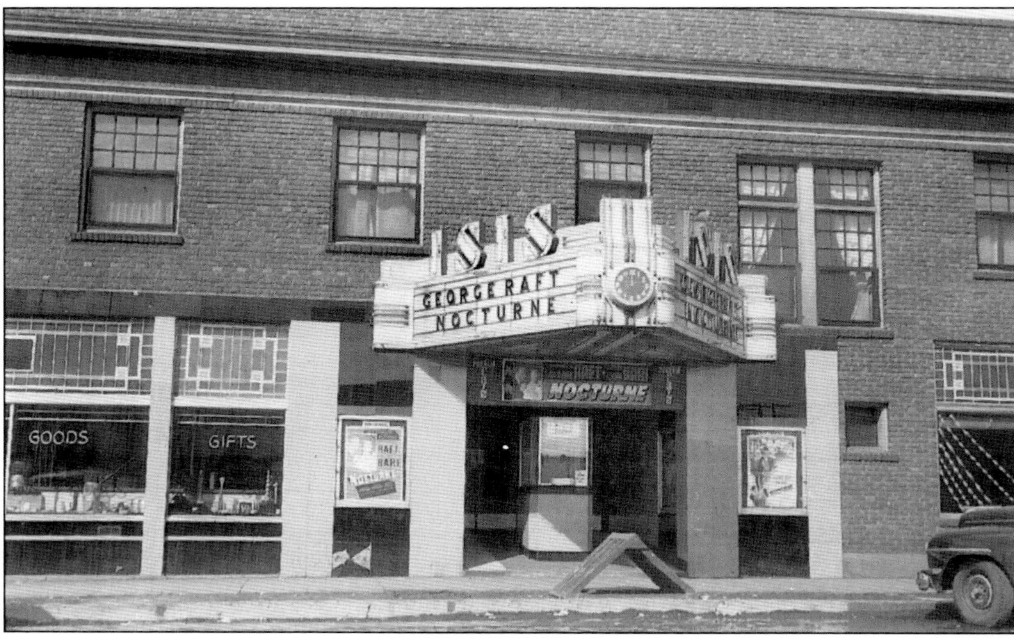

The Isis Theater, built shortly after World War I, was a favorite place for the youngsters of Green River to congregate. It is pictured here in 1949. The theater had racially segregated seating until roughly 1947, when a courageous woman of color, Estelle Crouch, decided to move from the back rows reserved for nonwhites into the center section and, by her action, ended segregation in the theater. (Courtesy of Sweetwater County Historical Museum.)

William Hutton was the custodian for the county courthouse between 1907 and 1965. Between 1910 and 1917, he and his wife, Hattie, occupied a homestead on the heights above Green River, an area still referred to as Hutton Heights. Hutton was a member of the fire department for 27 years and was chief for 5 years. He was also the U.S. weather observer for 37 years. (Courtesy of Sweetwater County Historical Museum.)

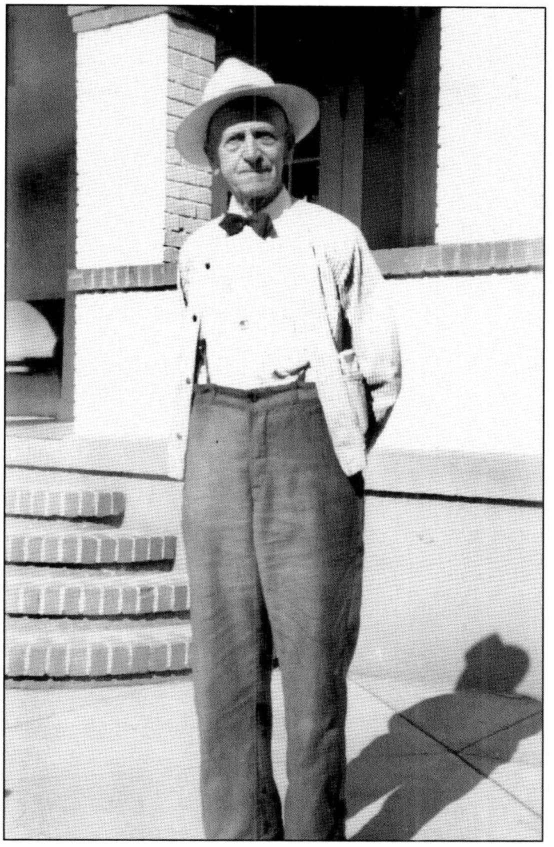

The year 1950 was a banner year for the Green River Eagles, who took first place in the Sweetwater County Basketball Tournament. They went on to lose at the Amateur Athletic Union tournament in Cheyenne. Pictured are, from left to right and by last name only, the following: (first row) Bamesberger (No. 5), Desmond (No. 4), Ringdahl (No. 11), Braden (No. 7), and Corners (No. 6); (second row) Paxton (No. 8), manager Kenney Pottoroft, Moore (No. 9), and Carroll (No. 3). (Courtesy of Sweetwater County Historical Museum.)

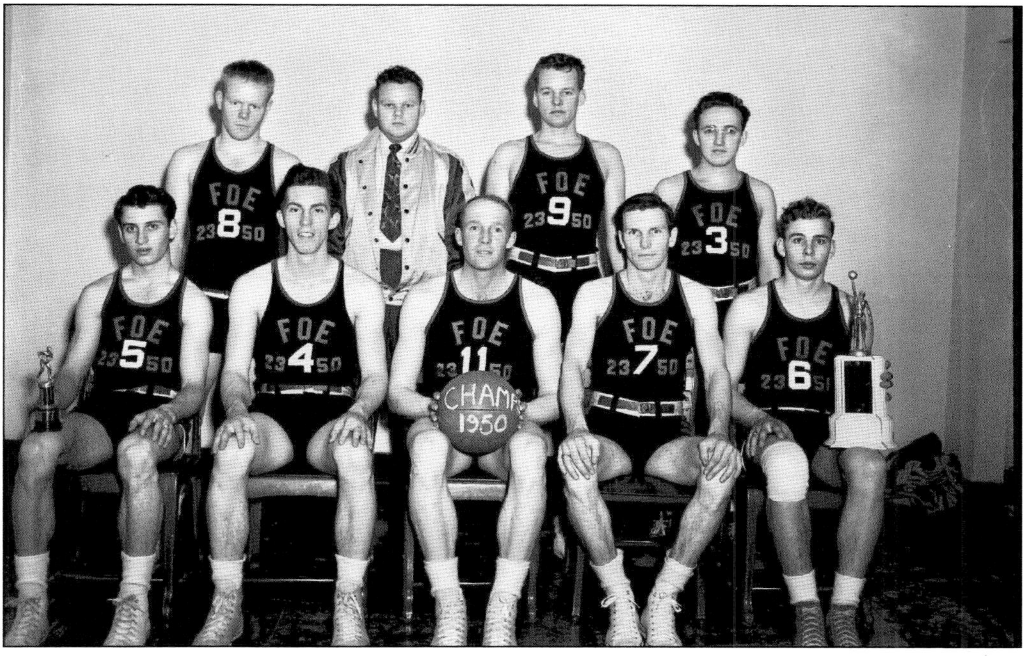

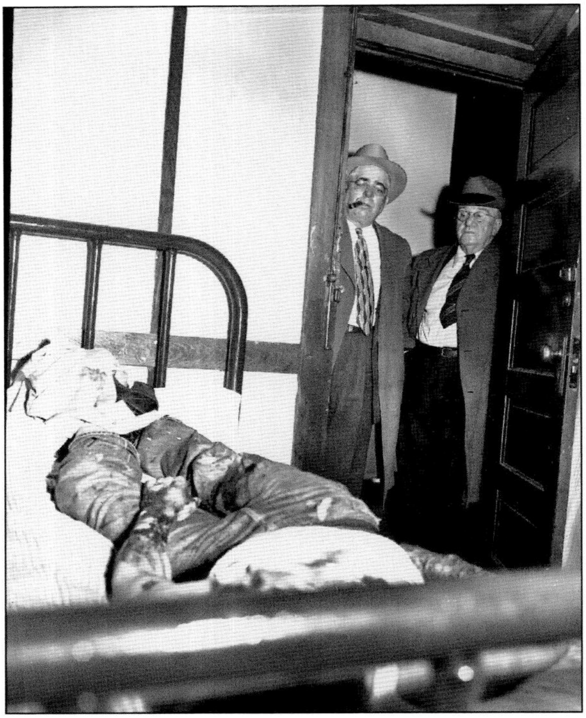

Standing in the doorway of room three at the Shanghai Hotel on December 29, 1949, are Sheriff Mike Maher (left) and another officer. The men were investigating the murder of Eugene Thompson, who was shot by his friend Charles Allen. Allen, seeing his wife in the room with Thompson, assumed she was cheating on him. Allen was convicted of manslaughter but served little prison time. (Courtesy of Sweetwater County Historical Museum.)

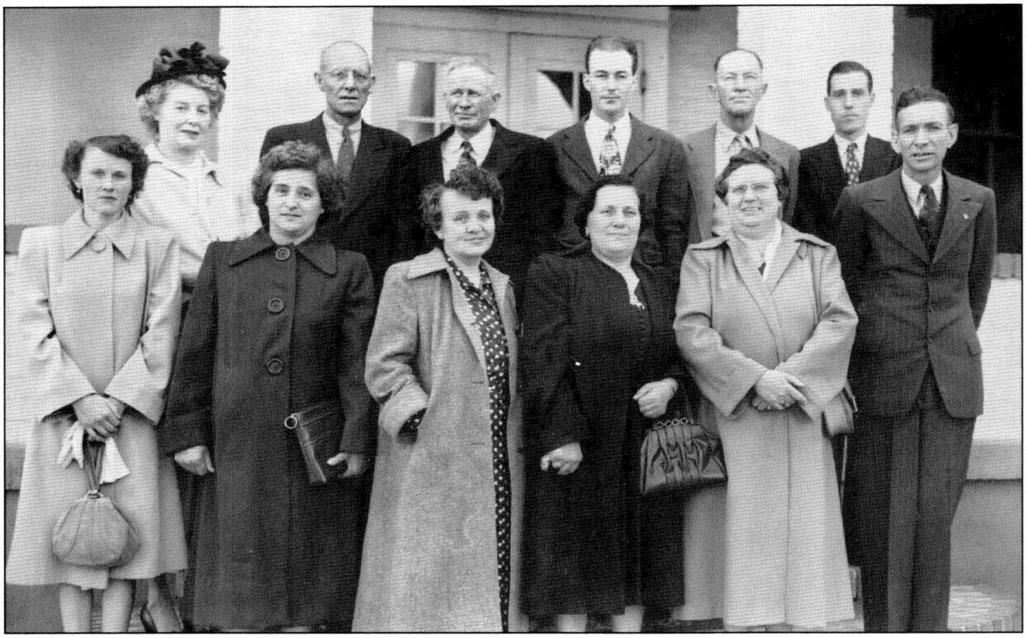

Changing times were reflected by the jury in the case of the *State of Wyoming v. Long*, a murder trial held in Green River in 1950. This jury was the first to include women since Wyoming earned its statehood. Louise Graf (front row, far right) was the first female jury foreperson. The case resulted in a guilty verdict, which defense attorney Walter Muir blamed on "those damn women on the jury!" (Courtesy of Sweetwater County Historical Museum.)

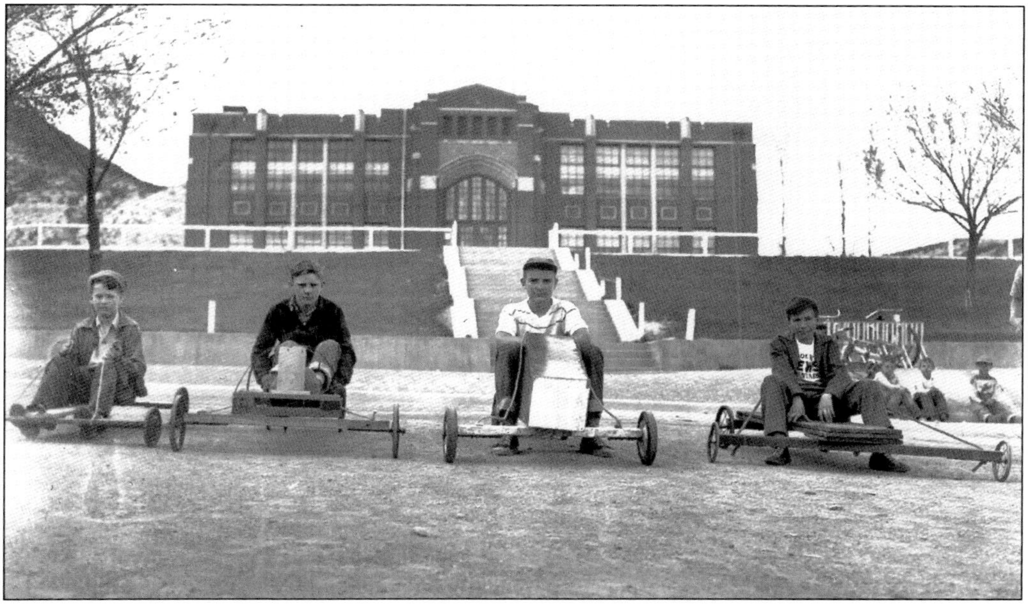

In this 1950 image by Edward Proctor, a photographer and teacher of biology and photography at the high school, soapbox derby riders begin their trip down the hill from the old Washington Elementary School. Tucked between the buttes and the river, the town's hills fulfilled the need for speed among the youth, whether they were riding derby cars, bicycles, skates, or sleds. (Courtesy of Sweetwater County Historical Museum.)

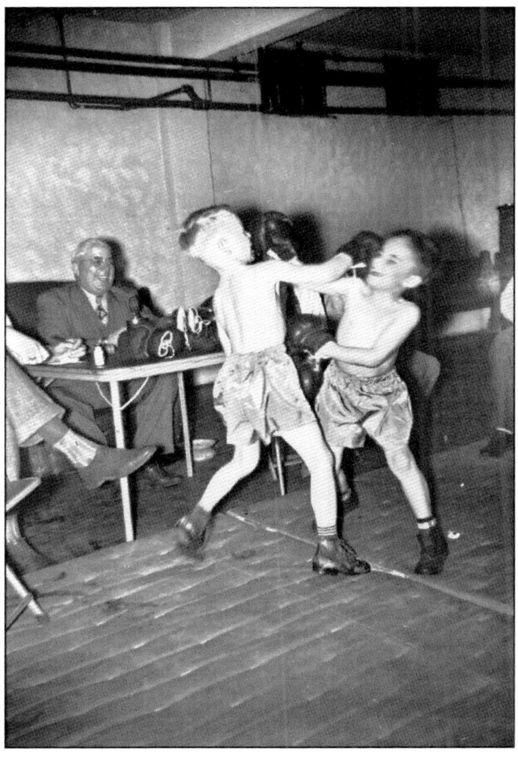

This is a 1950 image of young pugilists fighting. Sweetwater County sheriff Mike Maher appears to be judging the bout and perhaps announcing as well. The makeshift ring has no ropes, and the floor is covered with gymnasium matting. The location of this event is unknown, but it appears to have occurred in a basement. (Courtesy of Sweetwater County Historical Museum.)

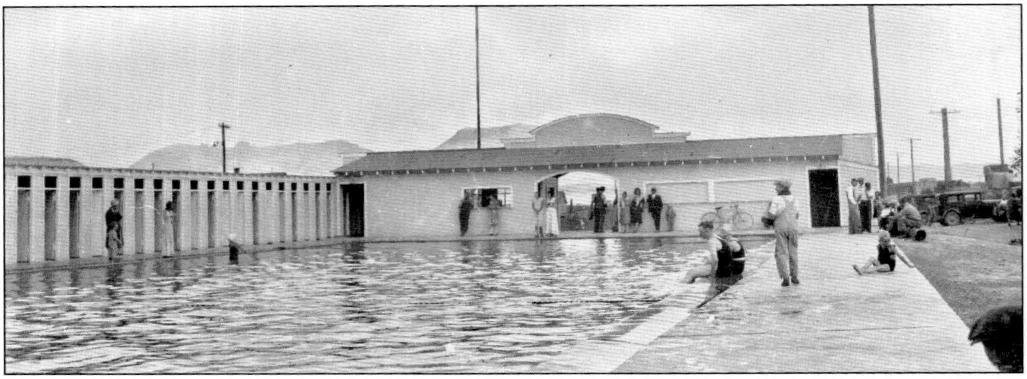

Green River's outdoor pool provided a haven from summer heat for both young and old from 1931 until the 1960s. The pool was closed once a week for cleaning and then refilled with river water. Cinders from the railroad tended to make the water muddy within a few days of each cleaning. (Courtesy of Sweetwater County Historical Museum.)

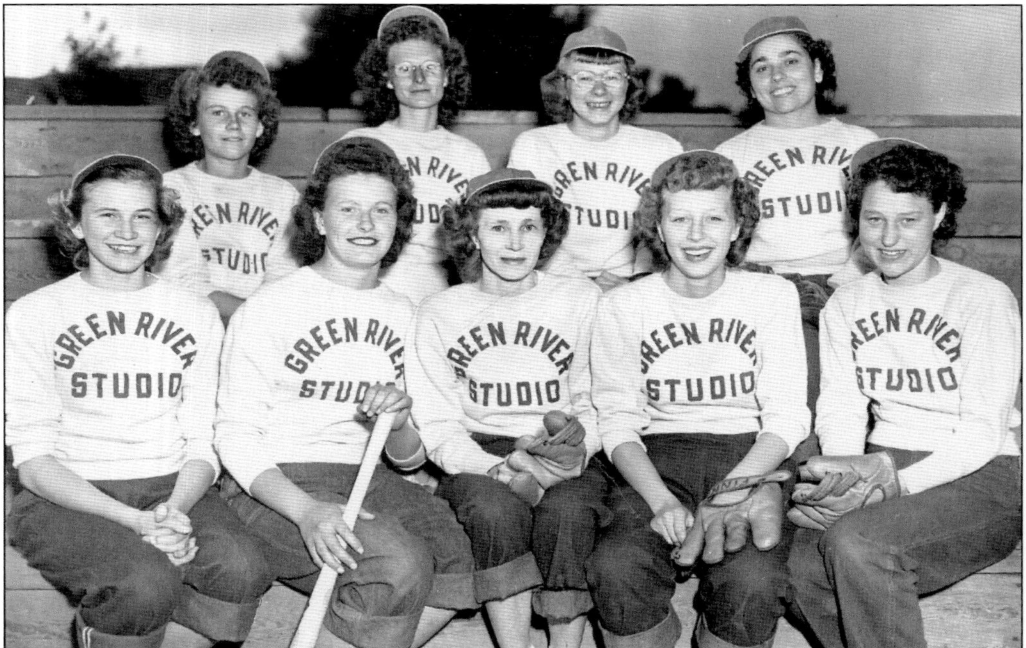

The Green River Studio "Snapshots" won their second women's softball league championship in 1949. Pictured are, from left to right, the following: (first row) Terry Melvin, Mary Seyerdahl, Mildred Finn, Darlene Finn, and Phyllis Twitchell; (second row) Phyllis Peterson, Evelyn Kinniburgh, Coleen Finn, and Virginia Brandner. (Courtesy of Sweetwater County Historical Museum.)

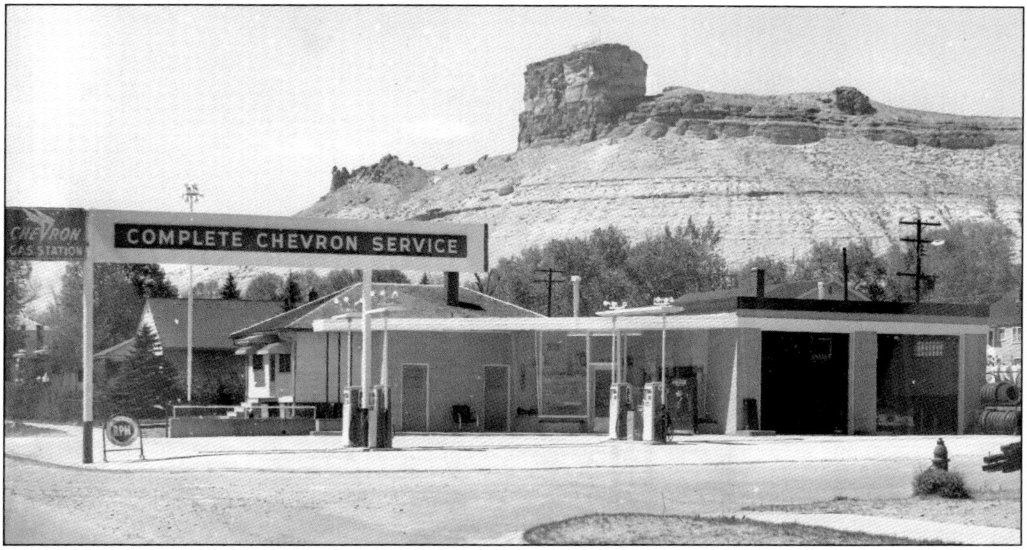

The Chevron Station on Flaming Gorge Way offered complete service to passing motorists. Full-service stations like this one were phased out in favor of self-service stations by the 1970s. This image appears to date to the late 1950s or early 1960s. Prior to the construction of Interstate 80, this station was located on U.S. Highway 30. In this image, Castle Rock has a flagpole and a sign declaring "Green River." (Courtesy of Sweetwater County Historical Museum.)

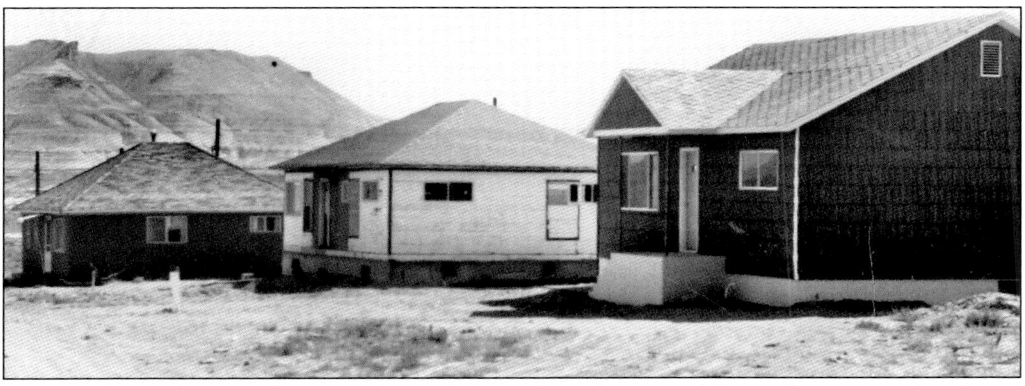

In 1957, the coal town of Winton, located about 30 miles east of Green River, was abandoned by the Union Pacific Coal Company and dismantled. Many of the homes were bought for a nominal fee and moved to nearby communities, such as Rock Springs and Green River. The houses traveled on large flatbed trailers via U.S. Highway 30. (Courtesy of Sweetwater County Historical Museum.)

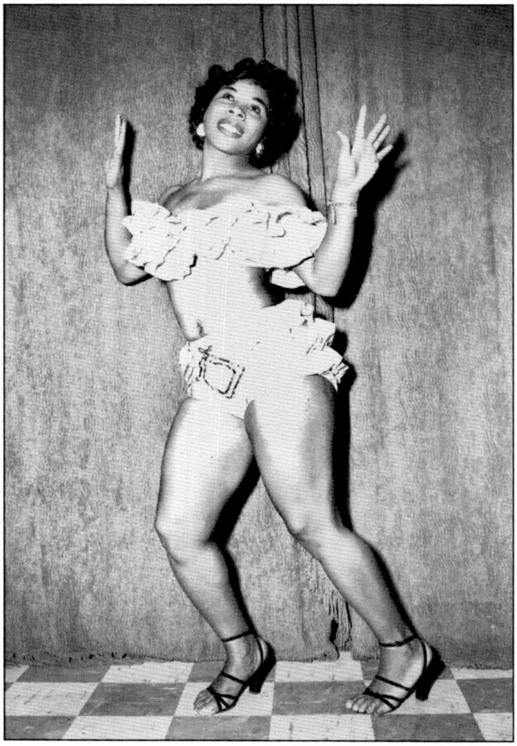

A dancer entertains her customers at a south side club around 1950. The neighborhood contained homes, stores, cafes, bars, and brothels. Angelie Scarpos, who grew up on the south side, recalled that the business district was rough, particularly at night. According to oral histories on file at the Sweetwater County Historical Museum, "There was this alleyway here . . . after dark you didn't dare walk up this alley . . . you didn't know if you would get your throat cut or not." (Courtesy of Sweetwater County Historical Museum.)

During the 1950s, a good time on the south side included liquor, gambling, pool, pretty ladies, and ribs at the Owls and the Oxford Clubs. In this image, Isaiah "Cat-Eye" Willis (left), the proprietor of both clubs, pours Jack Bivens a drink. Cat-Eye dealt with the segregation of the times by allowing only whites in the Oxford Club. The nearby Owls Club was for everyone else. (Courtesy of Sweetwater County Historical Museum.)

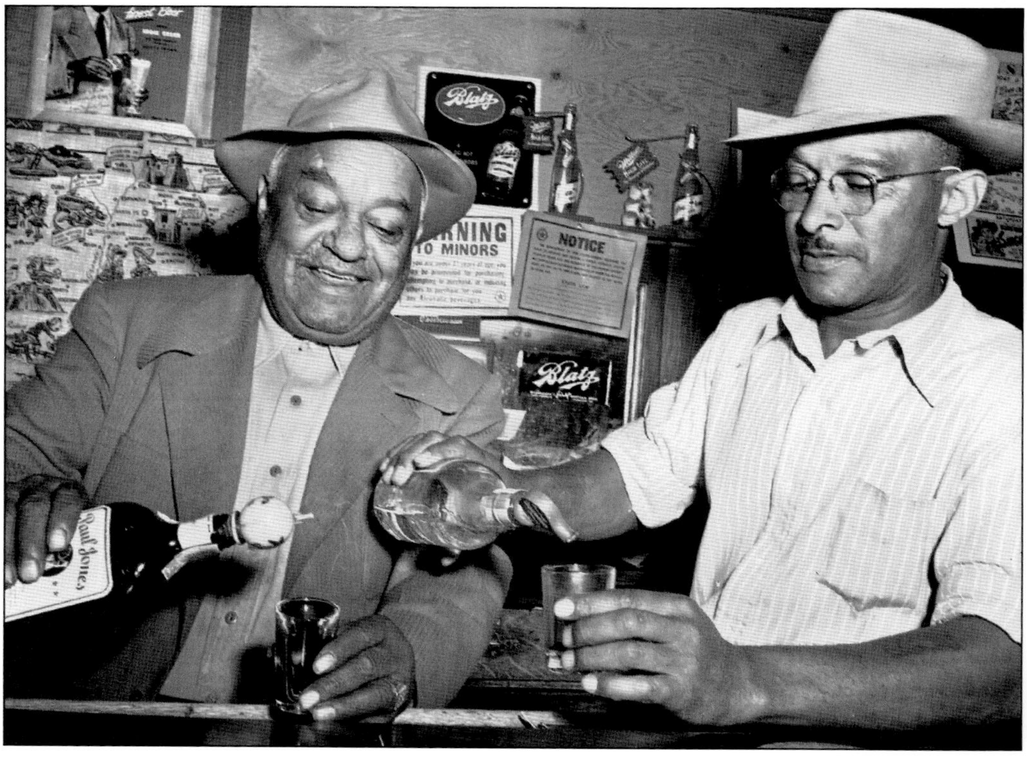

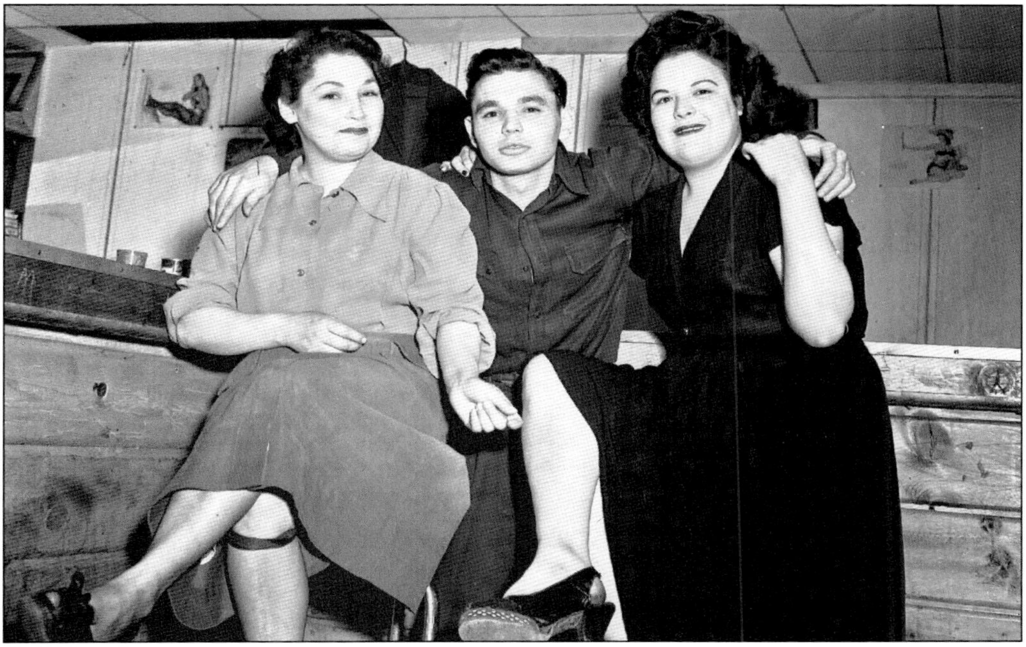

Longtime resident John Bacila is flanked by two unknown women in the Owls Club on Green River's south side around 1950. Bacila arrived on a freight train following his military service in World War II. Though just over 5 feet tall, he was a tough kid from Pittsburgh whose first job was as a bouncer at the club. (Courtesy of Sweetwater County Historical Museum.)

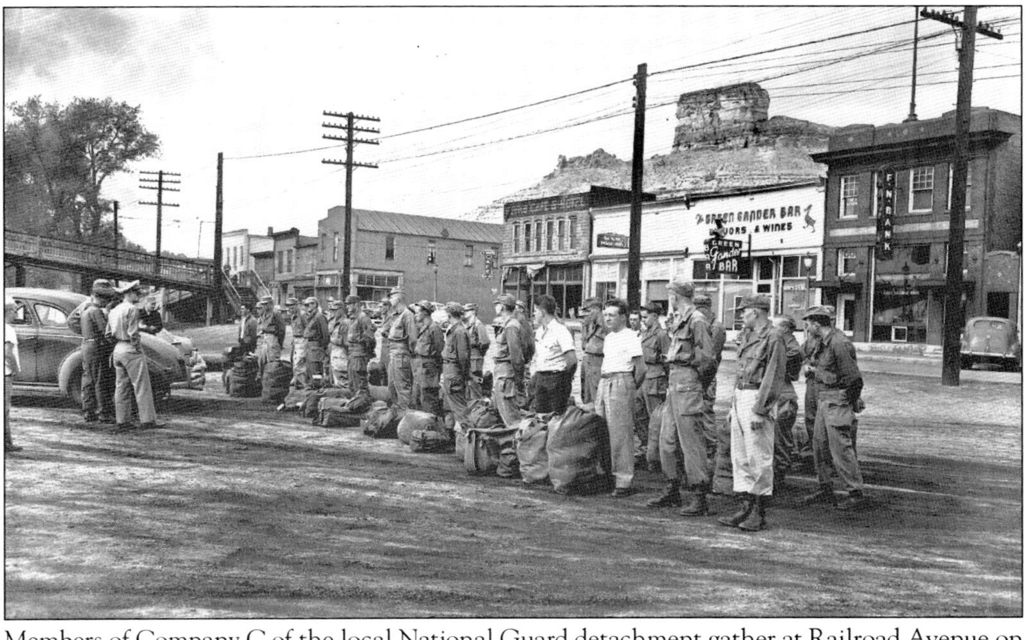

Members of Company C of the local National Guard detachment gather at Railroad Avenue on September 16, 1950. With the start of the Korean War in June 1950, readiness of military units became an issue. Here, Company C is preparing to journey to Camp Campbell in Kentucky for armored-tactics training. (Courtesy of Sweetwater County Historical Museum.)

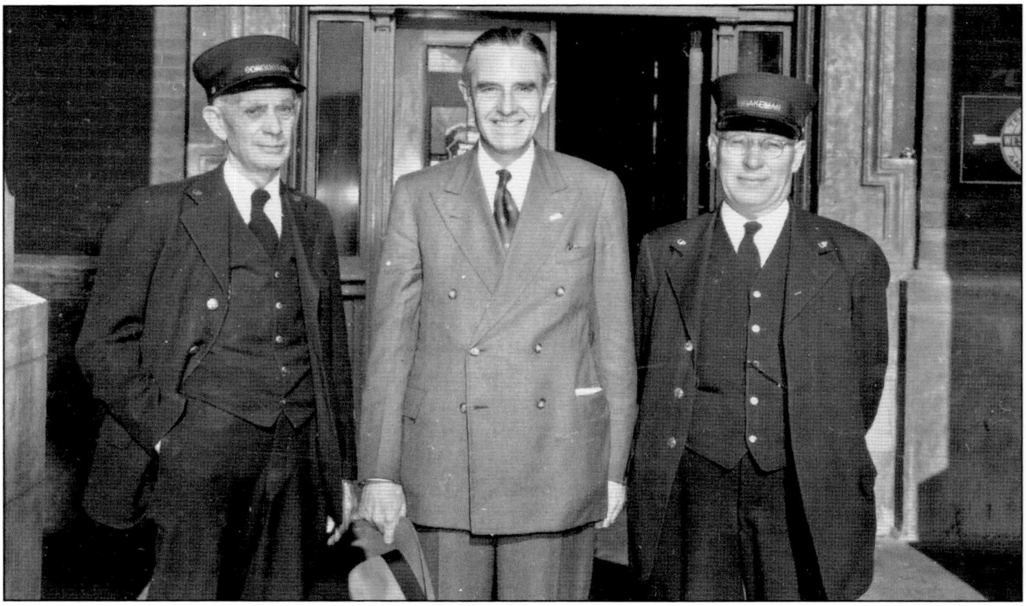

William Averell Harriman visits Green River on October 25, 1952. Harriman, the son of railroad baron Edward Henry Harriman, was vice president of the Union Pacific Railroad from 1915 to 1917 and was chairman of the board from 1932 to 1946. Harriman served Pres. Franklin Roosevelt as a special envoy to Europe, and he was the U.S. secretary of commerce under Harry Truman from 1946 to 1948. (Courtesy of Sweetwater County Historical Museum.)

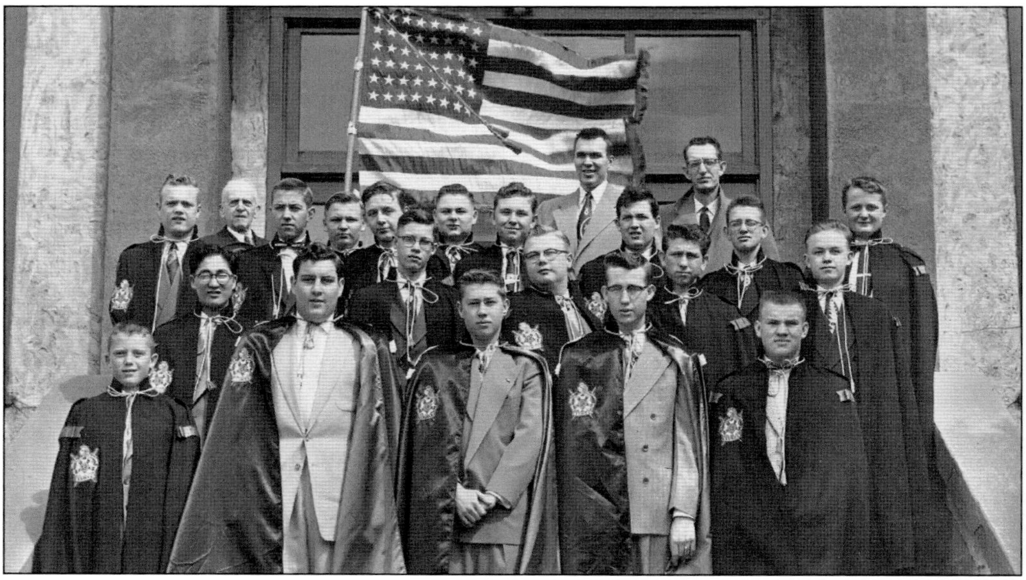

DeMolay was a Masonic youth organization. Pictured here in 1954 are, from left to right, the following: (first row) William Taliaferro, Loren Stone, Charles Jensen, Alfred Peterson, and Albert Stevens; (second row) Ray Sunada, David Whitney, Garth Foster, and Dean Larson; (third Row) Don Fowler, James Fox, Rex Keith, Michael Dankowski, Arnold Mabile, Harry Inman, and Howard Hagglend; (fourth row) William Hutton, Mr. Paxton, Brent Foster, John Wullschleger, and Divane Simpson. (Courtesy of Sweetwater County Historical Museum.)

Who says money doesn't grow on trees? Dell White (left), owner of Dell's Market at 95 East 1st Street North in Green River, shows off his "money tree" in this 1955 photograph. White used this promotional gimmick from time to time. The cash was awarded to a lucky winner chosen by a drawing. (Courtesy of Sweetwater County Historical Museum.)

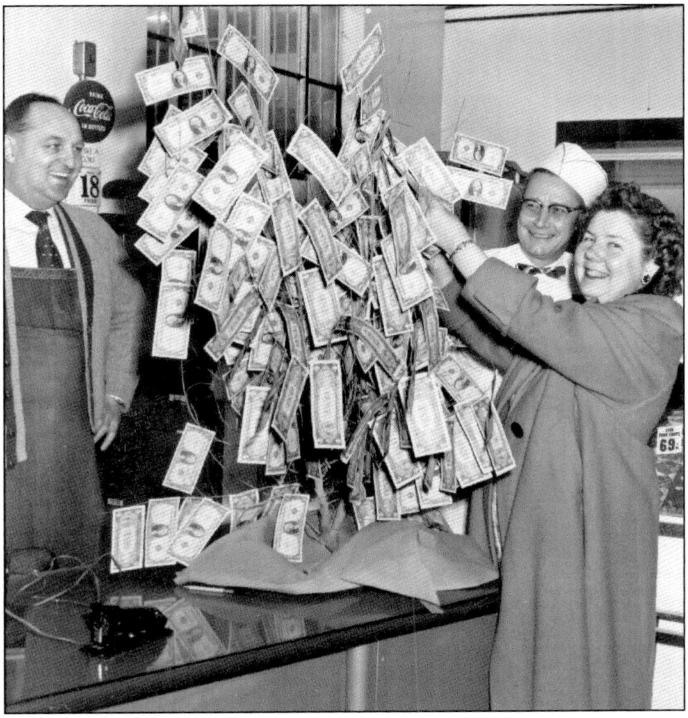

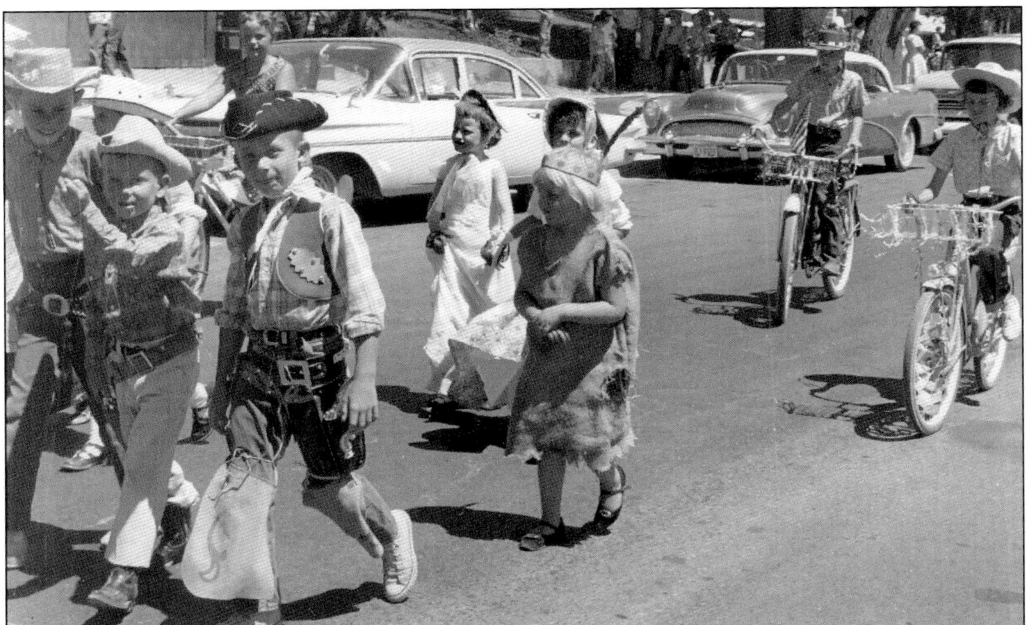

Children dress as cowboys, Indians, and settlers at the Pony Express Days celebration in July 1961. The five-day celebration culminated on the Fourth of July and included rodeo events. "Cowboy" culture is an important part of life in Green River. Various rodeos are held in the summer months. The Overland Stage Stampede remains a popular rodeo. (Courtesy of Sweetwater County Historical Museum.)

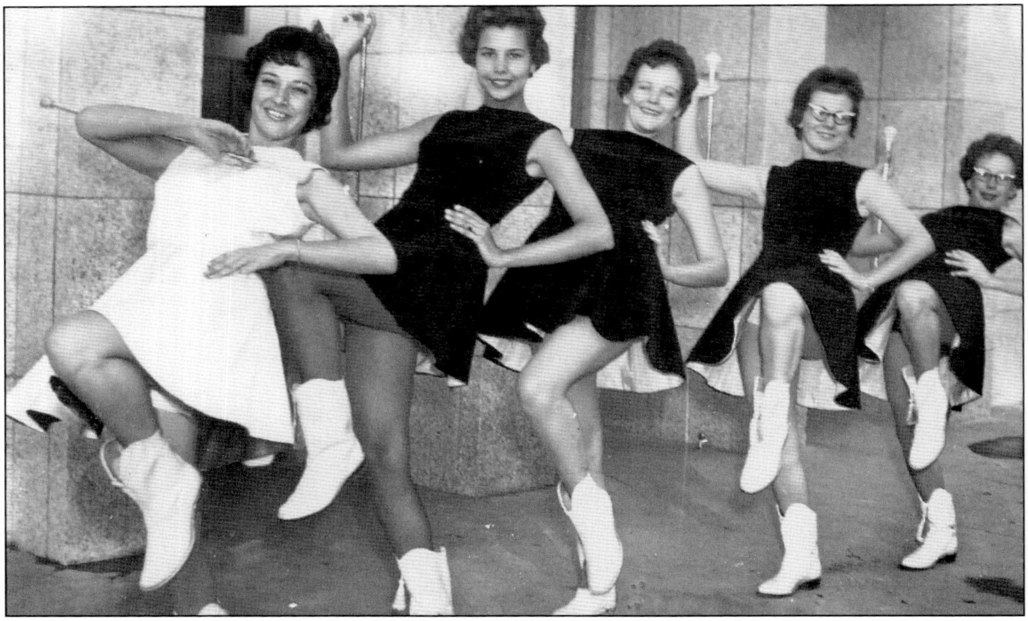

Members of the Lincoln High School Drill Team strut their stuff in 1961. All five girls were members of the Senior High Booster Club during the 1961–1962 school year. Called "the girls behind the goals," they provided the spirit for the Green River Wolves. Pictured here are, from left to right, Arlene Sorbie, Suzanne Bangerter, Alice Dunning, Vicki Gordon, and Nancy Biggs. (Courtesy of Sweetwater County Historical Museum.)

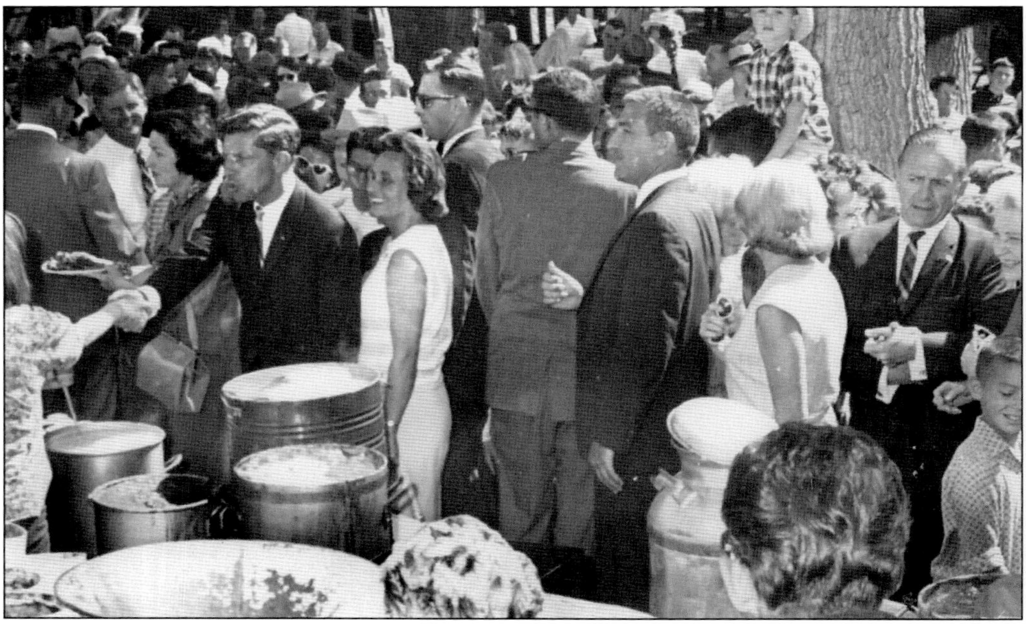

In 1964, Lady Bird Johnson, the first lady of the United States, dedicated Flaming Gorge Dam. According to the U.S. Bureau of Reclamation, the dam and pool alone cost $49.6 million. Lady Bird was a leader in environmental issues. In this image, she is visible at the left center, holding a plate heaped with Western barbecued food. (Courtesy of Sweetwater County Historical Museum.)

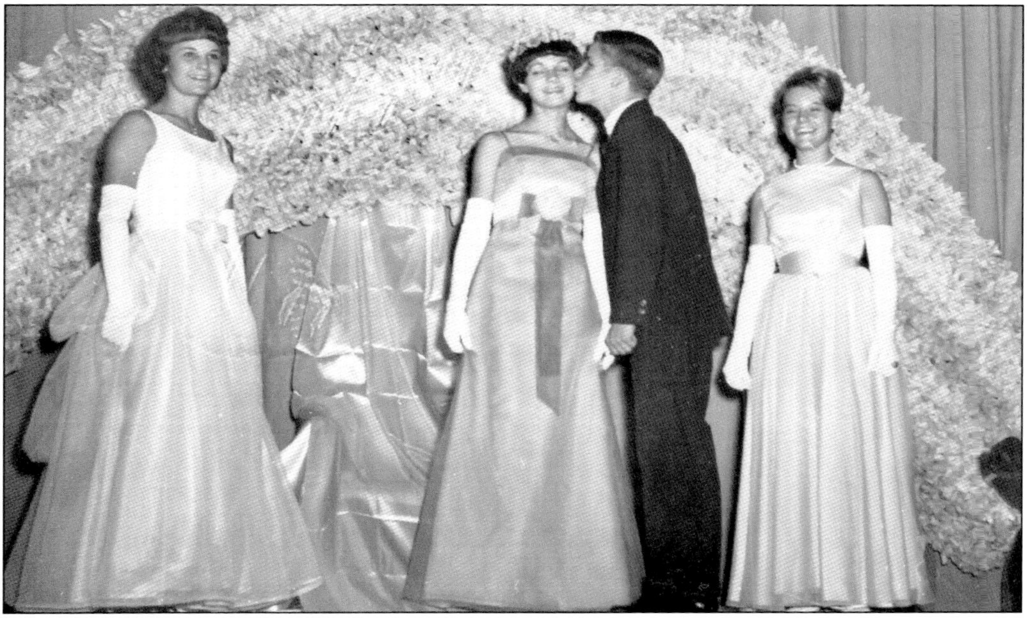

Lincoln High School's homecoming queen poses with her court in 1965. Casey O. Horton gives the queen a kiss. The ladies pictured are, from left to right, Sandra Kay Morrison, homecoming queen Debbra Dee Hardy, and Ellen Kay Sudman. (Courtesy of Sweetwater County Historical Museum.)

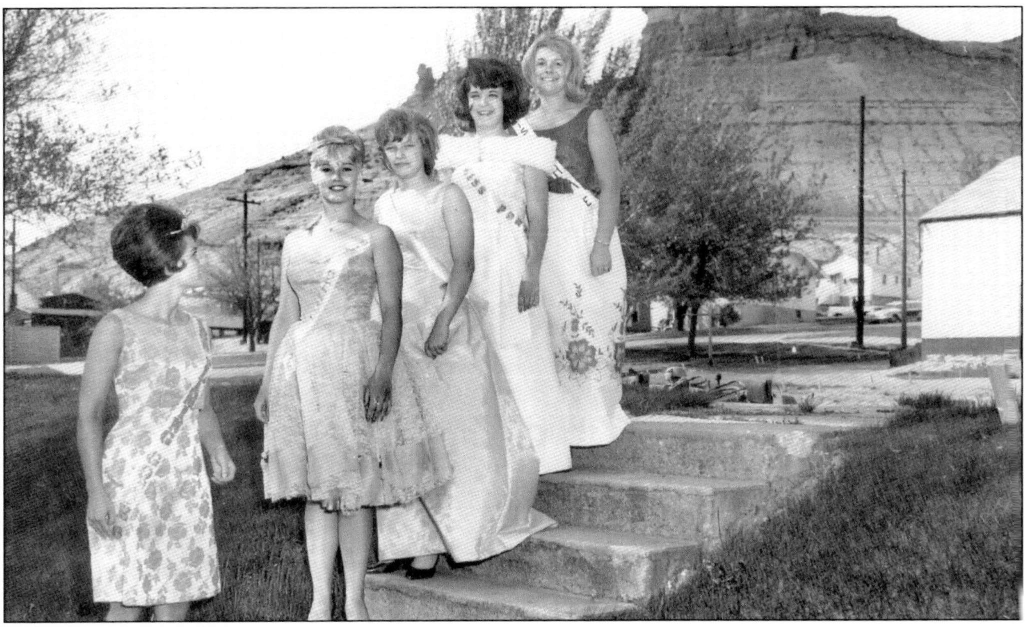

The reigning Miss Flaming Gorge of 1964 (at the bottom of the stairs) poses with several of the contestants in the 1965 pageant. Pictured are, from left to right, Jean Fox (Miss Flaming Gorge 1964), Dorothy Dichmueiler, Georgia Malicoa, Karen Porter, and Billie June Orme. The Flaming Gorge Days tradition was started in July 1963, coinciding with the completion of the Flaming Gorge Dam. (Courtesy of Sweetwater County Historical Museum.)

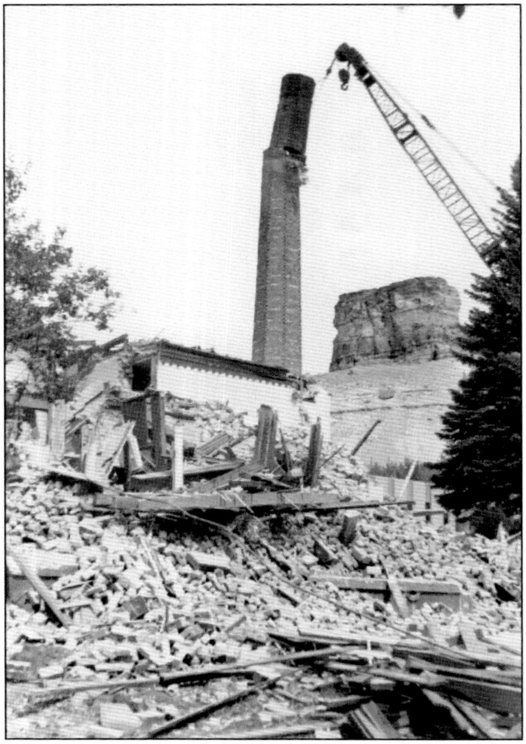

The remains of the 1876 Sweetwater County Courthouse fall to the wrecking ball. By 1956, the old brick building was decreed too small and decrepit for the growing county offices. A bond election held that year was turned down. It finally passed in 1965, and construction was completed in 1967. (Courtesy of Sweetwater County Historical Museum.)

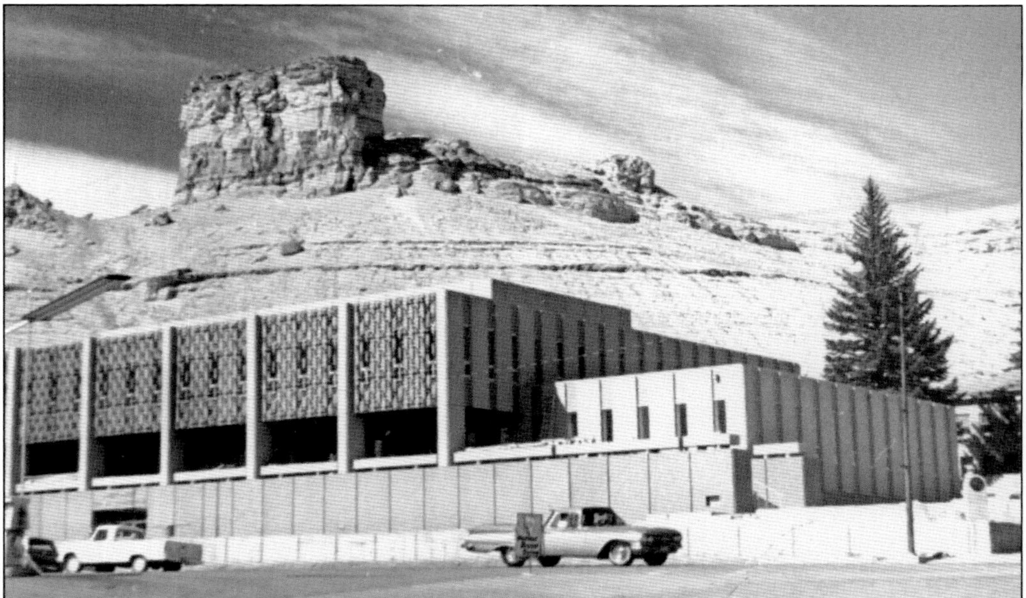

On August 13, 1967, the new Sweetwater County Courthouse was dedicated. This image dates to 1969, but it shows the courthouse much as it looked at the time of its dedication. At the time of the building's opening, it was too spacious for the needs of the county, and part of the building was leased to a bank. (Courtesy of Sweetwater County Historical Museum.)

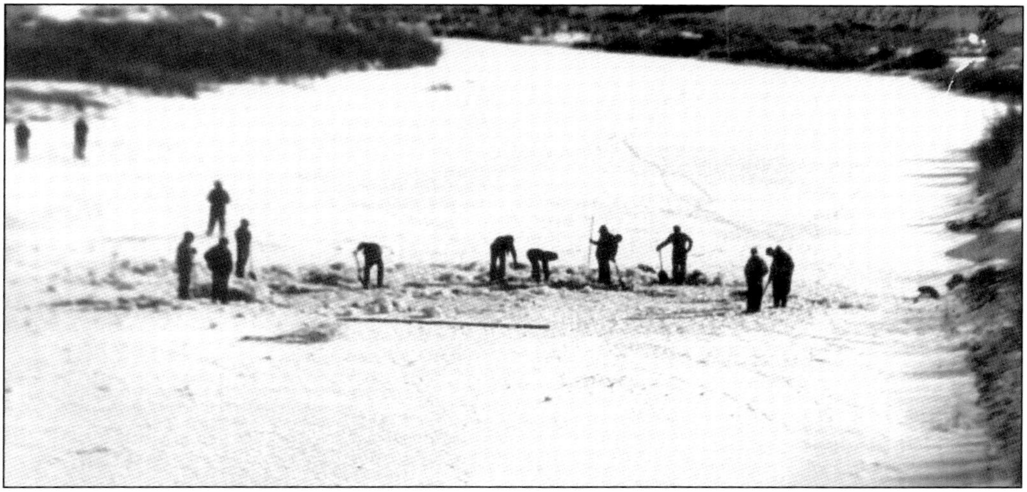

A crew takes on the grim task of searching for the body of a child under the frozen Green River. This 1960s image depicts the cutting of a trench across the channel in hopes of finding the body drifting below the ice. Such crews were supplemented by heavy equipment when the thickness of the ice permitted. (Courtesy of Sweetwater County Historical Museum.)

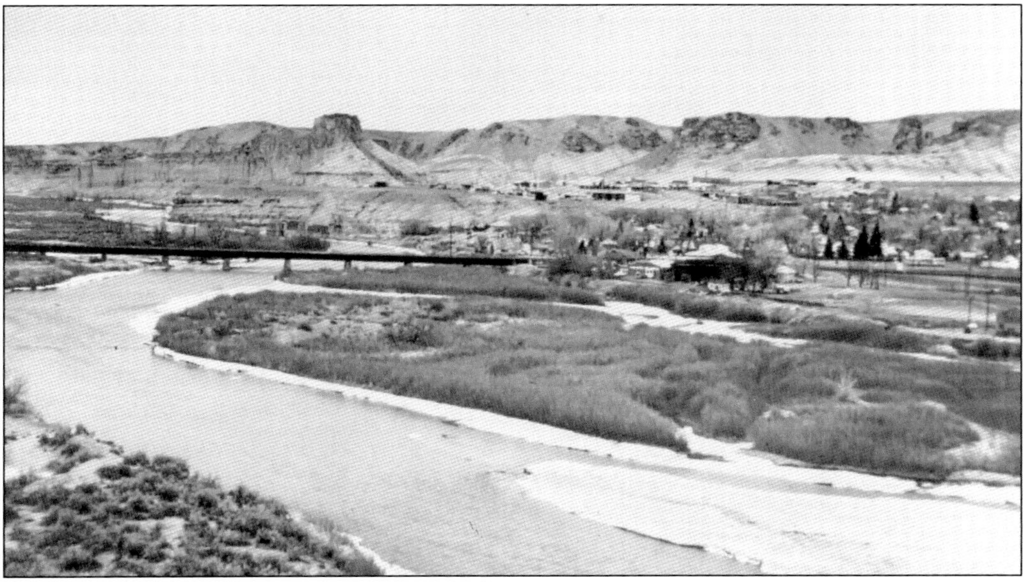

Green River is depicted here in 1975. The mid-1970s through the early 1980s were a "boom" time for southwestern Wyoming. Housing, groceries, and services were all at a premium as thousands of workers flooded into the area to fill new mining jobs. Law enforcement, fire protection, health care, and social services were stretched to their limits throughout the boom. (Courtesy of Sweetwater County Historical Museum.)

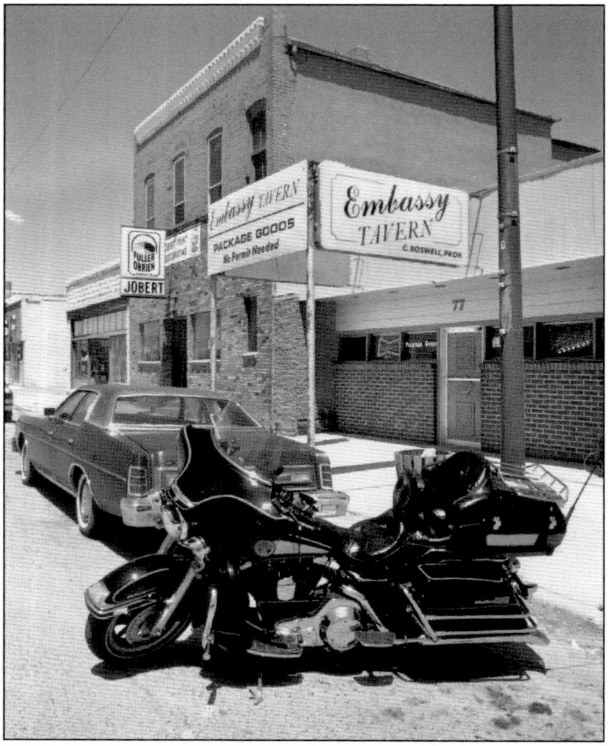

The Embassy Tavern was so named because owner Chris Boswell had a family member in the diplomatic corps. Constructed in 1870 as the Chrisman Drug, the building remained a drugstore through 1917. After that, a string of businesses occupied the building. In 1954, the Embassy Tavern, famous for its "world beer tour," took over the premises. (Courtesy of Sweetwater County Historical Museum.)

Green River mayor Richard Shuck opens the lock at the dedication ceremony and celebration for the Union Pacific Clubhouse. Also present are Union Pacific president Jack Kennefick (center) and Wyoming governor Stanley Hathaway (right). This image dates to about 1970. (Courtesy of Sweetwater County Historical Museum.)

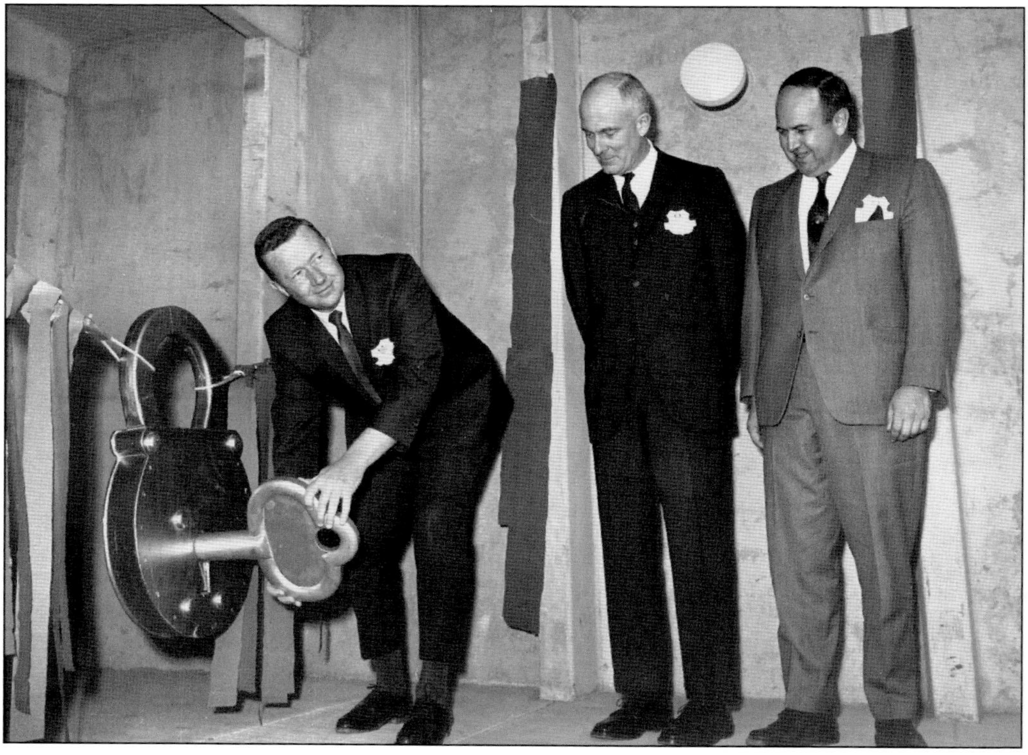

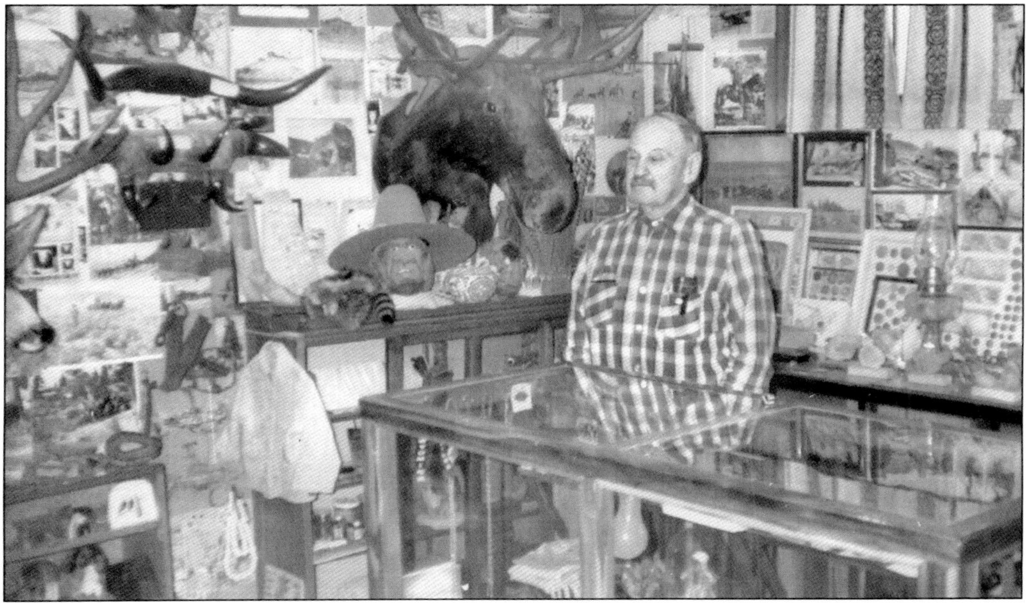

Noted collector George M. Stephens Jr. shows off his enormously popular private museum. Stephens, a son of early Green River residents, served as a Sweetwater County commissioner from 1947 to 1967. He also served as deputy sheriff. Stephens was a collector of historical artifacts. Upon his death in 1980, a portion of his collection was donated to the Sweetwater County Historical Museum. (Courtesy of Sweetwater County Historical Museum.)

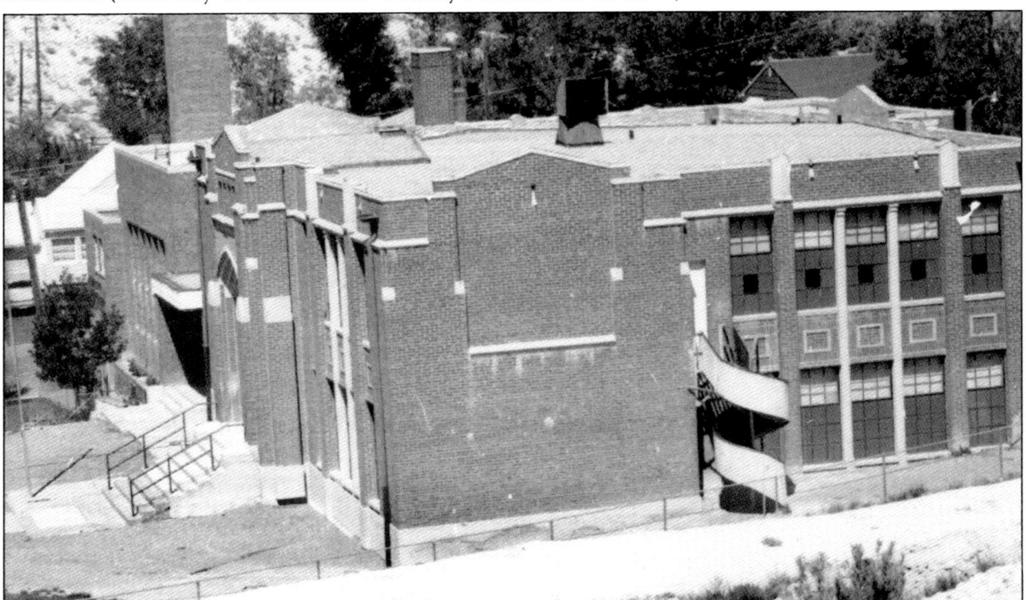

The Washington Elementary School, built in 1925, was the first school built solely for elementary grades in Green River. In 1978, a new school was built, and the old building was remodeled as an administrative hall. In the right center of this 1979 image is an unusual fire escape slide, the school's most-remembered feature. Many children got into trouble for using the large spiral slide for nonemergency purposes. (Courtesy of Sweetwater County Historical Museum.)

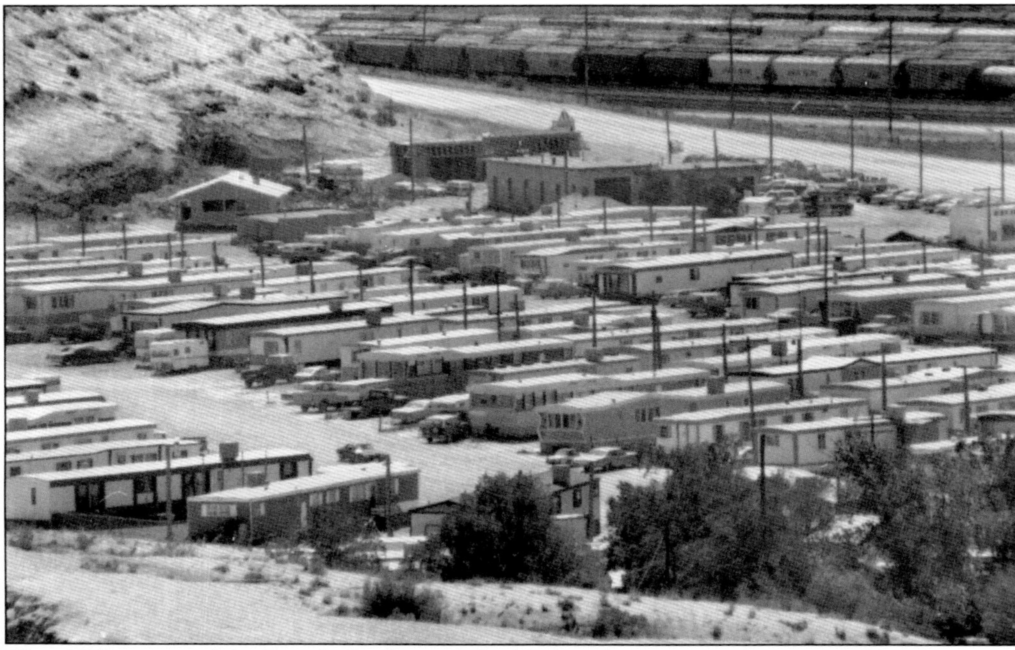

This 1979 image of the Routh Trailer Park highlights the overcrowding created by the energy and mining boom that took place from the late 1970s through the early 1980s. The trailer park predated the boom, but it rapidly filled with trailers as the housing market tightened. Green River's population grew from roughly 5,000 to over 15,000 during the rapid expansion. (Courtesy of Sweetwater County Historical Museum.)

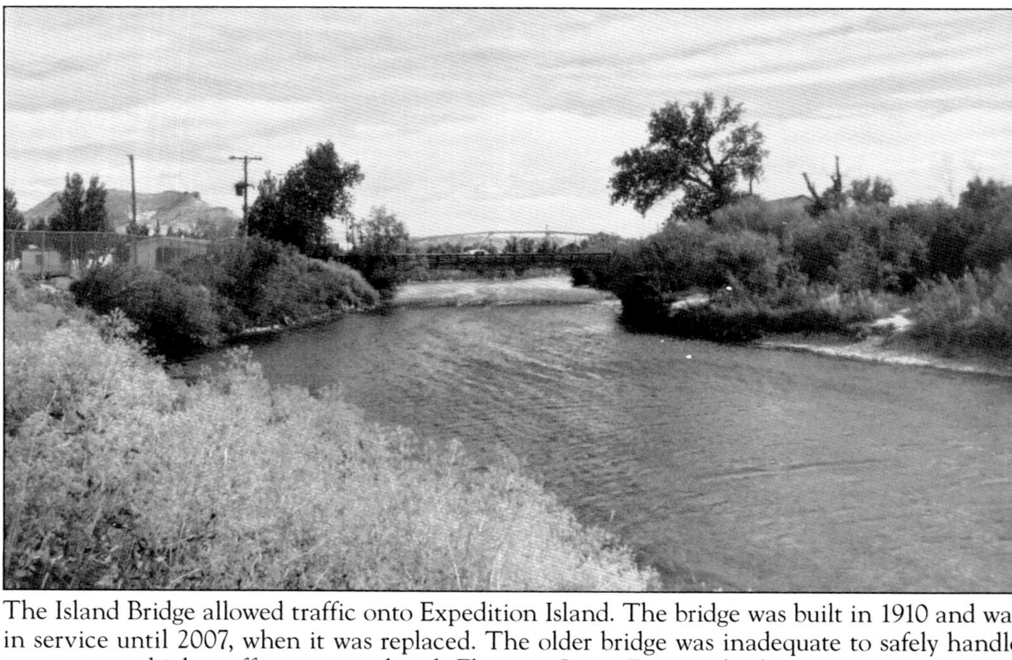

The Island Bridge allowed traffic onto Expedition Island. The bridge was built in 1910 and was in service until 2007, when it was replaced. The older bridge was inadequate to safely handle emergency-vehicle traffic associated with Flaming Gorge Days and other events. (Courtesy of Sweetwater County Historical Museum.)

Adaptive reuse of facilities is popular in Green River. For example, a former municipal swimming pool was filled in to make basketball courts. In the winter, as seen in this 1982 image, the courts were flooded and converted into a skating rink, which became a very popular winter recreation area. (Courtesy of Sweetwater County Historical Museum.)

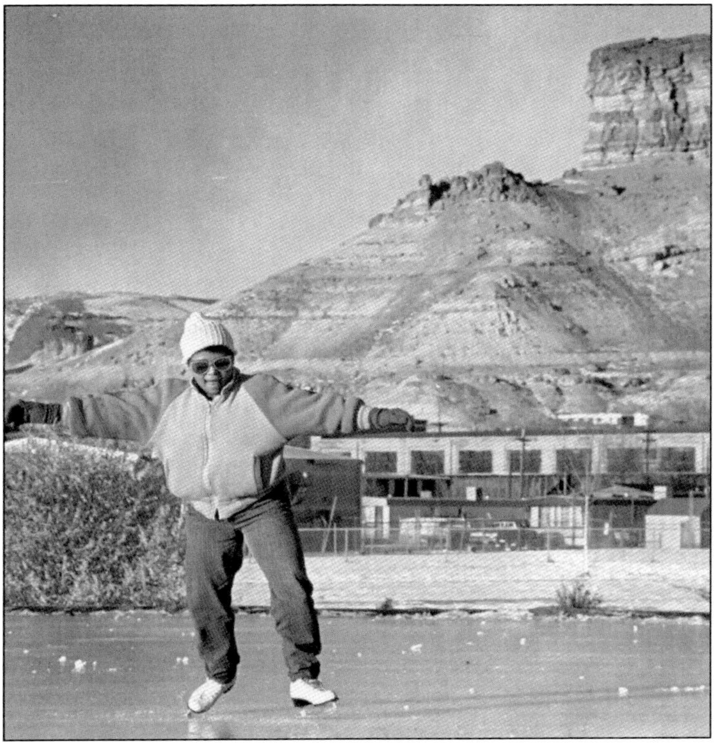

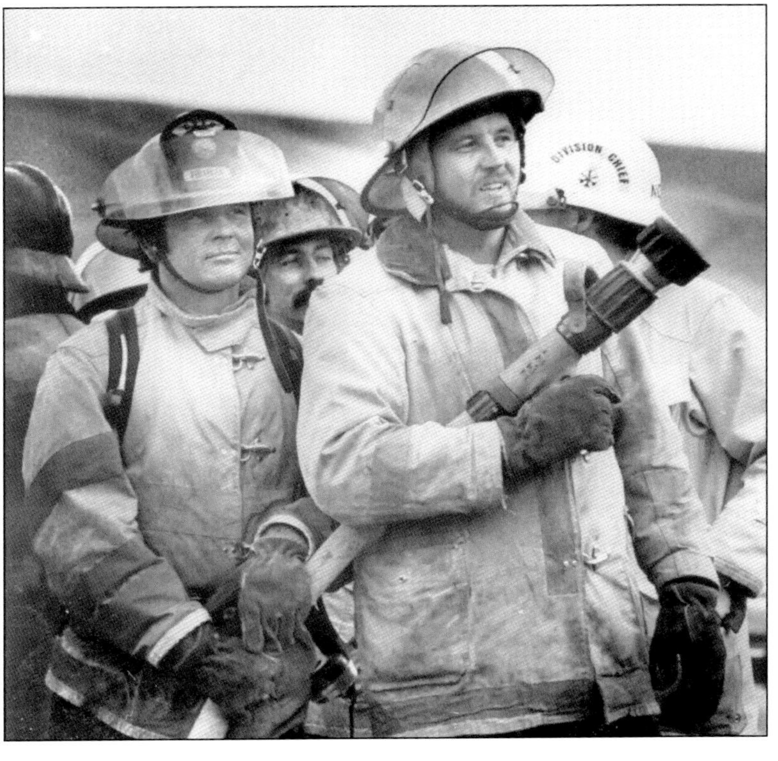

In 1982, three members of the Green River Fire Department traveled to Rawlins to participate in firefighting training conducted by the state fire marshal. Pictured here are, from left to right, Bob Clevenger, Neal Baldwin (partially obscured), and Barry Schunk. The department was founded in 1904 and has a long tradition of excellence. (Courtesy of Sweetwater County Historical Museum.)

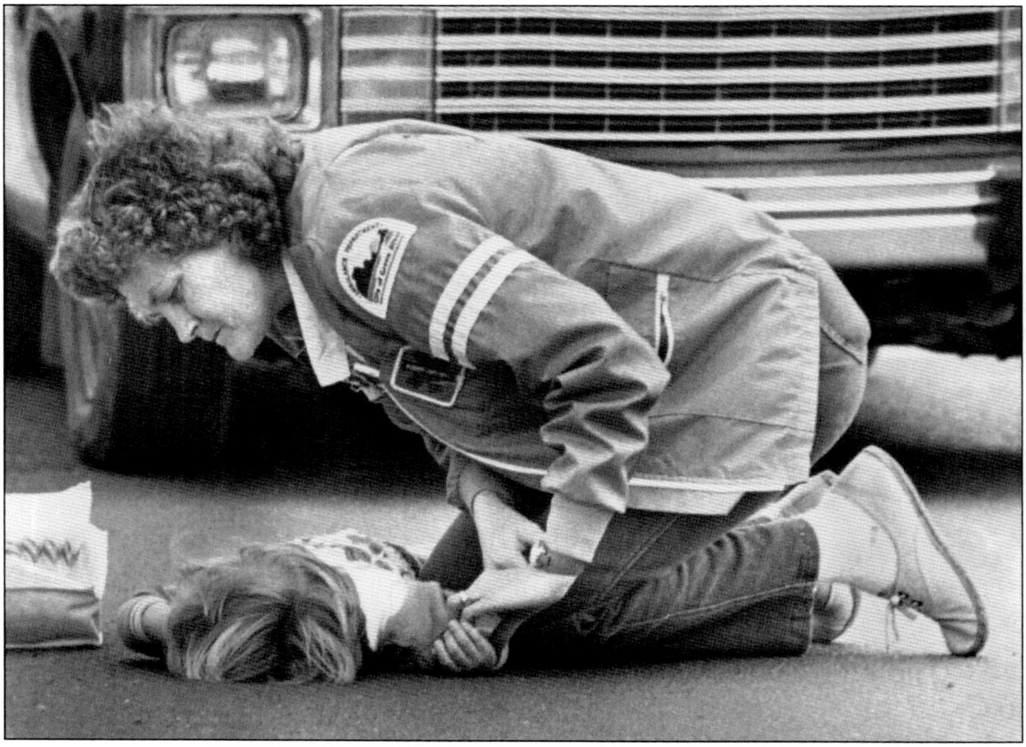

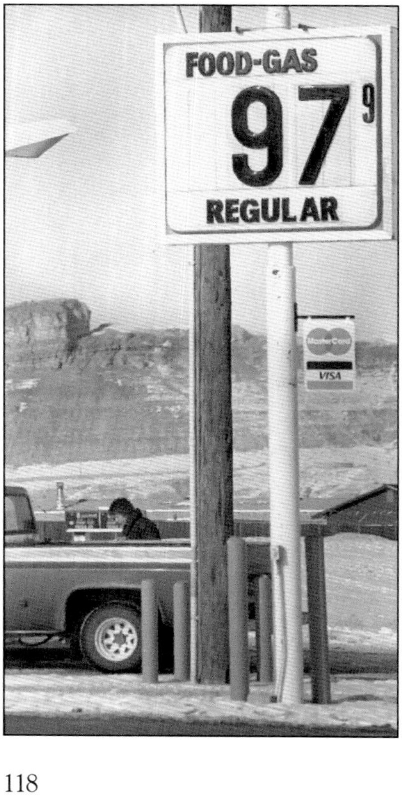

In 1982, Green River emergency medical technician Joyce Brazelton takes the pulse of Steven Hanson, age two, after the child reportedly fell from the pickup. The boy suffered a mild concussion and was released from the Memorial Hospital of Sweetwater County the same day. The Green River Ambulance Department formed in 1974. (Courtesy of Sweetwater County Historical Museum.)

Gas prices from the mid-1980s seem like reminders of the "good old days" in comparison to today's prices. This 1984 image of a convenience store gasoline marquee actually represents a time of high fuel costs. Gas prices for the late 1980s were lower than those shown here. Southwestern Wyoming's prices were lower than the national average, which for 1984 was $1.21 per gallon of unleaded regular. (Courtesy of Sweetwater County Historical Museum.)

Police rescue a wounded antelope at the Lincoln Junior High School. In this 1983 image, officers Randy Raetz (left), Ellen Dana (center), and David Hyer carry the stricken animal to safety; it was in danger of being killed by dogs. Roughly 5,000 antelope came to Green River during a season of particularly severe weather to escape the winds and cold temperatures of the hills. (Courtesy of Sweetwater County Historical Museum.)

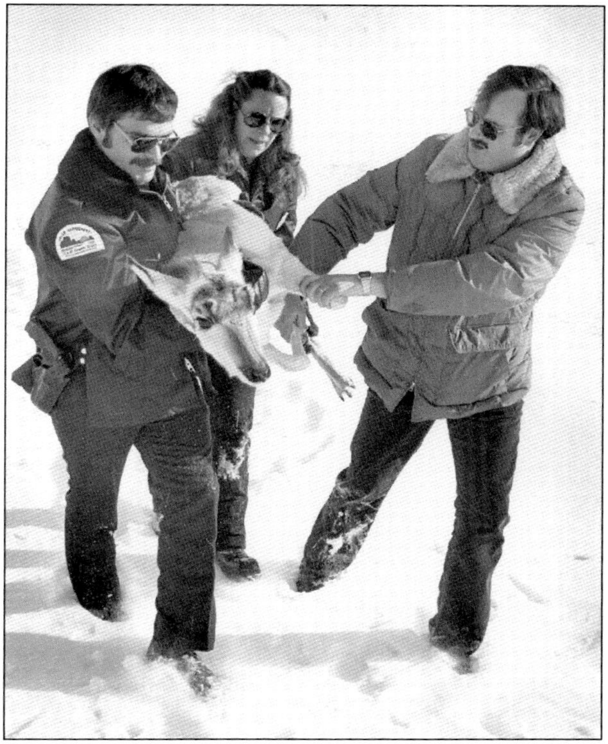

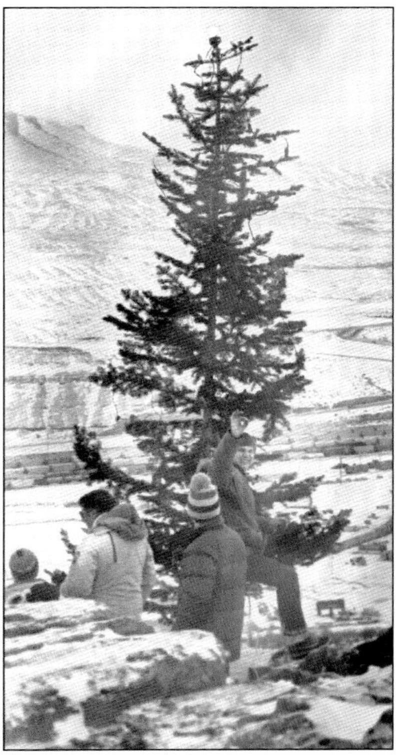

A Green River tradition is placing a Christmas tree atop Man's Face Rock. In this 1983 image, the Boy Scouts of America place the holiday tree. The light on top of the tree is visible throughout much of the community. (Courtesy of Sweetwater County Historical Museum.)

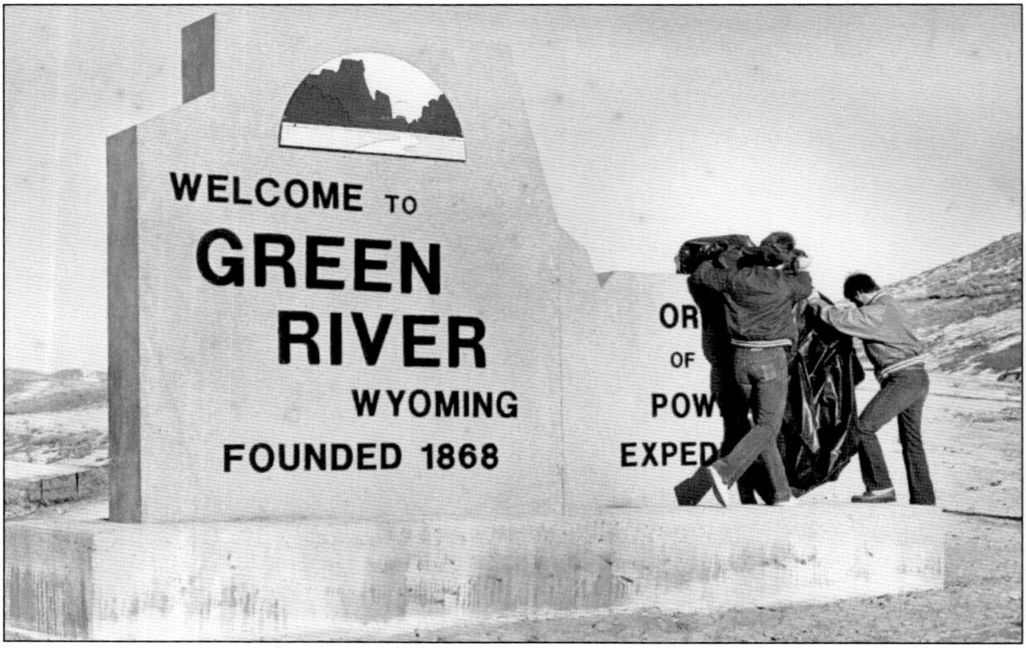

In March 1984, the City of Green River put out a new welcome mat in the form of a sign. Here, city employees Roger Moellendorf (left) and Eric Roosa strip the plastic covering off the new sign, which is located on the Interstate 80 exit ramp. (Courtesy of Sweetwater County Historical Museum.)

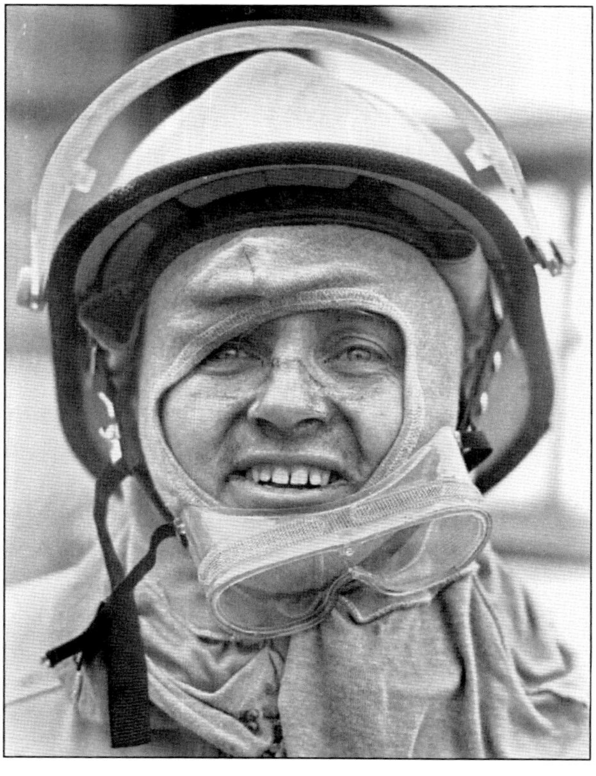

Glen McClean of Green River peeks out of his protective fire equipment. In 1988, Yellowstone National Park suffered a series of fires that burned roughly 1.2 million acres within the park. Firefighters from all over the nation, including a detachment of the Green River Fire Department, were put to work on the fire lines. (Courtesy of Sweetwater County Historical Museum.)

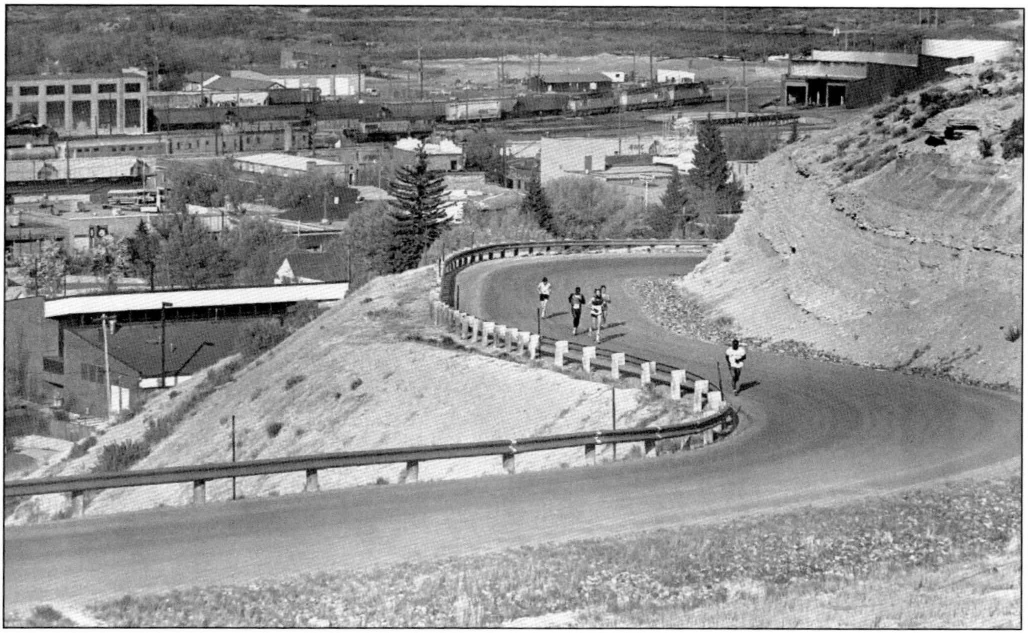

The city of Green River is viewed from Riverview Cemetery Road in this 1984 image of the Mountain Goat Run. This springtime event features a run from the city onto White Mountain. The 1984 winner was Amos Gibson of Rock Springs. Green River mayor Norm Stark (1995–2002) finished second in the over-40 competition behind Hal Stockton, also of Green River. (Courtesy of Sweetwater County Historical Museum.)

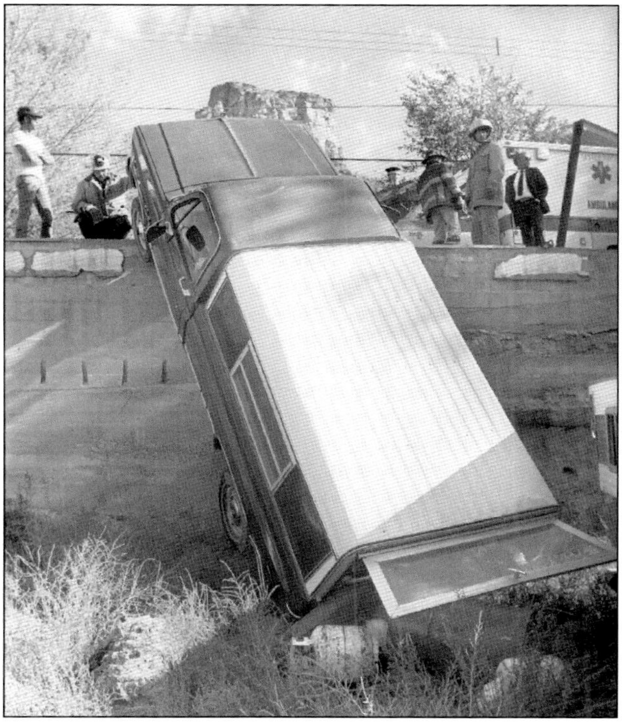

If one has to have an accident, it is best to do it at the body shop. In October 1984, this truck slipped out of gear behind Yeager's Auto Body. Truck owner Kalla Bame of Granger was injured while struggling to free her grandson from the vehicle. Green River firemen answered the call to deal with the propane tanks that ruptured in the crash. (Courtesy of Sweetwater County Historical Museum.)

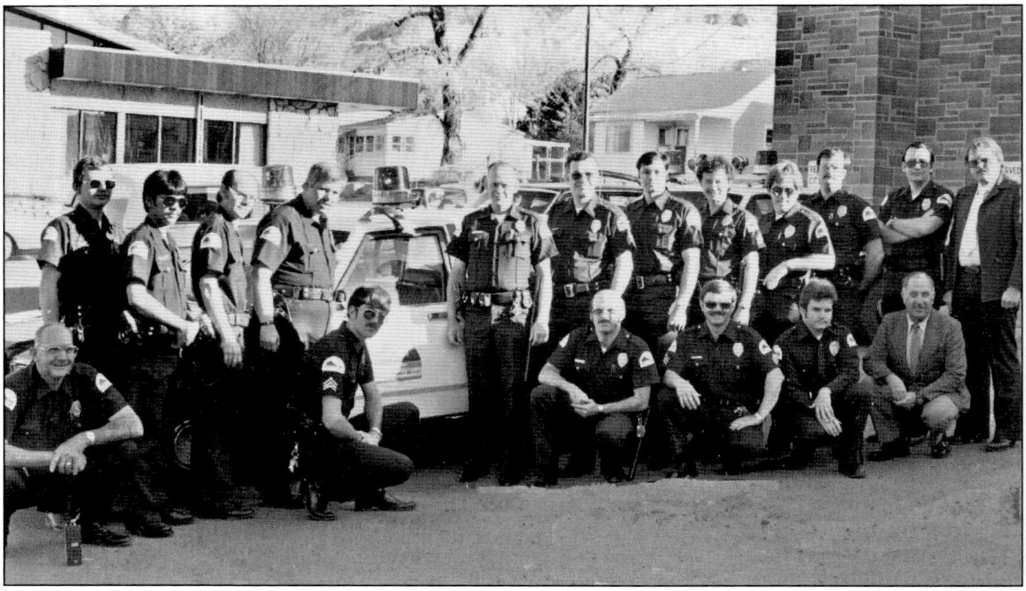

The Green River Police Department poses for a group photograph in 1985. The woolen police uniforms changed from brown to blue in 1980. In 1984, Green River became the first Wyoming city to incorporate the Drug Abuse Resistance Education (DARE) program. (Courtesy of the City of Green River.)

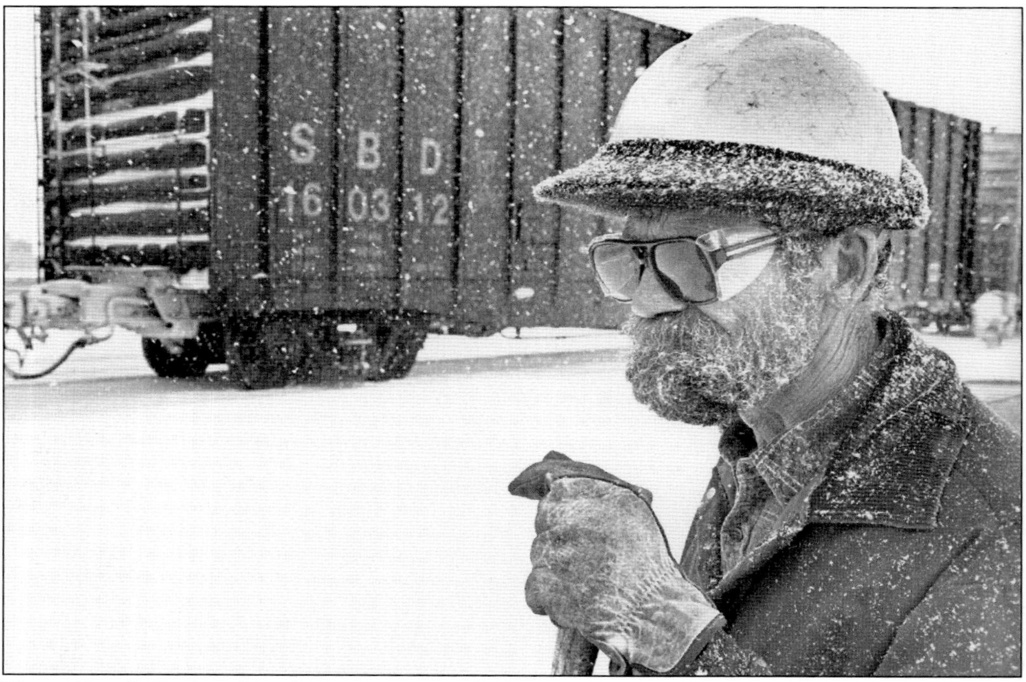

Union Pacific Railroad worker Dave Huston helps to keep the Green River rail yard operating in March 1988, when 15 inches of snow fell in a late-season blizzard. The snows were swept by winds of up to 30 miles per hour, creating whiteout conditions. Commercial air traffic was cancelled until the runways could be cleared. (Courtesy of Sweetwater County Historical Museum.)

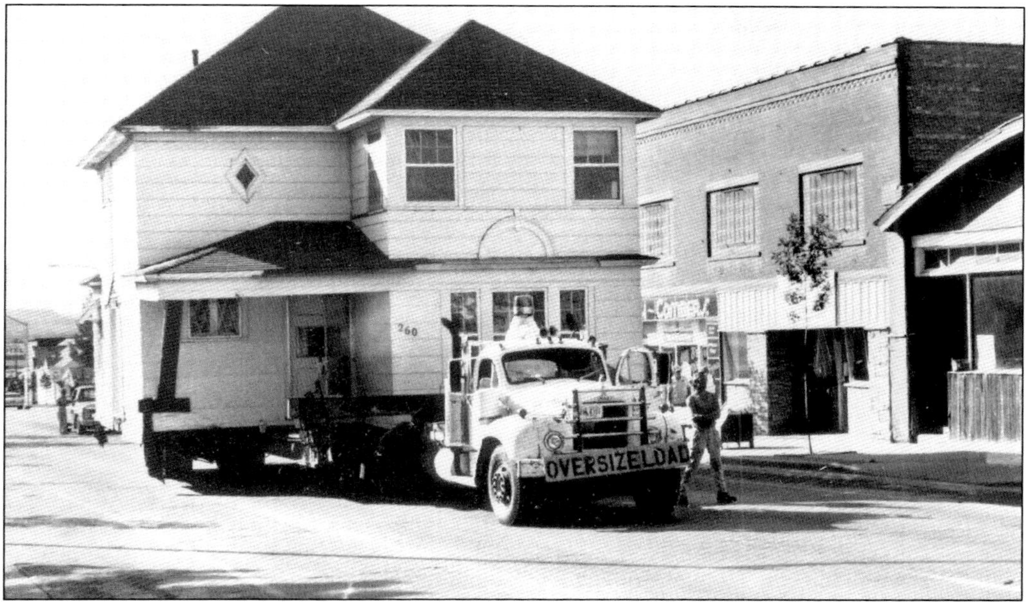

This 1989 image shows the old Union Pacific stationmaster's house moving through the downtown to a new location on South 5th Street West. This was the second move for this structure; it had already been relocated once in 1930 to make way for the post office building. (Courtesy of Sweetwater County Historical Museum.)

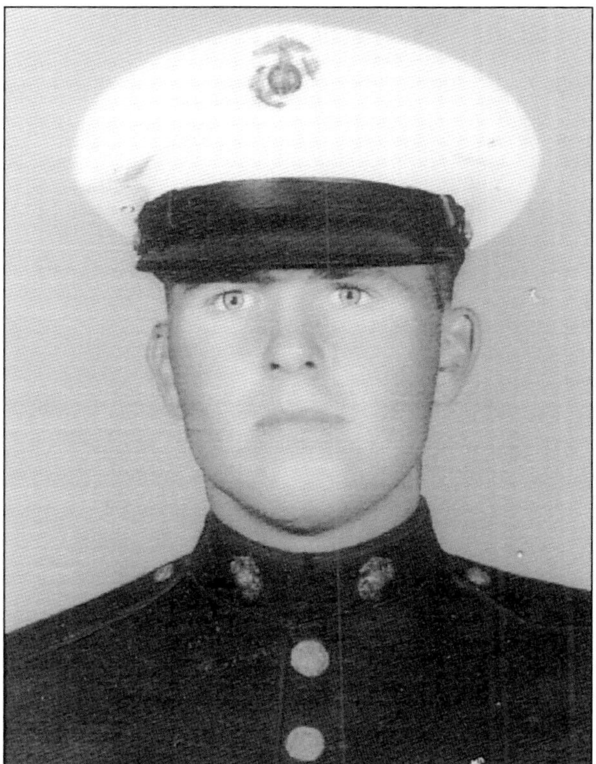

First Lt. Dennis D. King graduated from Green River High School in 1964. He served in the marines in Vietnam as a field artillery officer and was killed in action on February 20, 1968, in Quang Nam Province. Green River's other losses in Vietnam include Bennett E. Evans, Bruce A. Jensen, Robert F. Mauer, and Douglas E. Rogers. (Photograph courtesy Hays King.)

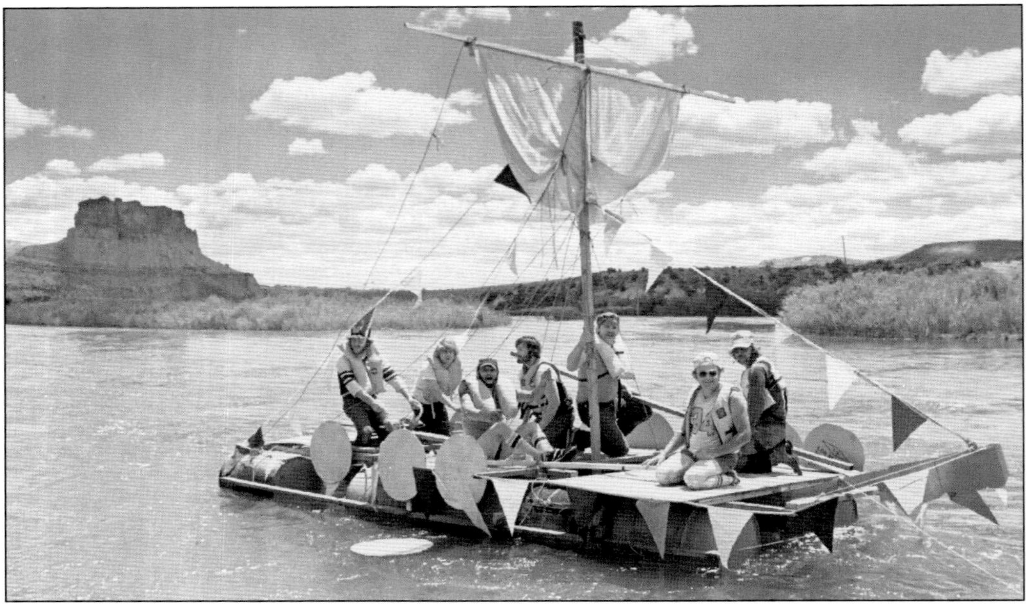

This 1982 image shows participants in the Green Garboon race. Contestants improvised river craft from a variety of materials. This craft, made by lashing metal barrels together, is falling apart as it starts the course. The Green Garboon race was a feature of Flaming Gorge Days until numerous injuries and mishaps resulted in its cancellation. (Courtesy of Sweetwater County Historical Museum.)

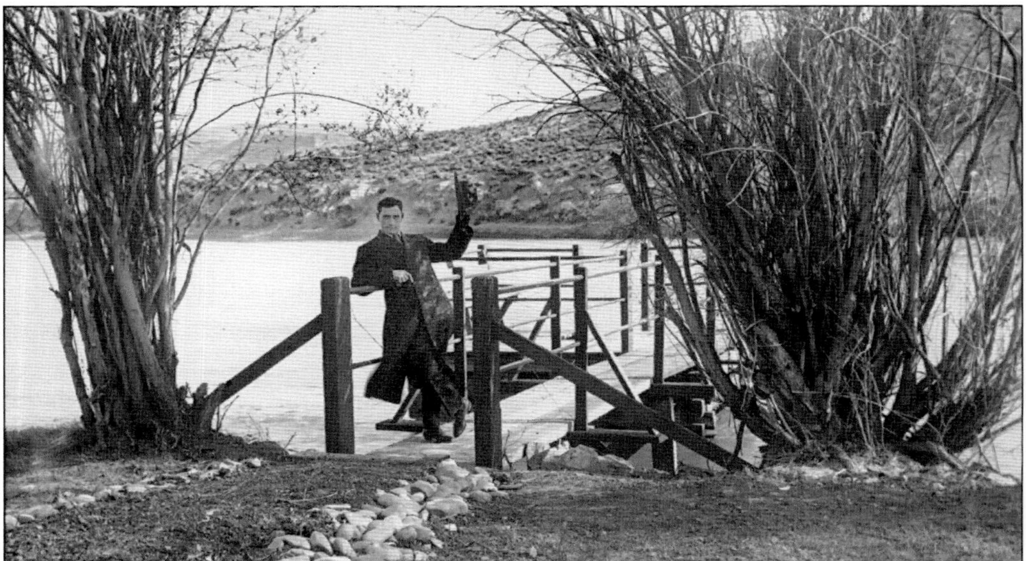

In this 1908 image, William A. Johnson bids a fond farewell while standing upon a pier on the Green River. A century later, we still share the moment. The meandering river and its sturdy palisades have quietly watched our small community grow and flourish. Millennia have come and gone under their patient gaze. How comforting to know that these age-old friends will maintain their vigil over our efforts and interpret them in terms of the long view. (Courtesy of the Sweetwater County Historical Museum.)

BIBLIOGRAPHY

Bell, W. A. *Philadelphia Bulletin*, Philadelphia, in *History of the Union Pacific Coal Mines 1868 to 1940*. Omaha: Colonial Press, 1945.

Dellenbaugh, Frederick S. A *Canyon Voyage: The Narrative of the Second Powell Expedition*. Tucson: University of Arizona Press, 1984.

Green River High School. *Rendezvous*. Green River, Wyoming, 1926.

Hebard, Grace Raymond. "Sweetwater County Fiftieth Anniversary: December 26, 1926."

June, James. *Sweetwater County History*, vols. 1-5. Sweetwater, Wyoming: Sweetwater County Historical Museum, 1990.

Green River Star, July 17, 1908.

Taliaferro, Thomas S. "Letter to W. S. Paxson, Green River, April 13, 1938."

Scarpos, Angelie. Transcription of oral histories on file with the Sweetwater County Historical Museum, 1997.

Shearer, Frederick E. *The Pacific Tourist*. New York: Adams & Bishop Publishers, 1884.

Stanton, Robert B. *Colorado River Controversies*. New York: Dodd, Mead & Co., 1932.

Yates, William. "Reminisces," unpublished manuscript on file with the Sweetwater County Historical Museum, n.d.

INDEX

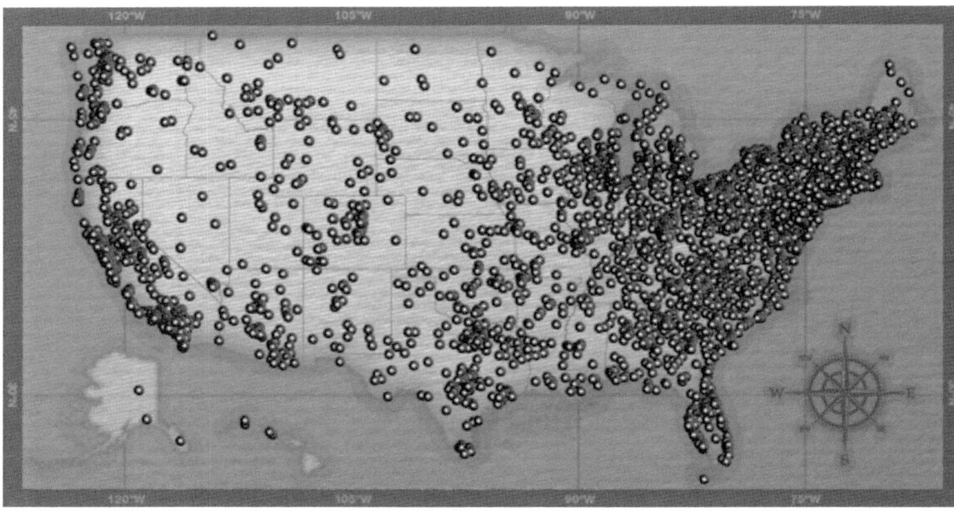

Consistent with our mission to preserve history on a local level, this book was printed in South Carolina on American-made paper and manufactured entirely in the United States. Products carrying the accredited Forest Stewardship Council (FSC) label are printed on 100 percent FSC-certified paper.

MADE IN THE USA